Brain Gym® and Me

Reclaiming the Pleasure of Learning

Paul E. Dennison

Brain Gym® and Me

Reclaiming the Pleasure of Learning

© 2006 by Paul E. Dennison

Book design by JLH Designs
Cover photograph by Cheryl Mac, PureImagePhoto.com
All photos of the movements by Laura Luongo Photography

The information included in these pages about the movement-based learning system known as Educational Kinesiology, including the Brain Gym® activities, derives from other published works of Paul E. Dennison and Gail E. Dennison.

Brain Gym® is a registered trademark of the Educational Kinesiology Foundation/Brain Gym® International, (800) 356-2109 from the U.S.A. and Canada and (805) 658-7942 from all other countries.
edukfd@earthlink.net
www.braingym.org

Printed in the United States of America

ISBN: 0-942143-11-6

Permissions Department
Edu-Kinesthetics, Inc.
P. O. Box 3396
Ventura, CA 93006-3396
www.braingym.com

A Notice to Readers

This book is intended for informational and educational purposes only, and should not be construed as a health guide or a manual for self-treatment. Before beginning any exercise program, it is always advisable to check with your physician or other professional healthcare practitioner.

Further, this book describes only a part of the vast movement-based learning system known as Educational Kinesiology, which comprises hundreds of curriculum hours among its diverse course offerings. The movements are simple yet potent, and used in more than eighty countries around the world. A qualified teacher can support you in accessing their many benefits. To find an instructor or consultant in your area, visit the website of Brain Gym® International at www.braingym.org.

Acknowledgments

I hold in deepest gratitude a group of people who sustained and guided me in the completion of this book. Their generosity and dedication to the project contributed much to its depth and scope, so—first—to each of them a big hug.

There is no way to sufficiently acknowledge Gail Dennison, my wife and partner and the cocreator of the Educational Kinesiology and Brain Gym® programs. Gail's meticulous reading and editing of this manuscript resulted in a broadening and development of each section. Her loving questions about my early life helped me to remember long-forgotten scenes and events. The result is a context to hold the complexity and diversity of the work. I love you, Gail.

Next I thank my Bear Clan brother Jai Collins, who interviewed me and many of my students and helped me envision the possibility of this book.

Special thanks to my friend Dr. Carla Hannaford, the neurobiologist and teacher whose explanations of the relationship of movement to learning have made our work more available to millions of people. Thank you, Carla, for appreciating the simple elegance of the movements and for opening people's hearts to hear in a new way.

I thank my dear friend and early mentor, the late John Thie, for his vision to make self-help technologies available to the general public, and for encouraging me to develop my educational work and share it with the world.

I warmly acknowledge Joseph Chilton Pearce for his understanding of the brain, and especially for his insights into the relationship between the power of the brain stem and the compassion of the frontal lobes to bring focus to the pleasure of learning. Thank you, Joe, for your friendship and mentoring.

I also thank Sydney Harris, Alexander teacher and dear friend, who shares my vision of the work. Your thoughtful reading of the original manuscript and careful questions helped to draw out my best writing.

A warm acknowledgment to Sonia Nordenson, our editor and friend since 1993, as "the woman behind the lines": Sonia, your clarity and directness have helped me to say what I mean. If God is in the details, you've helped make this work divine.

To Dr. Marilyn Lugaro, my student and friend: Marilyn, we met twenty-five years ago when I could hardly explain—let alone write about—the work. You learned it, taught it, lived it, and still inspire me to do ever more of the same.

To Richard Palmer, poet and community builder: Thank you for seeing my heart and modeling how to connect with others through nonviolent communications. It 's one thing to understand heart and another to commit to its rhythms. So I thank you, Richard, for teaching me how to check in with my heart.

I also want to acknowledge Alfred Schatz, my teacher, mentor, German publisher, and friend. Alfred and his associates, Beate Walters and Susanne Degandorfer, caught the unique vision of the Edu-K work and began translating it in 1983 for the German-speaking world, including Austria and Switzerland.

My gratitude also goes to Paul Landon of France; Tania McGregor of Australia; Glenys Leadbeater and Barbara Wards of New Zealand; Rita Edwards of South Africa; Renate Wennekes of Germany; Kay McCarroll of the United Kingdom; Rosmarie Sondregger and Bernhardt Studer of Switzerland; Hans Barth of Austria; and Svetlana Masgutova of Russia and Poland, to name just some of the International Faculty Members who have been instrumental in pioneering the work.

My thanks also to Colleen Carroll Gardner, Rose Harrow, Don Wetsel, Pamela Curlee, Sylvia Sue Greene, Sharon Plaskett, and Bonnie Hershey, our International Faculty Members in North America, whose focus and dedication keep the drawing-out model alive and pure within the Edu-K work.

Gail and I will feel gratitude always to the late Olive Liu of China, for her pioneering work in Taiwan and Southeast Asia. We are also thankful to Carol Ann Erickson for her wisdom, and for validating our work in the world of sports; to Joan Spalding for introducing the work in Russia; to Dorothy H. L. Carroll, Marilyn Lugaro, and Judy Grant for their leadership in organizing the nonprofit foundation to disseminate the work; and to Julie Newendorp, Rose Harrow, and Stephanie Badasci as the executive directors who have shepherded the work most recently, helping to keep up with the foundation's exponential growth. Warm appreciation, too, to Jeffrey Scharetg for his creative and technical contributions to my work and this book.

If space allowed, I would like to thank hundreds of others. You know who you are.

Contents

Preface

Movement Is the Door to Learning

In the last thirty years I've facilitated thousands of private sessions all over the world, using Educational Kinesiology—an in-depth system of movement-based learning—with people ranging in age from infants to elders. In coaching sessions in which we reorganize brain, heart, and movement patterns around a specific intention and purpose, I've seen countless individuals transform their lives.

I've also personally coached thousands of teachers in eighteen countries in Educational Kinesiology and its best-known component, Brain Gym, for these systems work cross-culturally. Brain Gym, developed by my wife, Gail, and myself, is taught in more than forty languages and used in homes, schools, and businesses in more than eighty countries. Gail and I are perpetually delighted to see individual instructors bring their own passion and innovations to the work, and we're thrilled by the remarkable results they achieve.

Many people write to us about the dramatic results they experience just by doing the basic twenty-six movements in *Brain Gym: Simple Activities for Whole-Brain Learning*, the little book we wrote in 1985.

As I'll explain in this book, all these seemingly miraculous results brought about by the Brain Gym program have a sound basis in neuroscience and in kinesiology, the study of movement.

I've long wanted to write a book about my understanding of the relationship of movement to learning, and I have a two-fold purpose in writing Brain Gym® and Me. I want to share the work—how we encourage people to reach for new possibilities, in a simple, intuitive, and elegantly structured process—and I also want to awaken my readers to an understanding of the interdependence of movement, learning, and brain development.

I want to convey how critical it is for movement—specific, conscious activities—to be included in daily life. I want to promote whole-brain neural networking for each and every one of us, for decision making and personal achievement of all kinds, starting in childhood and continuing through the life cycle. I want to promulgate the idea that learning doesn't have to be difficult, and that moving to learn can bring the health, intelligence, and fulfillment that we dream of for ourselves and our children.

A life made happy through the pleasure of learning is everyone's birthright. It's my vision that you, my reader, will wake up one morning in a place of curiosity and excitement and acknowledge to yourself, *Yes! My life is working.* These words will mean something specific and personal to you, and each time you say them you'll know that they herald another new beginning.

In my own experience, the pleasure of learning involves living on the edge, in a world composed of opposites through which I'm continually rediscovering my balance. While my sense of self navigates the course, I'm secure in the knowledge that, as I keep letting go, trusting, and finding my equilibrium in the midst of it all, I'm moving toward my goals no matter what life brings.

I remember being touched, as a young man, by the words of Karl Wallenda of the Great Wallendas. The Great Wallendas were a family of tightrope walkers who achieved fame with Ringling Brothers and Barnum and Bailey Circus and eventually became known as the Flying Wallendas. When asked why he risked his life daily on the high wire, Wallenda replied, "Walking the wire is living; everything else is waiting."

The pleasure of learning occurs on a similar balance point—the one between making it happen and taking it as it comes. It involves stepping into the fire, so to speak, in a space of waiting, yearning, and childlike expectation. In this state of moving to learn, we leave room for an unexpected future that is always fuller, more expansive, and more exciting than anything we could imagine.

The pleasure of learning begins in the body. We need to feel the tension of the opposites: the pull from the left and the pull from

2

the right; the pull forward and the holding backward; the safety or firmness of the ground and the thrill of flight through the air. When we experience a sense of balance in the midst of chaos, we can take a stand on our own two feet as we continue to develop our character and individuality.

How well I remember the first time I went to summer camp. As a ten-year-old child from the city, I didn't know how to swim. Going in the water with the other boys, I felt uncomfortable with all their splashing, whooping, and commotion, and almost gave up on swimming. I hated my bathing suit, which would fill with air like a balloon.

One day I heard that early risers could go skinny-dipping before breakfast. The next morning I went down to the lake, got into the warm, welcoming water sans suit, and began to swim. It was quiet and peaceful, the light filtering through the trees over the stillness of the lake. Miraculously, the water held me up. I felt my body take charge as I did the strokes I'd already learned—which had gotten me nowhere before. I swam and swam as the water opened up to my directed movements. When I had swum two laps, I heard my counselor cheering me. Unbeknownst to me, he'd been watching my progress from shore and now qualified me as being "a swimmer!"

Emerging from the water, I felt a new pleasure . . . the kind that derives from going beyond one's perceived limitations to meet a learning challenge. And it was in the Fall of that same year that I learned to read

Later, as a long-distance runner in California, I entered a ten-kilometer run in Beverly Hills. I had heard that Billy Rogers, winner of the Boston Marathon and a world-renowned runner, would be there, addressing the crowd before the race. It was said of Billy that, when he ran, his feet hardly touch the ground. Hundreds of men gathered to run the course in the park, and I had to decide before the gun went off where to seed myself in the pack, which would spread out as the race began.

Billy set the pace, taking off like a bullet. Having chosen a starting place better suited to a hare than to a tortoise like me, I got knocked down and trampled as the other men pushed and shoved their way through the melee. I stood up, brushed off my bruised body, and steadfastly ran the race to the finish, happy in the knowledge that I could go the distance in spite of a rocky start.

By the 1970s, as owner of the Valley Remedial Group Reading Centers in the San Fernando Valley, I was respected in the community as a professional educator and successful entrepreneur. I had developed a thriving business, helping people to read, write, and spell. After I wrote my first book in 1981, I began to receive international speaking invitations. Now there was a demand for training courses and for additional books and manuals.

When I was first investigating the phenomenal effects of movement with the students at my reading centers, other educators started telling me I should write a book, that I should start teaching this exciting work. And, sure enough, I was soon invited to teach in Europe.

Some of my family members said, "Don't be crazy! You're no expert on movement—who are you to teach about it?" I'd made risky choices before, and had taken my share of pratfalls. This time my heart was saying, *Yes, you can do this. It's right for you.* I listened to my heart and trusted it, and I went to Europe and began teaching about movement-based learning.

I had reached a crossroads in my life. I now needed to make the choice to give up the comfort and security of my reading centers and make a commitment to teach full-time about education through movement, as I couldn't do justice to both endeavors. I chose to take a stand for this new life, which meant letting go of the familiar and entering the unknown. Enveloped by a wondrous sense of being lifted up and held, I said to myself, *Yes, I will do this.*

A life of pleasurable learning involves taking matters seriously yet not being excessively serious. It's about working hard and hardly working. It's about relationships, honoring, and caring—not about having, owning, and controlling. Because my life will always reflect the way I engage with it, I choose to use my time well by being, doing, and caring.

I've learned that when I'm grounded in my body, I can trust an available knowledge greater than my mind can ever comprehend. The more present I am, the more safely I can take risks. When I'm able to be still and quiet, I can then dance and shout, love and be loved, and feel pain and empathy.

At the same time that it has reawakened my curiosity and sense of play, the Brain Gym learning system has helped me to release blame, shame, fears, and limitations that once compromised the expression of my individuality. When my life is more about service to others than about myself, I know who I am. Now I aim always to know that I've summoned all my resources and faced obstacles to the best of my ability, that I've played the game to the fullest, asked for help when I needed it, and felt gratitude for all that the universe has provided as it holds me in its arms. This, for me, is one of the chief delights of life: reclaiming the innate pleasure of learning that is everyone's birthright.

Introduction

Success with Brain Gym

In 1986, purely by accident, Brain Gym became a great part of my life when I was asked to work in the local intermediate school with alienated students as part of a nine-week pilot project. As a biology professor at the University of Hawaii, I used "Superlearning" techniques with my students, which the intermediate school principal thought might assist the Comprehensive Student Alienation Program (CSAP). I accepted the project with its nineteen students because it sounded interesting, even though I had no experience in counseling and it had been over twenty years since I had taught this age group.

Just before starting the project, I took a Touch for Health class from Fran Woollard, RN, who encouraged me to consider using Brain Gym with these students. She related a story about her son, Todd, when he was sixteen years old. Todd was a charming, intelligent boy who had struggled with learning, and especially reading, all through school. Because he was tall, the basketball team wanted him, but he was clumsy and tripped over the ball whenever he tried to dribble it down the floor.

That year Fran had attended a Touch for Health conference in California, at which Dr. Paul Dennison spoke about the Brain Gym program. Fran returned home with new hope for Todd. To encourage Todd to persist with the simple but unfamiliar Brain Gym movements, she had the entire family doing them every morning and evening. Within six weeks, Todd was reading at grade level and had become part of the basketball team as one of the key players. (Incidentally, Todd went on to successfully obtain a graduate degree in biology from a prestigious university—all the while using Brain Gym.)

I decided to see what Brain Gym could do for the CSAP students. In the background I played Baroque music as we did the Cross Crawl, the Thinking Cap, Hook-ups, and Lazy 8s before we began working on the difficult school subjects. Within two weeks, I had teachers asking me what I was doing with these students. They were seeing improved skills as well as delightful changes in the students' confidence and willingness to participate.

Half way through the pilot project, the principal was so impressed he invited me to give an in-service for all the teachers and then extended the pilot funding for the next four years! That spring I was invited to give a four-hour presentation on Brain Gym to all the principals on the island.

In November of 1986 I took my first Brain Gym course, which happened to be the In-Depth class. I witnessed neurological changes in the participants that I, as a biologist and neurophysiologist, "knew" could not occur. I needed to understand the underlying physiology leading to the research I later presented in *Smart Moves: Why Learning Is Not All in Your Head* and the more current research I included in *Awakening the Child Heart: Handbook for Global Parenting*.

Ultimately, if we didn't move, we wouldn't need a brain. Our entire brain structure is intimately connected to and grown by the movement mechanisms within our bodies. We are all natural learners, exploring and experiencing our world through our movements and intricate sensory systems, even before birth. How we take in and assimilate this learning is determined by the safety and challenges of that environment.

Because survival is paramount to our existence, it is the first variable. If we are in a survival state (stress, anxiety, frustration), the body goes into a reactive mode and only assists us in surviving. In this state, part of the brain shuts down—the part that sees and understands the whole picture; is able to plan complex strategies; can feel empathy, and altruism; is connected with music and play; and ultimately create new ideas. In this shutdown state, learning and memory are radically decreased and the joy and enthusiasm of life are diminished.

What the simple movements of Brain Gym have the power to do is to reactivate whole-brain function via the intimate connection with body movements. Brain Gym consists of integrated, cross-lateral, balance-requiring movements that mechanically activate both hemispheres of the brain via the motor and sensory cortexes, stimulate the vestibular (balance) system for equilibrium, and decrease the fight-or-flight mechanism. In this balanced state, it is much easier for us to think, understand, and come up with new ideas and solutions.

I have watched the phenomenon of people going from stress and survival to understanding. I saw this dramatically with an eleven-year-old Down syndrome boy in South Africa. His teacher had been working with him daily for three months in an attempt to help him learn his numbers: one through ten. She used a chart that showed the numbers, and the boy's task was to take laminated cards depicting the different numerals and match them with the corresponding numbers on the chart. As hard as he tried, he could not get it. He would pick up a three, say "Seven" and place it on the ten. When reminded it was a three, he would say "Three" but then lay it on a five. Both the boy and his teacher were extremely frustrated and stressed by this exercise.

I asked him if he would be willing to do Dennison Laterality Repatterning (which helps integrate the important cross-lateral movements of the body with eye movements and conveys the physical differences between new and familiar learning), which he was pleased and excited to do. His fellow students helped. This process became a game that took about fifteen minutes, with everyone laughing and enjoying the play of it. This young boy then he sat back at his desk and the chart, picked up a three, said "Three," and placed it on the three of the chart. He then immediately picked up a seven, said "Seven," and put it on the seven, continuing until the whole chart was filled correctly. I turned and saw the teacher behind me with big tears of joy running down her cheeks.

I have seen this same kind of shift occur with thousands of teachers, musicians, athletes, artists, dancers, business executives, students, and people with labels like "ADHD" or "dyslexia" in the thirty-some countries where I have taught the Brain Gym work since 1988.

In 1989, in Russia, a serious train explosion occurred outside Moscow. Svetlana Masgutova, director of the Institute of Psychology, worked with the severely burned and traumatized children who had survived the accident. Nothing she tried seemed to work. After three months, more than half the children had died and the rest were

8

symptomatically depressed, continuing to draw dark, horrifying pictures in their art therapy sessions.

Around this time, during a visit to the Moscow Institute of Pedagogical Science, Svetlana came across one of the small orange *Brain Gym* books I had left there in 1988 when I was a guest teacher of the Academy of Humanistic Psychology project to Russia.

Svetlana immediately started using the activities with the children, and within several weeks the pictures they were drawing had changed. Bright colors emerged, along with rainbows, butterflies, and depictions of children running through meadows. The doctors also noted that the children were now taking the skin grafts and healing. This so surprised Svetlana, the doctors, and the children's parents that at the end of six months she compiled her carefully kept records and wrote a professional paper. Experts throughout Russia were interested and invited her to give talks.

When I returned to Russia in 1991, now to teach Brain Gym, Svetlana had assembled fifty psychologists and medical doctors who, impressed by her results, had started using the Brain Gym work. They shared with me their remarkable success with people of all ages, and with every problem imaginable. Brain Gym is now being used in many areas of Russia.

That same year, in Botswana, I was invited to work with trainees of the Botswana Insurance Company who were preparing for their Insurance Exams. The pass rate for this formidable exam was less than 30 percent. I gave the examinees a six-hour Brain Gym session and showed them why it would help their studies and exam results. Three months later the group took the exam, and every single one of them passed. One man named Walks Tall had worried the examiner by spending the first thirty minutes of the timed test doing the Brain Gym activities. He was the first person in South Africa to achieve a 100 percent score on the Insurance Exam.

Other movement activities such as yoga, Tai Chi, the Alexander Technique, and aikido are integrated, cross-lateral movement, done slowly with balance, and thus they activate the brain in the same way. The beauty of Brain Gym is that it is profoundly simple, can be done easily anywhere without much space, works within the format of play, and has creative potential. The movements have been modified from many disciplines (kinesiology, occupational therapy, yoga, developmental ophthalmology, the meridian systems of Traditional Chinese Medicine, etc.) and are designed to affect the entire intellectual, emotional, social, physical, and spiritual body. Added to the movements are the elegant balances that take a person past their "stuck" places and into their full potential and joy.

Important brain research presented in 1999 showed that we continue to grow new nerve cells in the area of our brain that has to do with memory, until the day we die, *if* we feel secure, have an enriched environment with novel experiences, and, *most importantly, have cross-lateral physical activity.* New research even suggests that, in the elderly, regular dancing decreases the chances of dementia by 79 percent. Dancing is a perfect Brain Gym activity, and the balance experience that accompanies the movements provides the secure, enriched environment with chosen, creative, novel experiences.

My own life has become less "dramatic" and more peaceful over the years as I continue to grow through this work. With each new "aha" I feel more blessed to have this tool in my life.

It has been my great honor to read Dr. Dennison's manuscript of his personal story in bringing the Brain Gym work to fruition. I believe you will find Paul Dennison's book of great value to every step of your journey. This wonderfully readable book is full of heart, amazing stories of transformation and potentiality, a deeper understanding of the balance process from its originator, and a look into a most remarkable man who has overcome many obstacles and stands as a light of hope to the world.

—Carla Hannaford, Ph.D.

Chapter One

The Dragon's Treasure

It was New Year's Eve morning of 1940. In Europe, where nation after nation had fallen to the Nazis, there was now something to celebrate. The Battle of Britain had ended and the German invasion of England had been repelled. As champagne corks popped, no one could foresee that a year later Japan would attack Pearl Harbor and a new war would ensue.

For now, the news from Europe was good, bringing with it the hope that 1941 would be a better year. Yet the good news couldn't allay the fears of Bostonians, for Boston, the largest metropolitan area on the northeast coast, was the vulnerable seaport positioned closest to Europe. For more than six months, a blackout had enveloped the city each night. Even the golden dome of the state capitol had been painted black to camouflage it against a potential Nazi air raid.

For one young couple living in Boston's Brighton section, though, there was cause for celebration. In the previous night they had borrowed a car to drive across the Charles River to a hospital in Cambridge. There, during the citywide blackout, the couple's first child had been born.

Like every new infant, the baby boy was a miracle of creation—a bright-eyed being alert to the sights and sounds of his new surroundings. Tiny and helpless though he was, from the baby's eyes a fathomless intelligence shone, just as it shines from the eyes of every newborn. The child's parents, like innumerable parents before them, recognized that mysterious awareness with awe.

The war dragged on, and the American nation was soon actively engaged in it. The child's father did his part to support his country. Every night after dinner, he put on his jacket and took a bus to the shipyard. Wearing goggles and a riveter's suit, he was lowered over the surface of the water on a scaffold, to work all night securing sheet metal to the hull of a ship. Weary when morning came, he would return to the family's windowless, one-room apartment to sleep, while his wife and child spent most of each day being quiet. This way of life went on until the war finally ended, when the boy was nearly six.

The Formation of a Belief System

One of the child's first memories would be of holding his mother's hand as they climbed down the cement stairs to the boiler room located directly beneath their apartment. They were seeking the source of the strange sounds that rumbled up to their living space from below. The dark, oily air, the hissing steam, and the boiler's metallic clanging frightened the child, yet he needed to explore those mysterious sounds.

His mother squeezed his hand and said, "We're the luckiest poor people in Boston . . . at least we're warm!" Yet there was no joy in her voice, and in that instant he began to form a belief system.

The boy listened intently to whatever was said by this magical person who was everything to him. Observing that she often seemed sad and tired, he urgently wanted to respond to her, but was unable to speak. (He would be four before he spoke his first halting words.)

When the boy was two, an evening bath-time incident formed what would be another vivid memory. He was splashing around, scooping water and pouring it over the floating soap bar, when his mother stepped out of the room. For a while his absorption in play distracted him from the fact that he was alone. Soon, though, the water grew cool and he noticed his fingers getting white and wrinkled.

He called out for his mother. There was no response. He called again, and the house was still. After calling a third time, he made a tearful decision: he would get out of the bathtub without help. If he couldn't rely on his mother, he would have to take care of himself. He clambered out, pulled down a towel to wrap around himself, and headed for his parents' bedroom, where he was surprised to find that his mother had fallen asleep.

He felt a strange mixture of exhilaration and despair. He had taken a first step toward autonomy and self-sufficiency, and yet it hurt to feel abandoned. As he climbed onto the bed and snuggled up to his napping mother, he couldn't know that a host of new ideas had just swamped his young psyche. These beliefs would influence him again and again in adulthood: *Life is uncertain; I may be abandoned at any moment. I'm responsible for my own survival. I can't be sure that anyone else is going to help me. I'm on my own . . .*

Starting School

When finally the war ended, the economy began to improve. The boy's parents decided to move the family (which now included a second son) to the more upscale area of Brookline, where the schools were among the best in the country. They hoped their older boy, who would soon be starting school, would thrive in this environment of academic excellence where most parents were college-educated—many at Harvard. They reasoned that, given the tremendous pressure on teachers in Brookline to coach every child to learning success, their two sons would receive the kind of education that could lift them out of poverty.

Three months before the boy's sixth birthday, his mother took his hand to accompany him on that daunting journey in which children leave the safety of home to start their first day of school. For this shy newcomer who hardly spoke, it felt as if that first day would never end.

He'd been hoping for quiet play, hearing stories read aloud, and getting to do coloring and crafts—things he was familiar with at home. But the other children constantly fought, shouting names at one another. The teachers appeared exasperated and angry, and every youngster in the school seemed to take a turn pushing and shoving him. The new boy didn't understand any of this.

As the first few years of his schooling passed, the boy foundered completely. When most of his peers could read and write, he was still barely able to hold a pen correctly or read a simple sentence on

13

the chalkboard. He wanted to please his teachers, but his best efforts failed; anyone who stood at the front of the classroom eventually became impatient with him. He wanted to make friends with other boys, but few of them wanted to make friends with him. By the time he was in third grade, life was dismal at best, and he often wept silently as he walked home from school.

A strange paradox was occurring. Since the war, his home life had become filled with music, dance, and the arts. The many topics of frequent and passionate discussion included drawing, design, opera, and plays. Yet the boy felt no connection between the creative longing inspired by his family and the word "learning," which seemed so elusive at school.

One day Mrs. Clifford, the third grade social studies teacher, was conducting an oral quiz.

"Class, what was the first tool?"

The boy knew the answer, and raised his hand in school for the first time. The teacher called on him, surprised.

"The thumb," was the boy's shy but confident response.

The other children howled with laughter, and Mrs. Clifford removed her glasses and gave him a pitying smile.

"I'm sorry; that's not correct."

Embarrassed though he was, somehow the boy still knew that his answer to Miss Clifford's question had been right. He couldn't yet know that his answer was a wise message from his body, meant only for him: he was being given a glimpse of his own future and purpose.

More than three decades later, this incident would reveal itself as a key to two areas of his work: the physical skills of writing and the influence of hand position on the eyes and brain.

Trying Hard and Failing

The competitive environment of school was hardly the place for a boy like this to make a longed-for breakthrough. Unable to read, write, or do math, and rarely speaking, the boy was bewildered by school and continued to fail abysmally. His teacher would often rant at him while the other students giggled nervously.

The boy's mother was now in full despair. One night, after her

14

first-born had gone to bed, she went into his room. Believing him to be asleep, she sat down beside him and began to cry. "What's going to become of you?" she whispered. The boy held his eyes tightly closed, afraid that they would open and his mother would realize he had heard her. He knew he was a good person, and something told him that one day he would be able to learn, when the time was right. Silently, as he feigned sleep, he promised his mother that he would try harder.

But the harder he tried, the harder it was to succeed and the angrier his fourth grade teacher became. One day, in absolute frustration and in the manner of an old-fashioned educator, Miss Newton grabbed the boy by his shoulders. Perhaps, like her namesake, Sir Isaac, she wanted the universe to be a precision mechanism like a Swiss watch. Children who didn't fit this paradigm seemed to bring her torment. In a fury, she dug in her fingers and shook him back and forth.

"Why can't you learn!?" she hollered, her face just inches from his. Her breath smelled of coffee. "What's wrong with you!?"

He could hear laughter from the other boys and girls. Shamed and bewildered, the boy began to sob. In that instant his natural genius, which had been gradually receding through the years, went completely into hiding.

What exactly *was* this natural genius now dormant in him? It was that limitless intelligence and creativity that had sparkled in his eyes at birth. It was his intense curiosity, his thirst for understanding, his humor, ingenuity, and playfulness. It was all the many attributes with which babies are universally endowed . . . the gifts that somehow combine to make children uniquely who they are. In short, it was everything the little boy was meant to be—his true potential that, fully expressed, would allow him to discover the pleasure of learning and the beauty of life.

What the Dragon Guards

As you have probably guessed, I was that little boy. It took me many years to reclaim my power and my natural ability to learn, and the process continues to this day.

Yet I don't regret the wounding that sent the finest part of me into hiding. I have found that one's pain and one's gift are located close together in the deepest part of the self. In mythology, a dragon guards these two aspects of our being in a treasure-filled cave. Just as the hero must stand up to the monster to find the gold, so must we confront our darkest wound in order to discover our gift. This has certainly been true for me. From my hurt emerged my work, my message, and my mission: to bring to the world community a new way to educate our children so that they can learn without failure.

The previous summer I had gone to camp for three weeks, enrolled in a special program for children from low-income families. There, in a cold lake, under a canopy of beautiful trees, I had learned how to swim. I had discovered the wonderful feeling of moving my whole body at once, moving in the water with direction and purpose as I coordinated my breathing and swimming strokes. This had been my first experience with a sport and with physical activity. I had learned that I had a body and that I could learn with it. My success at learning to swim had been profound, and it continued to profoundly influence all other areas of my learning.

When fall came, because of that miserable year in Brookline, my parents transferred me to another school. Since I had been flunked and I had to repeat the fourth grade, they wanted to spare me the pain of seeing my classmates move on without me. That decision proved to be one of the greatest blessings of my life, for at the new school an angel came down from heaven to help me, and I was now ready to respond to her guidance.

Marie Paquette was full of warm regard for all of the children in her class. She paid special attention to me—a quiet, curly-haired boy who was happy to be with younger children who didn't judge him. Working at an easier pace than I'd previously known at school, with the recent benefit of whole-body movement experiences, and in an atmosphere of respect and cooperation, I was now ready to learn. Mrs. Paquette managed to teach me, at age ten, how to read. What she may have lacked in technique, she more than made up for in kindness and patience, and I began to blossom as a student.

At the end of the year, Mrs. Paquette revealed a secret: she was one of my father's cousins, and they had been close friends in junior high school. Knowing who I was, she had made it her personal mission to watch over me. At the end of the school year, she introduced herself and her family to my parents. I remember my mother hugging Marie Paquette and whispering, "Thank you." I knew that she was thinking, *You saved my son, and I don't have the words to express my gratitude.*

As the years went by, the art and culture in my home life continued to sustain me, yet I was a mediocre student. Without any pressure or impetus to succeed, I didn't know how to do more than gradually take interest in each subject and catch up at my own pace.

By high school I had actually begun to enjoy my studies. At fifteen, while in the middle of my freshman year, I got my first A in French and began to see myself as a capable learner. Good teachers and counselors now encouraged me, as they began to recognize my gifts.

I sailed through high school and was accepted at Boston University, which I could afford to attend because it was close to home. I culminated my scholastic career by returning to the topic that had tormented me in my early years: reading. Along with a doctorate in Curriculum and Instruction (I specialized in reading) from the University of Southern California, I received a Phi Delta Kappa award there for my research on the relationship of speech and thought to beginning reading achievement.

My Faith in the Natural Love of Learning

I became skilled in teaching reading to young children, and opened a chain of eight reading centers throughout the San Fernando Valley, north of Los Angeles. Anyone who had known me during those painful early years in Boston, and especially my mother, could now hardly believe what I'd managed to make of myself. At a relatively young age, I had become a recognized expert in my field. People called me "the Reading Doctor of the Valley," and my business thrived.

But this wasn't enough for me. I wanted to understand even more deeply the process of learning and the factors that inhibit it. I wanted to see if I could find a way to help my students access more of their potential—that part of each of us that loves to learn and has something unique to offer the world. So I immersed myself in a study of the literature on reading and applied brain research. I knew I had now mastered the foundations of this work, and now I wanted to ask questions that hadn't been asked by educators before. This was the beginning of trusting my intuition, of seeking answers that would lead to further discoveries of my own.

I saw how young children, prior to any school experience, naturally delight in learning that is strongly movement-based, exploring life with a curiosity and zest that few adults can equal. I also saw how school-age children too frequently fall behind, then continue to flounder in the classroom environment. I became familiar with the ways in which educators have typically addressed the dilemma of failure in our schools: by devising programs to drill, entice, condition, motivate, and reinforce children, so as to "stamp in" learning. These programs may succeed in raising test scores, yet they don't address the question of why some children do well in school while others do not.

I discovered that some children try too hard to cram in information and, in so doing, stop movement and switch off the natural brain-integration mechanisms necessary for complete learning. What I came to realize is that, for educators, effective teaching isn't about presenting the information and letting the student passively take it in, but about connecting the information to the movement of the body in an active way. Data and information is received by the senses as an "impress," but without active movement this data is inaccessible to the prefrontal cortex as an "express." This inability to participate by expressing in their own words what is learned and held inside, locks students in a failure syndrome.

Discovering How to Stop Trying

Through the last twenty years my wife and partner, Gail, and I have continued that research I began so long ago, refining Brain Gym and what we call the balance process to a point where we can truly say that no child need ever endure the shame of failure. Only ignorance stops us, as a society, from guiding every young person to learning success.

Not every child will become a lawyer, engineer, nuclear physicist, or even a Web master, but the world needs many forms of genius. There are so many ways for us all to contribute to society that it is completely unnecessary for any child to be traumatized at school and made to feel dumb or "less than." Every child has limitless capability, just waiting to blossom in its own way. When I work with a child, I don't want to hear how he has a "problem" and I have no desire to "fix" or change him. The essence of Gail's and my work is to help people discover how to stop trying and simply do their best.

From my own early struggle to speak in public, I've learned a lot about the effects of negative stress. I see so many young people failing simply because they're trying too hard. When I hear teachers or parents tell children to try, I realize they don't know the meaning of the word, nor do they understand its deleterious impact on the physiology. The Brain Gym work shows that asking children to try harder is asking them to make a stressful effort—to go beyond their natural ability. What a difference when parents are able to say, "I believe in your abilities, and I just want you to do your best."

I see parents and teachers sometimes wanting to "fix" behaviors or eliminate those they don't like in their children or students. Yet this inadvertently teaches those young people that aspects of themselves aren't worthy of love or compassion. We need, instead, to offer them a way to heal, to integrate, and to learn from the deeper meanings in their behaviors. Brain Gym provides the tools with which to do this.

The problem lies not just with children. It seems to me that most adults who try hard to succeed still lead lives that are a mere shadow of what they might be. Many of us are out of balance in mind and body, with our heads often disconnected from our hearts. Brain

Gym offers a way to rediscover our natural balance and renew the connection between mind and heart, so we can let go of "trying."

When this balancing and renewal happens, we become wiser, more peaceful, more joyful, more sensitive, and more compassionate. Life flows easily and we manage our affairs with greater effectiveness and less stress. Moreover, we can now tap into the creative part of our nature, turning our lives, no matter how difficult, into works of beauty and joy.

Fear of Public Speaking

Brookline, Massachusetts, the town where I grew up, is a community that cares about culture and the arts. It was there, when I was about seven, that my mother, a dancer, painter, and sculptor, and my father, a poet with a bold, stentorian voice, developed the Dennison Marionettes. Their wonderful puppet shows for children, accompanied by twenty members of the Boston Symphony Orchestra, were performed at the Brookline High School auditorium and often featured in youth concerts.

One of our best shows was *Peter and the Wolf*, narrated by Augustus T. Zanzig, Brookline's music director and the author of the music books we used at school. An esteemed elder within the community, Dr. Zanzig was a tall, robust man with a full head of white hair. He came many times to our apartment, where his presence filled the living room as he practiced with us for the performance. From my place in the corner, I watched in awe as he spoke in his deep, rich voice the lines I knew so well: "Early one morning, Peter stepped out through the gate into the deep green meadow." Dr. Zanzig was like a grandfather to me. I adored him, and I loved to imitate his bass voice.

As a reticent ten-year-old, I played a Native American chief in my own first public performance. In this part, I traded corn for jewelry with Paul Bunyan, the famous giant (played by my father).

"How much?" I asked, seeking to elicit from the giant his best offer.

Paul Bunyan made an offer of jewels and then asked, "Do we have a deal, Chief?"

"How much *more*?" I asked emphatically.

Paul placed more jewels in my palm. "Now, do we have a deal?"

"Heap big deal," I replied, emulating Dr. Zanzig's mellifluous tones and tasting the joy my own voice could bring me. With those three short lines, my public speaking career was launched.

As music director, Dr. Zanzig would periodically organize a town sing-along in which all the schoolchildren would participate. When I was twelve and in the seventh grade, he and I had an encounter that would continue to affect my life. Having repeated the fourth grade, I was a year older than my classmates, and my voice was the first to deepen. As I sang along with the group, a basso amid tenors and sopranos, Dr. Zanzig singled me out, asking me not to sing out loud because I was spoiling the sound. "Just move your lips," he suggested.

Our voices hold much of our fire, so it was a pity that this otherwise exemplary man could offer no better way to bring me into harmony with the other singers than this unintended slight. The experience only added to my already considerable fear of speaking out in public.

The Essence of My Work

Yet, as my career progressed, circumstances forced me to face my fears. Life kept challenging me until finally I was able to experience the pleasure of using my voice. Today I write, speak, and otherwise publicly share my passion with equanimity. How strange life is! It so often happens that, as youngsters, we are wounded in the very area where, as adults, we will be asked to excel.

No matter how many people tell you not to speak or sing or otherwise expose a weak area, I encourage you to persist in following your dreams. Where you see your greatest obstacles, there also you'll find your highest potential and your greatest opportunity to experience the joy of learning.

As I struggled through the fourth grade, terribly embarrassed by my failure to read and write, I desperately needed someone to believe in me, take special interest in me, and help me in practical ways.

That's why, through this book, I'm going to introduce you to ideas and practices that can help you to love yourself, believe in yourself, and alleviate whatever is blocking your progress. When this happens, your natural genius will reappear—perhaps tentatively at first, and then with increasing confidence. Its qualities of curiosity, playfulness, creativity, and joy will then become yours to delight in.

You'll begin to live and learn in a deeply creative way. You'll enjoy what you do and become skilled at it. You'll find that it can be fun to learn. There will be a new fire in your life, and everything will become warmer and brighter in its light. Your body wisdom will be activated, your intellect will return to its rightful (subservient) place, you'll connect with your innate intelligence, and your heart will be open. You'll find out in a deep, experiential way who you really are.

Encouraging you in this movement toward authenticity is the essence of my work. I believe that we all have a special gift to give to our community, and that—when we express this gift—there is less misunderstanding, less destructive competition, and more compassion and cooperation. Out of facing the dragon of any pain, loss, or wounding that may occur in life, it's possible to feel our fire . . . to find our mission and turn it into a passion. Then living, playing, and learning become the great pleasures they were always meant to be.

Chapter Two

Learning Just for the Pleasure of It

Exquisite
(Past participle of Latin *exquirere*, to search out, to seek)

Grounded by physicality and the senses
Accompanied by delight and feeling
Showing subtle understanding
Pleasing through beauty
Precious and rare
Illuminating
Masterful
Ingenious
Excellent
Flawless
Yielding
Esoteric
Skilled
Vibrant
Delicate
The juice
The ecstasy
beyond the pain
The yes in yesness

—Paul and Gail Dennison

"I don't know why movement works, but it helps us *get at* the problem," my friend and colleague, Dr. Richard Sowby, confided to me one afternoon.

Dr. Sowby, a developmental optometrist, shared office space with me at the Burbank location of my Valley Remedial Group Learning Centers. We were in the Lion's Club together, and often exchanged our views on children's learning as we drove to and from meetings. It was the early 1970s, and I was working as a remedial reading specialist with people of all ages.

Dick and I became good friends. I referred children with vision problems to him, and he sent me children who were having challenges in school. My friend was innovative; for several years he had been including the walking of a balance beam and other physical components in his visual therapy practice. As an educator, I was always fascinated by his stories of children's visual and related academic improvements and ideas about perceptual abilities.

Dick Sowby sometimes invited me to observe his work with clients, and I was highly influenced by his creative approach. One weekend he held an in-service on vision training for his staff and invited me to attend. I didn't understand the terminology used, but I saw the interesting ways that Dick used movement to help people develop their visual skills. He included many contralateral activities, such as hitting a ball on a string with one hand while hopping forward on the opposite foot.

Around this time, Dick Sowby introduced me to his longtime friend and colleague Jerry Getman, and the three of us went to lunch together. I was fascinated to hear Dr. Getman's stories of clients, and impressed by his understanding of the relationship between the eyes, hands, and brain. It suddenly dawned on me that this man was the renowned G. N. Getman, O.D., from whose book, *How to Develop Your Child's Intelligence*, I had learned the bilateral drawing activity that I had been using in my remedial work. (This bilateral drawing would later inspire a Brain Gym activity known as the Double Doodle.)

Soon after my in-service with Dick Sowby, I began to adapt (without use of lenses, prisms, or other optometric equipment) some of his activities for use with my own students. I anticipated that adding movement to my program would be useful to learners. Yet, within weeks of beginning the new movement program, I was dumbfounded by the changes I saw. Ten-year-old Robert was suddenly reading more fluently, and no longer pointing at each word with his finger. Jennifer, age seven and previously unable to hold a pencil correctly, was writing on the line and no longer making letter reversals. Marshall, age nine, wrote all his spelling words, then proofread and corrected his errors on his own. I could clearly see that my students, who did such activities as Lazy 8s, bilateral drawing, and the Cross Crawl, as well as rebounding or walking a balance beam, were approaching their academic assignments with a new interest. In fact, they seemed like different children.

I heard a new delight in the voices of the parents when they picked up their kids. "I don't know what you're doing with Sam," one father told me. "He could never catch the ball—never wanted to play. Now he can't wait to play catch with me on the front lawn almost every evening."

Another dad told me that his son was now getting ready for school on time, and even brushing his teeth, without being asked. Dad was feeling happy that he no longer had to nag his child all the time.

Yet another parent confided to me, "I just have to say it's six o'clock and Brian goes to do his homework. There's no more fighting about it."

Not only children but adult clients, too, reported huge shifts taking place, not just in their ability to read, write, do spelling and math, and learn but also at work, in their personal lives, and in their level of energy—their ability to relax, concentrate, and communicate. What I saw happening for these people was a shift beneath the level of effort—a change in their ability to "own their own movements" and to take positive, personal action from a place of intrinsic motivation and curiosity.

How Children Actually Learn to Read

Adding movement to my teaching repertoire opened my eyes to other academic connections, as well. For my Ph.D. dissertation, I had completed a research study with first graders that was focused on the relationship between children's ability to think without speaking aloud and their ability to master beginning reading.

Most children think out loud with overt speech until they're about five to seven years old—about the same age that reading is introduced in the school curriculum. At around this time, they begin to acquire the ability to think silently (which ability is also known as silent speech or covert speech). This is a developmental skill, meaning that most children learn it without being taught. One day they're talking aloud as they work and play; the next they're quietly exploring.

My research involved a short-term memory/concentration game in which the children had to remember and match cards printed with pictures of objects. Some of the names of these objects didn't rhyme (like ball, dog, and fish) and could be easily remembered by the picture clues alone, while some of the names (like cat, hat, and rat) rhymed, as well. The purpose of this game was to infer which children were developing silent speech (known as "covert thinking") and which were not.

My thesis was that, if a child's hearing of the similar rhyming words undermined his ability to match those words with the corresponding pictures, the child was already thinking silently and the linguistic clue was confusing his memory of the word. If the child did equally well with either set of cards, we could conclude that, even though the names rhymed, he was still using only the picture clues.

Working one on one with the youngsters, I deepened my understanding of the importance of both auditory and visual skills to learn sound-and-symbol correspondences in beginning reading. I saw how some children learn better through sight recognition of words— by identifying their letters and word shapes—and some prefer to learn through the sounds and rhythms of words—their phonetic analysis. Ultimately, a good reader needs both skills.

At the time, my primary interest was the improvement of reading skills. Through my research, I began to realize that a person's reading process—how he engages his body, eyes, and ears with the printed page—could affect not only his level of visual stress but even his ability to concentrate, to think and remember, to organize information, or to communicate with others. I further realized that a person who lacked certain physical skills of reading might experience specific muscular tensions—in the neck, shoulders, or hips, for example—that could affect the blood sugar level, the autoimmune system, and even lifelong health.

I began to feel strongly that to teach beginning reading is to teach much more than word recognition and listening skills—it is to teach beginning visual skills, and even to teach basic life skills pertaining to health and well-being.

Reading is not merely about the identification of words and letters. I define it as an active rewriting of the text in which the reader simultaneously decodes the words and hears herself telling the story. Reading is an educated guessing game in which the mind anticipates what will happen, yet is—at the same time—waiting to see whether the guess will be supported. The more the reader's eyes, ears, movement, and sense of touch are relaxed and coordinated, the more she can scan for information to support her guess. Attention is the reader's ability to know where she's going, so that her senses can support her journey instead of distracting her from it.

Yet good reading can't happen without a whole set of physical abilities, such as:

- binocularity (using both eyes together in the visual midfield)
- convergence (moving both eyes together to see something that's nearby)
- tracking (moving both eyes together to cross the visual/auditory/ kinesthetic midline for reading from left to right)
- sustained attention and concentration
- directionality and motor planning
- hearing and matching graphemes (symbols) and phonemes (speech sounds)
- thinking (silent speech)
- memory of sounds and shapes
- the visualization of letter patterns and word shapes
- eye-hand coordination
- timing, rhythm, and phrasing of speech patterns

What I was discovering through my research was that it isn't just the mental skills, but also the physical abilities that we take for granted, that prepare us to be good readers.

Stu and the Elephant: We Can't Read Until We Can Listen

Stu was one of my more challenging clients. As a building contractor, he had used his sense of visual aesthetics to amass a small fortune, even though he had never learned to read beyond the first-grade level. One of Stu's greatest desires was to read to his six-year-old grandson, Devon. As an adult nonreader, he was able, with some difficulty, to recognize words by sight, yet he didn't discriminate speech sounds as he read or understand that he needed to listen and speak simultaneously as he responded to symbols. He could read "hat"; however he didn't hear the difference between this word and the word "mat." This ability to "hear" and use sound to help us discriminate words as we read is a function of the temporal lobes, which is why this part of the brain is important in learning how to read and spell.

Watching Stu stare at the letters on the page, I realized that he was so visually stressed that he couldn't hear or move at the same time that he looked. His large neck and shoulder muscles inhibited his ability to turn his head left and right; in another context one might have seen him as "bullheaded" or overfocused. I wondered if there was a connection between head-turning skills and the ability to listen.

So I taught Stu how to do a Lazy 8—tracing a large 8 on its side with first one hand and then the other, the eyes following the hand at a slow, relaxed pace. Although this movement visibly relaxed Stu's eyes, it didn't seem to affect his reading. Stu's deep dedication and longing to make this work stirred me to search for new answers.

In the middle of the night, I would sometimes think about my students and ponder how to help them. One night I awoke with a middle-of-the-night hunch. I knew that readers often tense their throat and neck muscles when they subvocalize the words as if saying them. I now realized that Stu's inability to listen, remember, and read definitely had something to do with the tension in his neck and the way that tension was affecting his ability to turn his head. I imagined doing the Lazy 8 in a new way—moving the whole body while keeping the neck muscles still. (Years later, when Gail and I wrote *Brain Gym: Simple Activities for Whole-Brain Learning*, we would call this new movement "The Elephant.")

When I next saw Stu, I asked him to turn his head, which he could hardly manage. I then shared with him my new movement discovery, and we did it together. Afterward, Stu was dumbfounded to realize that he could turn his head more easily and was now able to focus on words in the book without tightening his neck. Suddenly he was able to see, hear, think, and remember, all at the same time. The words on the page began to make sense to him.

Once he was able to see the sound and symbol correspondences, Stu quickly learned to read. Now, when he read to his grandson, Devon would teach him words and he would help Devon with words that were beyond his vocabulary. Instead of pretending to read as he had previously done, he now had the exquisite joy of sharing the learning process with his grandson. And when he brought Devon in to meet me, I had the joy of seeing them do the movements and hearing them read and laugh together.

Stu's commitment to learning had a profound impact on his own life as well as that of his grandson, and his vulnerability and willingness to explore his process also had a deep impact on *my* life. Because of his longing to read and my eagerness to explore all avenues to help him, I, too, improved my head turning, listening abilities, and reading skills. And I would soon realize that, thanks to Stu, I'd made a breakthrough discovery: that a major physical cause of reading disability is tense neck muscles, and—further—that, once the physical stress is released, the mental act of learning can be quickly mastered.

When I opened myself to inspiration regarding a student, as I had for Stu, an answer would usually come to me in the form of some new idea about what to do. Over the next few years, an intriguing phenomenon took place: clients with the same needs would come to me in waves, which meant that I always had enough people with whom to explore and perfect a particular movement. It seemed that whenever I felt confident that I'd discovered a key movement that unlocked the answers to a specific learning difficulty, a client would appear for whom the established movement didn't work at all. I would then renew my search for a way to support the new client.

Graphemes and Phonemes

I now experienced what I had previously been taught in theory: that reading is a complex linguistic process. That is to say, reading is about language.

New readers know language as a spoken communication, involving speech and listening. Learning to read involves "listening" to one's own voice speak an auditory (phonological) code that has been written down as visual symbols. These symbols, called graphemes, must be first recognized visually and then processed auditorally as phonemes (speech sounds).

For reading perception and mastery of the code, successful physical processing of sound-symbol correspondences is a necessary preliminary. The code is phonological regardless of whether one approaches it as a "look-say" (sight-word) process or from phonetic analysis. To put it more simply, writing is talk written down, and reading is listening to that talk through a visual code.

Once integrated, reading becomes more of a visual skill (as in speed-reading) and attention to the auditory code is minimal. Research shows that the temporal lobe (which among its other functions processes auditory information) fires less as we mature in our reading skills.

Paradoxically, in order to read we need to learn to listen, so that we can learn the letter sounds—the auditory code—only to eventually, as mature readers, let go of the code and read visually.

The Physical Skills of Learning

In those days, brain research was evolving rapidly. There was much excitement regarding hemispheric specialization in the brain and about our ability to identify specific neural locations that govern specific behaviors. The prevailing view was that the brain was the seat of the intellect and that, as far as learning was concerned, the rest of the body was pretty much irrelevant. In fact, one of my college professors, a renowned author of reading textbooks or "basal readers," taught emphatically that, "Reading is a mental act. It has nothing to do with the body!" My experience told me otherwise.

I recall spending a day at a local school and seeing my professor's viewpoint manifested in its full regalia. Movement in the classroom was kept strictly in check, and many students were uncomfortably confined in chairs too big or too small for them. The children received instruction that was primarily verbal, and were required to spew this back in undigested form—a process supposedly arrived at by deductive reasoning, but closer to rote memorization and regurgitation to please the teacher.

In this way, not only was learning restricted to the brain but it was also limited to just one part of the brain: the left hemisphere, which is associated with linear, coded, step-by-step sequences and analysis— the breaking down of information into small units.

I saw this then, and still see it today, as evidence of a terribly misguided view of learning. The assessment of classroom achievement usually depends on tests that measure the acquisition of information. In such tests the body may appear to be superfluous, but it plays an intrinsic part in the learning process, for real learning must *always* involve movement and concrete experiences. Until we are building, organizing, and creating something with our eyes, ears, and hands working in concert, no thinking or learning has actually taken place.

Reading a book is as much a physical act as it is a mental activity. As such, it can be pleasurable when the body is engaged and terribly stressful when it's not. When the physical skills of learning have been mastered, the mental part can take care of itself.

We can easily observe a parallel process when we watch a child learning a physical activity such as riding a bike. She begins by balancing herself over the bike, then coordinating her feet on the pedals while exploring the steering and developing a reflex movement of the brake.

It's somehow more difficult to observe the physical proficiency involved in reading, working at a computer, communicating with a partner, or memorizing historical facts. Yet these activities all involve such physical skills as coordinating the body for sitting, focusing and moving the eyes; coordinating the hands; or activating the ears for listening, thought, or speech.

Physical movement stimulates brain function. Toddlers, as they learn to walk, speak, and socialize, require very little teaching. Amazingly, by the age of three most children have mastered a new language as well as all the nuances of hand and facial gestures and the social interactions that provide the language context. They've also learned to walk, run, and balance themselves in gravity. And they learn all this through movement and play. If children are allowed to explore, their learning is enjoyable, and the same goes for grownups. Anyone of any age can use a natural movement process to learn more easily. Sure, we all fall down sometimes. Yet most often we can't wait to take another risk in order to keep learning.

Important Connections along My Way

In 1977 I had the privilege of meeting Dr. Richard A. Tyler, a kinesiologist who was the father of two of the students at my learning center in Studio City. Dr. Tyler shared with me several techniques from a remarkable system he was studying with a Dr. George Goodheart from Michigan, called Applied Kinesiology—a system of tests and processes that studies various movements of the muscular system with the aim of improved well-being and physical comfort.

I was intrigued by the possible applications of this work to the perceptual training I was undertaking with my reading students. Richard Tyler and I would later work together to compile data regarding the relationship of movement to neurological integration and reading achievement.

In 1979, in order to learn more about Applied Kinesiology, I enrolled in a Touch for Health course in Pasadena, where I explored in greater depth the relationship of wellness to muscle response, meridian energies, and lymphatic massage. I was deepening my own physical skills of learning.

It was in that year that I first met John F. Thie, D.C., author of the Applied Kinesiology textbook *Touch for Health: A Practical Guide to*

Natural Health with Acupressure Touch. John was an extraordinary pioneer in the field of wellness—a giant of a man and a master teacher. His vision was to make self-help techniques available to the lay public to enhance living, loving, and learning. It was he who encouraged me to develop my work and share it with the world, and at John's inspiration I published two articles in *In Touch*, the journal of the Touch for Health Foundation.

John and his wife, Carrie, soon became my dear friends and mentors, and remained so through the years. One of John's last acts of kindness was to write an endorsement of this book. Not long after, Gail and I were immeasurably saddened to learn of his death.

Gail and the Birth of Brain Gym

In July of 1981 I was invited to speak at the Touch for Health Annual Meeting in San Diego, where I had the opportunity to address more than three hundred leaders in Applied Kinesiology who had assembled there from around the world.

Here I introduced my first book, *Switching On: The Whole-Brain Answer to Dyslexia*. In the audience that magical summer evening was a young woman—a dancer, artist, and movement teacher—who would soon capture my heart and become my life partner.

My cocreator, mentor, and spouse, Gail Dennison, has taught me how to see, laugh, play, and be in community. Her love of nature, music, and poetry has been an inspiration to me and to all of our students. Gail and I have co-taught more than five hundred courses, and have coauthored fifteen books and manuals on Educational Kinesiology and natural vision. We love to work together, whether we're writing stories, exploring movement sequences, or designing new programs. Our collaboration represents the joy of the meeting of two unique minds and souls as one—a whole that is much more than the sum of its parts. I believe it is Gail's gift for seeing and creating systems that has helped to make "Brain Gym" a household term around the world.

Into the late 1980s, Gail and I continued developing the movements and adding new ones. We drew inspiration from dance, long distance running, various movement programs, Applied Kinesiology,

Developmental Optometry, and our own inventiveness. More and more, we realized the value of this particular collection of movements that so effectively facilitate learning, enhance the enjoyment of daily life, and help individuals attain more of their potential.

As we traveled and taught together throughout Europe, Canada, Australia, New Zealand, and the United States, Gail's and my greatest joy, beginning in the early 1980s, was to teach together an in-depth process we called Educational Kinesiology: Seven Dimensions of Intelligence. At that time we often stayed over in one location for a few days after teaching a course, to give private consultations. We would end a session by suggesting a few movements from our repertoire as homework.

One afternoon we had the good fortune to work with a seven-year-old boy, Danny, who had cerebral palsy. During the session, Danny improved his hand-eye coordination with his right, previously shortened and "useless," arm, which through muscle-relaxing activities now appeared the same length as his left. We played catch with a crumpled paper "ball" and asked Danny to write his name and draw a picture. By the end of the session, Danny's eyes had come to life and he read fluently for the first time. His mother listened with tears streaming down her face. We laughed and chatted with Danny, confident in our good rapport, for we had become pals.

Then I mentioned homework, and Danny promptly got up and left the room, not to return.

It was at this moment that Gail and I, realizing that our movements deserved a more playful and appealing name, coined the term "homeplay."

In the context of the educational system of the '70s and '80s that referred to learning challenges as "minimal brain dysfunction," and perhaps anticipating the '90s and "the decade of the brain," and also given my understanding of the relationship between the brain and the rest of the body, the name "Brain Gym" came to me. Gail and I both immediately liked the name. "Brain Gym" clearly speaks of what our work is all about: bringing together the thinking intelligence and the coordination of the body.

An Experience of Brain Gym

What is Brain Gym, and how can it guide a person to the pleasure of learning? Neuroscience tells us that all learning involves movement, and Brain Gym is about learning through movement. As my friend Dr. Carla Hannaford explains in her introduction to this book, Brain Gym is a movement-based system in which enjoyable, easy-to-do physical activities are used to enhance the ability to learn, process information, and respond to the world around us in a pleasurable, loving, and effective way.

You can experience for yourself this increase in pleasure, even as you read this book. From now on I'll be describing key, progressive Brain Gym movements as we go along, and I invite you to choose one or more of them to do before each reading session.

Lazy 8s

A Lazy 8 forms one of the most mysterious symbols in the universe: the infinity sign. Decades ago, *National Geographic* published photographs showing a time-lapse study of the sun, taken over the course of a year, in which the sun appeared to be moving along the trajectory of an infinity sign. Evidently the whole universe moves in this elliptical orbit, turning and turning in this "Lazy 8" orbit shape.

Following this horizontal motion across the body's vertical midline is a natural and elegant movement for us, as it follows the innate diagonal motions of the four limbs. In Edu-K, the Lazy 8 naturally defines distinct left and right visual fields, as well as the midpoint between them. It invites the development of the two eyes' cooperation, bringing our focus to the center of our experience. It also encourages the minute, automatic saccadic motions that relax our visual system, giving it relief from its commonly entrained mode of pointing at stationary objects.

Before we get into the Lazy 8s activity, let's do a pre-activity.

Take a moment to notice how your eyes feel just resting on this page and taking in information. Do they feel relaxed and comfortable, or are they tense? How does your neck feel? How quickly and easily are you reading?

Now cup one hand and cover one eye. Notice how the other (open) eye rests on the page. How clearly can you see the letters and words? Repeat this with the other eye.

Now slowly trace the Lazy 8 three times with the tip of your left index finger, then with your right index finger, then with both together. Notice any differences as you cover your eyes, one at a time, and look again at the page. Finally, look once more at the page with both eyes open.

Like many people who do the Lazy 8s activity, you may notice an immediate relaxation of your eyes, improved comprehension, greater reading speed, or a sense of pleasure of which you might not previously have been aware. It is small, sweet pleasures like this that guide us as infants to be exploratory learners, curious about our senses and about what they tell us of the world and our relationship to it. I encourage you to pause to do some Lazy 8s any time your eyes feel tired or stressed. Like the Lazy 8s, each Brain Gym movement offers a way to bring our sensory experience to the learning process.

Drawing Out Learning from Within

The word "education" comes from the Latin *educere*, meaning "to lead forth"; kinesiology is the study of muscles and movement. Brain Gym is the entryway to a burgeoning field of endeavor called Educational Kinesiology, or the drawing out of learning through the study of movement.

Movement and learning go together; we can't really have one without the other. Movement-based learning is truly nourishment for the brain, and the joy we feel at the moment of learning something new—making it our own through movement—will be ours for life. The kind of learning I'm talking about is natural, authentic learning that lasts, not just a process of memorizing information that will be forgotten tomorrow. This true learning is based on patterns and rhythms that we hear, see, or feel as we move and interact with our environment.

As humans, we naturally seek a single, organizing rhythm, whether it be—during infancy—the mother's heartbeat, her walking rhythm, an exchange of voices, or the sounds of nature, or—later—the pace of words as we read, think, or write, or our own rhythm as we go about our daily activities. At any given point in time, our senses are bombarded with possible points of focus. We find the ground for new learning when we resonate with one distinct object of focus and tune out distractions. This dynamic is the crux of an exquisite natural system: the learning process.

Parents and educators often construct a playful situation, through toys or sounds, to hold a child's attention. How do we, as adults, focus our own attention? Is attention merely part of our survival system, or is it something so integral to life that it can emerge naturally? Neuroscience tells us that both kinds of attention exist.

In early childhood, we develop two primary ways of paying attention. I call the first one *purposeful attention*, a state that occurs when we're in equilibrium—relaxed in the moment and simply being. We reach this state through our resonant connection with what nurtures us, for this connection invites sustained attention and a movement forward toward the things that attract us. The other way of paying attention is one I call *reactive attention*, a state that manifests "trying" and effortful behavior. We reach this state through our fight-or-flight response to any stimulus that throws us off balance, resulting in an urgent movement away from anything that frightens or upsets us. As we explore our world, intense or unusual stimuli (such as loud noises or bright lights) or even an absence of stimuli can distract us from purposeful attention and from the focus that arises from playful interaction with the environment.

Purposeful attention that is focused in an active search for structure is stimulated by our frontal lobes and brings us integration, helping us to learn and organize new information in a useful way. Reactive attention that derives from fear, strain, anger, or distraction is actually a search for safety, stimulated by the brain stem. This kind of attention is hard-wired in us for survival, and when we fall into it we stay in reactive patterns, unable to access new learning.

Children are sometimes described as inattentive or "attention-deficit," yet the fact is that children in a waking state are always paying attention to something. When we watch youngsters at play, we can see what natural learners they are. Their curiosity impels them to sustain a particular point of focus—with both their attention and their whole body.

So how can we, as parents and educators, support a child in finding out how to use this natural ability? At certain times, when a child is already in a state of purposeful attention, we need to be such good observers that we can discover what is already drawing the child's attention and join him there. For example, when he pulls pots and lids from a kitchen cupboard we may kneel beside him to explore the different properties of his objects of interest. Or we may invite the child to join us in a focus that we deem significant, such as reading a storybook or putting away toys. At other times a child may be in a clear state of reactive attention—perhaps in an overtired state and pitching a fit for a desired object on a supermarket shelf. Such trying times may be resolved only by the sweet release of a nap in the car seat on the way home. In any case, as we support children in discovering how to restore their physical and emotional balance when they feel tense or distracted, we can help them return to a positive search for structure.

As you can see, reactive attention leads to survival-based learning, and the difference between survival-based learning and natural, creative learning is vast. To learn for the sake of survival, we must have our attention pulled away from what actually interests us. We then move into a fight-or-flight stance so that we can overfocus on what someone else has decided is important for us. When the Brain Gym movements are part of our learning experience, we're less likely to learn through stress-based associations and more likely to discover our purposeful attention and natural, exploratory learning process.

The way we look at words, listen to ourselves think, and move as we read can set an easy pleasing rhythm for us or a halting, analytical one—and there may be a time and place for each. The important thing is this: are we able to return to the joyous and restorative rhythms of movement or do we become stuck in stressful and unbalanced behaviors, such as allowing the pleasing rhythm to become a rote singsong or the careful decoding to devolve into a discordant fragmentation? The Brain Gym activities can help us to restore a natural, more integrated, learning rhythm.

How the Body's Three Dimensions Support Learning

When we do Brain Gym activities, we reconnect with our concrete, three-dimensional experience. From my studies in the field of brain research, I hypothesize that Brain Gym works by establishing neural learning pathways in the three-dimensional body.

Gail and I describe the first pathway through which we learn as being related to the back-to-front neuropathways and associated back-to-front movements of the body, a system called the Focus Dimension. This system refers to signals coming to and from the brain stem, or old brain, and the frontal lobe—the newest part of the cerebral cortex. During the development of this level of intelligence, we learn to move toward or away from a stimulus, fine-tuning the muscle proprioception that tracks our movements in space and gives us a sense of boundaries. This is our kinesthetic, physical intelligence, and it provides the spatial qualities of *whereness*—the sense of *Where am I and where am I going?* Without an intrinsic knowledge of safety in the space where we are, we have no other intelligence available to us.

The next learning pathway that Gail and I identify in our work is related to the top-to-bottom brain system and associated movements of the upper and lower body, called the Centering Dimension, which refers to signals put forth by the vestibular system that help us discover balance and our relationship to gravity. Objects, when endowed by the midbrain with emotional content, take on new meaning, and we thereby develop a relationship with them. In any moment that we experience balance, we are automatically centered and can coordinate the two sides of the body. The Centering Dimension encourages coordination of the eyes, hands, and body movements and the sense of organization, as well as the qualities of connection and belonging. As we begin to sense our center of balance, we ask the question *Where is it* (i.e., any external focus) *in relationship to my body?*

The third pathway through which we learn is related to the movement between the left and right cerebral hemispheres and all associated movement between the left and right eyes, ears, and sides of the body. This system is called the Laterality Dimension, and refers to the neocortex or new brain, where symbolic language is processed so that spoken or written communication can take place. It is through this pathway that our concrete experiences can be coded into language. Language is a remarkable gift of our humanness: we can encode any experience (store it as a symbol, as in writing) and then later decode it (from the symbol back to the meaning, as in reading). We can return to this experience years later, reflecting on its meaning to us today, and even share it with others in conversation. The development of the two interrelating cerebral hemispheres that make up the neocortex helps us to identify qualities of *whatness: What is it?* and *What do I mean to say about it?*

When these three dimensions develop naturally, the midbrain, housing the emotional centers, connects our automatic physical movement (the reflexes of the old brain) to the conscious, verbal directives of the new brain. Learning is once again imbued with feeling and restored to the natural process it was meant to be.

When reading instruction is built upon this experiential base, children easily and naturally seek out symbolic language as a way to further explore what is real to them. The goal of reading instruction need not be that children "learn to read." Rather, it should be that children "read to learn."

Five Principles of Learning

The Brain Gym® work is based upon the premise that, when learning engages the sensory system rather than compromising it, curious, caring, and respectful behavior is a natural outcome. To elaborate, we see that dynamic learning emerges from the student's engagement of three learning dimensions.

We understand the Focus Dimension as the bridge between the brain stem, the oldest area of the brain and the part that keeps us safe and holds our most ingrained survival habits and patterns of movement, and the prefrontal cortex, the newest and most risk-taking area of the brain and the part from which our noticing, intention, and possibility thinking arise. This "bridge" of the Focus Dimension enables us to take action from responsible choice and to access our most intelligent social responses.

We see the Centering Dimension as the bridge between the emotional midbrain, which pulls us into the fight-or-flight reflex of fear, anxiety, or anger, and the rational cerebral cortex, which helps us to defuse those reactions so that our higher instincts of love, forgiveness, and compassion can emerge and we can live in relationship. Moment to moment, this dimension helps us to maintain equilibrium.

We designate the Laterality Dimension as the connecting bridge of the left and right cerebral hemispheres, joining our skills of distinction and detailed analysis with those of context and synthesis, and supporting eye movement for visual skills; head turning for auditory skills; and the skills of coordination and directionality for ease in academics, sports, and other activities.

From this fundamental understanding of neural function, we've established the following five learning principles as central to the Brain Gym work:

Draw Out: Intelligence Is Inborn
Focus: Attention Follows Intention
Notice: We Learn What We Actively Experience
Move to Learn: Growth Is a Search for Balance, Imbalance a Search for Growth
Interconnect: Each of Us Is Affected by Every Other

Applying the Five Principles

Draw Out: Intelligence Is Inborn   The process of learning through movement begins in infancy with the acquisition of developmental skills and congruent sensory functioning as a basis for healthy focus and attention. This congruency exists on a continuum, and it is dynamic rather than static; each new goal invites the emergence of associated movement abilities. As movement educators, we respect and attend to this natural process for ourselves as well as our students, creating a space for moving and learning with a sense of safety and curiosity.

Focus: Attention Follows Intention   Ideally, teachers engage students at their levels of interest and ability and support the students' growth by helping them cultivate a learning context based on their needs and self-selected goals.

Notice: We Learn What We Actively Experience   New learning is anchored by self-observation and discovery. The conscientious teacher encourages students to notice what has been truly learned and what has not yet been learned and integrated into function.

Move to Learn: Growth Is a Search for Balance, Imbalance a Search for Growth   As learning challenges arise, we seek movement to provide equilibrium. The proficient educator offers movement and performance skills that correlate with successful accomplishment of the student's goal, including a Brain Gym® movement menu that gives access to the balance needed for successful functioning. As students do the movements to attain each new skill level, they naturally discover their own sense of body congruency.

Interconnect: Each of Us Is Affected by Every Other   A sense of exploration and play keeps the action lively. When learning is offered in a collaborative, community-based style, one in which learners are encouraged by each other's explorations and discoveries, the students find ways to generalize the learning to everyday life situations. And when students learn through cooperation in this way, it means that everyone wins.

Play and the Role of the Heart in Embodied Learning

In the animal kingdom, play is the natural ability to interact sportingly with the environment or relate lightheartedly with another living being. In humans, it's an essential component of what we know as love. Brain Gym represents an invitation to play and to be more fully in one's body without fear of failure. In essence, it activates the loving heart space that is so essential to an infant's earliest building of movement patterns. To an infant, movement and learning are one. Brain Gym completes learning by bringing back to education the physical aspect of play, so often overlooked or taken for granted, that is such an indispensable element of both learning and life.

When we move and play we're naturally curious, exploring experiences with the relaxed rhythm of the heart as a backdrop for our movement. Watching children at play, we see the intrinsic relationship of movement and learning. In our modern world, we have been strangely reluctant to admit play into the classroom or workplace. And yet, without the ardor and enthusiasm of play, we can become dry and impotent. What is more, our ability to learn, grow, and adapt to our environment becomes severely compromised.

Doing the Brain Gym movements not only builds and reinforces effective neural connections and pathways; it relaxes us and activates centralization and focus along the midline. It also opens the heart, inviting us to interact. When the mind, body, and heart are active and integrated, people blossom. They learn easily, they become creative, they are compassionate and friendly, and most importantly they find meaning in their lives and are happy. I'll always remember the young woman who approached me in a workshop and said, "Dr. Dennison, thank you for teaching me this work. I use it with my husband and children. It's helped us come together as a family. For us, Brain Gym is another way to say, 'I love you.'"

In recent years, scientific research has confirmed that the heart is an integral part of the intelligence. Scientists are beginning to prove what some nonscientists never felt needed proving: namely, that the heart is not just an organ for pumping blood. I refer to the heart's intelligence as the core of our "body wisdom." The body has a mind of its own, and this mind communicates with the brain. In fact, according to Paul

Pearsall, more messages flow from the heart to the brain than the other way around. Moreover, evidence is appearing that the heart has a large electromagnetic field; thus, by way of our hearts, we are all influencing one another in invisible ways.

As we'll see in later chapters, in our modern society, people too often stand "beside themselves," unable to access the "yes" of the body's intelligence. We must bring the *body* back into our homes, classrooms, and places of work. We must reinstate the *heart* as being central to all that we do. With the heart open and connected, we're more effective and organized in all aspects of our lives, and more joyful. We get better results with less effort.

If the 1990s were the decade of the brain, the 2000s must be ushering in at least a whole century of the heart. And if you believe, as I do, that human relationships are more important than money and technology, then the opening of the heart becomes essential. After all, it's the "brain" of the heart that gives us empathy and compassion—two forms of emotional connection that serve as the foundation of joyful human interactions.

Taking More First Steps for Yourself

I'd now like to share with you more about how Brain Gym's repertoire of movements can support you in deepening your experience of your own life.

We might liken true learning to a before-and-after photography sequence. Somewhat like the makeover photos you might see in a magazine, this work helps people notice how they perform a skill—for example, read a paragraph—and then notice how things feel and seem to them after the intervention of a few Brain Gym movements. As we engage and interact in the learning process, gathering new skills as we gather experience, we notice what has worked to produce positive change.

"Balancing," a term to which we in Educational Kinesiology gave a new meaning, refers to the entire Brain Gym process, including having a specific goal for each session; performing the action you're intending to improve (or some activity symbolic of same); experiencing the joy of movement; and noticing what works for you. Balancing is not something that we do once and then we're "fixed." Just like tightrope walkers, we continually go in and out of balance.

In the way that small children naturally learn through a dynamic continuum of balance, imbalance, and movement, the Brain Gym activities stimulate the brain in specific ways that connect the individual with that same easy, pleasurable learning. Being balanced means that we're always able to return to equilibrium. After being out of balance, we often feel a sense of exhilaration when we rediscover our center.

What follows will be like the Lazy 8s you learned earlier in this chapter: a brief process that will give you a physical, whole-body experience of Brain Gym . . . a personal glimpse of what Brain Gym can do.

Hook-ups

As a pre-activity, close your eyes and scan your body. How are you feeling? Are you tense, relaxed, or somewhere in between? Is anything causing you anxiety? How strong and clear do you feel? What do you notice about your heart? When you think of other people in your life, how does your heart feel then?

When you've done this, do the following Brain Gym movement.

The Hook-ups activities reactivate our balance-related muscles and sense of equilibrium, relaxing tensions and reconnecting us to that heart space where we can feel the joy of learning.

Cross your left ankle over your right. Next, extend your arms and cross your left wrist over your right; then interlace your fingers and draw your hands up toward your chest. Hold this position for one minute, breathing comfortably, with your eyes closed and the tip of your tongue resting on the roof of your mouth.

Now uncross your ankles and place both feet on the floor. Put your fingertips together at chest height and breathe deeply for another minute, again closing your eyes to gain a full experience of relaxation.

Finally, repeat the scanning you did in the pre-activity. How do you feel now? Is your mind clearer? Are you more relaxed? Is anything still bothering you? What do you now notice about your heart? If you had to perform a complex task, would you do it better now than before you did the Hook-ups?

As you continue through these pages, you'll begin to appreciate the fact that simple movements of this kind can have a huge impact on your life. It takes the brain only seconds to learn something new, and people who do Brain Gym movements say that the addition of even just a few minutes a day of these simple activities—at home, at work, or in a classroom—makes an enormous difference in how they learn, feel, think, remember, and go about their daily lives.

The Brain Gym movements have been designed to activate various cognitive functions, including communication, organization, and comprehension. The movements are effective because they activate the brain in specific ways that ready us for learning. Brain Gym strengthens the physical skills involved in the learning process, and when we feel physically prepared to meet the day, the mental aspect of our learning comes more easily.

An Invitation

This book is an invitation to you to use the techniques of Brain Gym, as outlined above and in the following chapters, to integrate your mind, body, and heart so that you can express more of your magnificence.

What would it mean for you to manifest your full potential? Only you can discover this. For me, it means to walk joyfully on this earth in the service of a higher purpose. It means to work creatively, to have the ability to give and receive love, and to know more deeply than ever before who I am and what I'm here to do. All this amounts to the sweet pleasure of living life to the fullest.

I believe that our lives can be transformed in each moment that we make the shift from a fragmented to a more integrated state, which we do by learning to balance our mind, open our heart, and activate our body. In the fragmented state, we operate at a fraction of our abilities. Once we release the blocks to our own integration, we discover an energy and creativity we never imagined possible.

Exactly how this happens will vary from one individual to another. Perhaps your work will become immensely rewarding, both financially and emotionally. Relationships that have been dysfunctional for years may become sources of extraordinary fulfillment. You may discover that your body, once you bring it back into the equation, has a wonderful ability to heal itself.

Though we all express our higher potential in different ways, I believe that people have two fundamentals in common. First, everyone has a purpose. When we have a deep sense of who we are and why we're on this planet, life soars. It's a wonderful feeling to know that we matter in a cosmic way—that we're in this world for a reason bigger than our individual needs and ambitions. Secondly, life is supposed to be joyful. We weren't meant to live a stress-filled, anxious life punctuated by brief moments of relaxation and happiness. We're supposed to wake up every morning thrilled to be alive and appreciative of every instant of our existence. Once we find ourself moving wholeheartedly toward a goal, a tremendous amount of power, from both without and within, makes itself available to us.

Brain Gym is grounded in the premise that movement is life. As we learn to move more fully, we experience more of the joy of being fully alive. We then offer a precious gift to those around us, by bringing joy into every facet of our life: family, work, school, and play. Joyful people are appreciative, loving, confident, humble, patient, supportive, kind, and generous . . . When we *are* these qualities, then we get to *have* everything we've ever desired.

"Fight, Love, Give"

Life is not about having things and looking good; it's about doing and being. The joy of life is in the moving and living of it. It's about experiencing the delectable euphoria of mastery, of overcoming handicaps and personal limitations, of setting personal goals and surpassing them in unimaginable ways. To be fully alive means to have a vision, to know who you are in that vision, and to put your whole heart into it. You can't hold back; you must "spend it all" to make your dream come true.

As a young child, I learned that I couldn't learn. Once my self-confidence as a person who could learn had been shattered, I felt awkward and clumsy, and I failed in every area of school. But something in me never gave up, and I finally discovered the most important thing in life: how to transcend my perceived limitations. I learned how to break down the walls of my early conditioning and recreate myself.

The boy who couldn't read went on to earn a doctorate in education; the boy who had no self-image of athletic prowess grew into a man who ran three marathons; the boy who couldn't speak became known in many countries for his public speaking.

Whatever you may perceive as your own particular limitations, you too can break through them. This will require you to get in touch with your dream and live as if it has already come true. And you must move in your own way. In your movement you'll find the resources and abilities to do your best, as you learn how to obtain the skills necessary to reach your full potential. And along the way, you'll enjoy the process!

My mother was my first mentor. With her commitment to excellence and beauty and her ability to overcome the hardships that seem an inevitable part of life, she taught me from an early age to live the exquisite life.

When I was about thirteen, I fractured my skull in a serious bike accident. For the first time, I realized my own mortality—that someday

I would die. After I left the hospital, I went through a period of morbid depression in which I stayed in my room and cried for days. Finally I approached my mother about it.

"What's the point of going on," I asked her, "if we're all going to die anyway?"

"The point of living," my mother replied, "is this: to guide others through the same journey *we* are on, and to help them deal with the same issues."

Then she gave me a phrase to hold close to my heart: "Fight, love, give." She meant "fight" in a positive way: to make my life everything it can be . . . to fight to realize my potential so that I might live fully and make a difference. By "love" she meant to love myself and others and, in so doing, discover that it's my true nature to give back to my community.

I'm now passing my mother's phrase on to you, as encouragement for you to find your own unique ways to fight, love, and give.

Chapter Three

We Learn by Noticing

The essence of ignorance seems to be a failing to notice and then failing to notice that we fail to notice.

—Sidney Callahan
Commonweal Journal

My fingers shook and my eyes ached as I tried to print the letters of the alphabet and stay on the line, as the other kids were doing so successfully.

As she walked around the classroom, my second grade teacher, Miss Murphy, would make quiet comments about each student's work. "Stephen is making beautiful, round *o*'s . . . I like how Sylvia is holding her pencil . . . what perfect, even, neat circles Nathan is making for his *o*'s."

Miss Murphy never commented on my work, though, and I knew that this was because my *o*'s were never round enough, no matter how hard I tried.

I felt bewildered during writing lessons. Everything went so fast; I couldn't seem to slow time down enough to master and control the pencil. When I tried to coordinate my eyes with my hand movements, I would often get stomachaches and double vision.

I wondered how the other children moved so quickly. They made it look so easy! What was wrong with my *o*'s? My work just didn't come out the way I wanted it to. In my mind's eye, I could see the *o*'s as smooth and round; yet, on the page, each one I drew came out jerky and uneven.

Observing My Own Experience

I tried to shut out much of what I experienced in school, for it didn't seem of any use. My wooden desk, too big for me, was uncomfortably hard and awkward to sit in. I felt lost in it, my feet barely able to touch the floor. Things and people in the room felt far away, and I longed to move and use my muscles. My stomach often hurt, and the most I could hope for was that no one would notice me.

As a left-hander in a right-hander's world, I always felt that I was swimming against the tide. In my inner listening, I could sense Miss Murphy and the other children moving together in a rhythm all their own—one that was foreign to me. I felt myself falling behind, and tried to move more rapidly to keep up.

I still hold vividly in my memory that long-ago struggle with the pencil. As that particular second-grade lesson transpired, I suddenly began to notice myself and my anxious situation with the detachment of a kindly observer. This was a pivotal, living-dream memory that I sensed would stay with me, like a jewel in a treasure chest, for the rest of my life. Although I still felt alone and helpless in my awareness, this moment was a gift.

As each new lesson took place, I now began to experience my situation and notice the whole scene taking place before me. This ability to self-observe was my prefrontal cortex—the brain's center of self-awareness—in action.

The brain's prefrontal cortex holds the essence of our humanness and is an integral part of every learning experience. When we can witness our behavior and evaluate it, we can act on it and change it. Otherwise, we keep repeating the same behavior ad infinitum and never learn. These frontal lobes of the cerebrum develop simultaneously with the rest of the brain as we grow through childhood, through our teenage years, and on into adulthood. As we learn to sense, move, feel, and think for ourselves, thanks to the prefrontal cortex we're able to notice and code our experience of these various functions.

I couldn't know, back in Miss Murphy's class, what I know now— that, when I picked up the pencil, I was focusing too hard on that one fragmented piece, unable to sense or feel the whole spatial context of my body and hand motions, unable to stop and think. I was still in a stressed state—withdrawing and contracting as if I were trying to become invisible in the room.

I was experiencing common stress responses: dizziness, muscular tension, breath holding, increased heart rate, a sense of accelerated time, and, as the pupils of my eyes dilated, an inability to access peripheral vision.

As my tension increased, I remember tightening my grip on the pencil. I was seeing more and more of what stressed me—the pencil moving on the page—and experiencing less and less of myself. Everything seemed reduced to a fast moment—one with which I could never catch up. I repeatedly felt the sense of something rushing toward me—the teacher; noisy, pushy classmates; or a test—yet I could never work quickly enough to feel ready for what was coming. Years would pass before it occurred to me that I could never, ever go fast enough to get ready for learning, and that what I really needed was to slow down. My attention was too much on time and not enough on space.

Until that first moment of self-aware noticing, I had felt completely overwhelmed and unable to follow what was going on in the classroom. Soon after my new experience of self-reflection, I began to examine my abilities, plan my own learning steps, and take responsibility for teaching myself. And this was only the beginning: within the next three years I would discover how to connect this noticing with my sensory processes. For instance, such things as the movement of my hands and my tactile experience as I formed letters would eventually help me with my handwriting, and there were innumerable other instances of such useful new connections.

Spatial Time vs. Artificial Time

Movement is our first and most natural teacher. From our earliest spatial explorations as infants, our movement teaches us through our search for balance. We are not static beings. Through our body, we constantly seek a dynamic sense of balance, constantly rediscovering ourselves as the ever-moving center point between left and right, front and back, top and bottom. To walk and run means to continually fall and right ourselves in gravity, in a state of dynamic balance.

As we move on foot, we learn to coordinate the rhythmic and symmetrical interplay between left shoulder and right hip, right shoulder and left hip, opposing arms and legs, and the reciprocal joints of elbows and knees and wrists and ankles. Whether we walk, skip, run, jump, dance, or simply gesture, we impel our bodies from an internal sense of the balance and counterbalance of opposing forces. Our noticing of the personal movement pattern in which all this occurs is our kinesthetic awareness.

Babies are natural learners who live in real, kinesthetic time. For my infant granddaughter, the day begins when the sun comes up. When I watch her attempt to stand up, she does this at her own rhythm and pace. First one hand reaches out as she begins to pull herself up, then a foot pushes until she wobbles but gets her balance, the other hand and foot grounding her. Oops—a fall. That was interesting. Time to start over again; there is no rush.

The joy on my granddaughter's face comes from her fulfillment of an intrinsic need for physical interaction with reality, not from how quickly and efficiently she may have accomplished a developmental skill. Soon she'll take her first step, and will likely fall again. It is by sensory-based noticing of the subtle and momentary experience of balance (before we fall) that we learn how to stand up and walk unaided in gravity.

All learning, from crawling to walking, talking, sitting, standing, and holding a pencil, and not only for children but also for adults, depends on our ability to notice and be aware of our movement in space over time. And when our muscles are relaxed, the proprioceptors—the brain cells in our muscle tissue—provide a pleasurable sense of our own movement, as well as wonderful feedback about the size, shape, and mass of our body—about how we move in space. What this means is that real learning, in real time and real space, is pleasurable.

It was Albert Einstein who reminded us that "Knowledge is experience; everything else is just information." Until quite recently in our long history, human endeavors were more physically based. A young person might become a farmer, a blacksmith, or a tradesman; regardless of their field of interest, most people learned by doing things with their hands and bodies—by trial and error—or as an apprentice under the watchful eye of an expert. People took as much satisfaction in their workmanship as in their accomplishments, and didn't pride themselves on how quickly projects could be finished.

Today's world is a less grounded one in which technology has eliminated much labor that was done by hand in the past. Yet the emphasis on production and on speed for its own sake often separates the individual from his roots in the concrete, tactile, and kinesthetic world of real time and space.

Oscar the Monkey and Kinesthetic Learning

Around the same time that I was struggling with my o's, I recall watching Mama, one evening after dinner, as she filled a bowl with starch and shredded newspaper. She stuffed one of my father's socks with the wet paper and worked the sock until it was as smooth and round as a small balloon. Concentrating deeply, she then began to push and mold the sock with her thumbs.

I was amazed to see that the sock now looked like a head, with chubby cheeks, two large round eyes, and a turned-up nose. Mama was in a serious mood as she studied the face, seemingly perplexed as to how it should look. Then suddenly she smiled as she held the shape aloft, and found a safe place for it to rest as it dried.

Over the next few days, I watched in awe as Mama deftly painted large, curious blue eyes, rosy cheeks, and a playful smile. Using balsa wood, my father added a torso and moveable arms and legs. Mama then carved beautiful balsa wood hands, and sewed black pants and a tunic of gold, yellow, and green. Finally she added wooly yarn, giving the marionette a shock of bright yellow hair. A look of serene satisfaction came over her face as she hung the three-foot puppet high on a hook in our living room, in a special place with the others.

I wanted to play with this friendly-faced boy. I loved the way he smelled, with his fresh wood and paint. But I could see the risk of

54

getting his strings tangled, so I quickly learned not to handle this new friend. Like my little brother, this marionette was named Peter, and he and his friends—a bird and duck—were to play a large part in my childhood.

Imagine my delight when Mama gave me the materials to make my own puppet! That little boy who couldn't draw a round o, who appeared at school to be clumsy and lacking in eye-hand coordination, now made a beautiful hand puppet with a lovely round head. When I had completed Oscar the Monkey, he was eighteen inches tall and painted all brown.

Mama helped me paint the face. She showed me how to mix the colors to make Oscar's cheeks look bright, round, and red as apples. His small black eyes peered out mischievously from under an organ grinder's cap. My father made the wooden links for Oscar's legs, and helped me attach a fine papier-mâché tail that I had made with great care.

And Oscar wore a flowing red cape that I had proudly sewn myself, in my left-handed way, in nice straight lines just like Mama's. My twelve-year-old cousin Lois could hardly believe my skill: "Look— Paul can thread a needle!" Learning to sew was one of my major accomplishments in second grade. I learned to do it all kinesthetically, by following my mother's movements and exploring these same movements on my own. I couldn't read, but I could sew.

Oscar was all mine, and I played with him endlessly. Creating that monkey puppet gave me an experience of my body and movement patterns in real time. It gave me a way to explore and practice my hand-eye coordination and the pleasure of my senses—touching, looking, creating, and learning about spatial relationships as I choreographed the puppet's movements in ways that pleased me. During my parents' rehearsal times, as the music played and the marionettes spoke and fluttered across the stage, I could experiment with Oscar, making him leap and hop, swing from branch to branch of a tree on the set, and dance into mysterious life.

This three-dimensional play taught me a lot about how to plan and coordinate movements. It also taught me to stop time. In the expanded space of my movement, I could breathe, relax, and find my own rhythm. To my great relief, the noise and dizzying speed of the classroom melted at night in the quietude and imagination of my play.

Children Are Losing Their Sensory Skills

Children learn what they live, and today the hours of many young people are too rigidly scheduled, with little allowance for play and exploration and little or no time spent outdoors. What free time may exist is usually given to passive engagement with the flat, two-dimensional images presented by television, computer games, and DVD movies, rather than such three-dimensional experiences as running, hiding, climbing, building, exploring nature, and engaging in imaginative play.

This is an age of artificial time, when speed and fast reactions are immediately rewarded. A boy I know, "Marshall," was at age ten a technological expert who had mastered the Gameboy™ and could navigate the Internet more quickly and expertly than most adults. Yet, like many young people of today, he had information without knowledge, facts without abilities. Worst of all, Marshall seemed to lack a sense of wonder.

For millennia, the natural world of trees and stones and grasses, creeks and rivers, birdsong and animals, has provided humankind with a rich apprenticeship in the visual, auditory, and other sensory modalities. The sense of wonder depends upon curiosity—a quality of receptivity of the unknown. This receptivity is encouraged by the many surprising shades, surfaces, and textures found in nature.

I vividly recall stepping out in my back yard as a child one morning, just as I had done the day before. On this day, though, I encountered something that hadn't been there yesterday: a large face peering over the fence at me from the neighbors' garden. It belonged to a beautiful, full-grown sunflower that seemed to reflect all the brilliance of the sun. It appeared to be looking over the fence in search of a friend, and I was only too glad to respond. I ran across the yard to see it more closely, and studied the intricate whorled design of its countless seeds. For as long as that flower lasted, it made me feel happy whenever I saw it.

Even such small encounters with the natural world help children to develop the sense of awe and wonder that will keep them exploring and learning.

For Marshall, as for many children like him, the idea of camping or walking a nature trail was either scary or boring. "I don't do outside," he told me early in our friendship.

Marshall avoided exercise because it made him breathe hard and he thought he "might get warm." He was bullied at school, as I was, for being a nerd and not fitting in, and he compensated by reading a lot and excelling at competitive tasks. After several months of doing Brain Gym movements with his father and participating in both family and individual balances, Marshall (his father told me) had started enjoying outdoor play with his siblings in a way he'd never done before.

In his groundbreaking new book *The Executive Brain*, Elkhonen Goldberg discusses what it means to be "smart" and the relationship of decision making to the prefrontal lobes. He explains how that area of the brain gives us our interpersonal abilities and plain old common sense; for example, the ability to "read" situations, discern the meanings of facial expressions, and anticipate the consequences of various actions. To take Goldberg's idea further, too many of our children are passively "downloading" their education as Marshall was doing. New information must be integrated with concrete, three-dimensional exploration for balanced learning. Otherwise, how can children learn to make active use of their intelligence?

From Maria Montessori to Jean Piaget, many extraordinary educators of the last century recognized the importance of actual, concrete, experiences to a child's sensory development. Brain-imaging techniques now verify this need for children to physically experience the world in real time before they code it into information and proceed to read or talk about it. Yet many of our new century's youngsters are so overstimulated by external input that they're missing the sensory input of their own body wisdom.

Another way to say "noticing" is to say "being curious and interactive." We may remember that, when we ourselves were children, we were naturally inquisitive, wanting to touch, look, listen, and otherwise explore the world. In Brain Gym, we invite this natural curiosity, along with a kindly sense of nonjudgment, to our experience.

Dr. Montessori taught that it is the child's work in the world to discover that water is wet, that materials have weight, shape, volume, and texture. She understood that children will naturally explore the physical world if given an environment in which they can move and interact with its properties.

We must not assume that today's children feel the same sense of safety in nature or love of discovery there that we may remember and retain. As we've seen, passive experiences have replaced nature and the backyard for many children, who sit for hours in front of an electronic distortion of reality. A flat screen displays a "reality" without real properties: there is no weight, mass, or texture to the images displayed. Because adults aren't mentoring them into the sensory complexities of the natural world, many children are losing the brain integration they need to really enjoy or interact with nature.

Facing the Neurocognitive Breakdown

My friend and mentor the educator Joseph Chilton Pearce describes in his lectures and books (such as *The Crack in the Cosmic Egg*, *Magical Child*, *Evolution's End*, and *The Biology of Transcendence*) how our children are not developing their sensory perception.

In a 1999 interview with Chris Mercogliano, Dr. Pearce spoke of how the German Psychological Institute had conducted a twenty-year study of four thousand children per year, children who by the age of six had watched an average of five thousand to six thousand hours of television.

As Joe Pearce explained, the researchers found that as recently as twenty years earlier young people could distinguish between 360 different shadings of a single color category such as red or blue. By the end of the study this number was down to about 130—an almost two-thirds loss of the ability to detect shadings of color.

This is one small example of what Dr. Pearce calls the neurocognitive breakdown taking place in our children. A more serious change uncovered in the German study was a breakdown of the brain's ability to cross-index its whole kinesthetic/sensory system. That is, the sensory systems of more and more children are acting as isolated components in the brain, rather than as coordinated whole gestalts.

Are we teaching our children to rely on constant external stimulation? When the researchers put the children raised on TV into a natural environment containing no high-density stimuli, the children grew bored and anxious and tended toward violence. And the final disturbing finding of the German study was that there had been, over the same twenty-year period, a 20 percent reduction in the children's awareness of their natural environment.

Pearce explains that this fits right in with the 1980s studies of anthropologist Marcia Mikulak on evolution, in which she discovered a 20-to-28.5-percent reduction in the ability of children in the United States to register environmental sensory signals when compared to children from preliterate, nontechnological societies. So the German studies cited by Dr. Pearce confirm what previous research has told us: Children exposed to excessive and overstimulating images from such sources as television and computers are lacking in sensory skills.

Thought and the Opposable Thumb
When we hold chopsticks in the traditional Japanese manner—between thumb and forefinger—we're seeing "the opposable thumb" in operation. If we hold a pen in the manner of our forefathers, we're again making use of the opposable thumb. Anthropologists theorize that the opposable thumb is one of the flowering achievements of human evolution, occurring concurrently with the development of thought, language, and the ability to hold an idea in memory in order to act on it over time. Yet, in our modern Western culture, the neural pathways that support this function are not being developed because of insufficient physical play and other movement activities.

What my wife, Gail, and I have observed over the last twenty years is that, whether it's a chopstick or a pen, people are no longer holding common tools with precision. Instead, they use something called the power grip. (The terms *power grip* and *precision grip* were coined by Frank Wilson in his book *The Hand: How Its Use Shapes the Brain, Language, and Human Culture,* which can tell you everything you might want to know about the subject.)

The evolution of the opposable thumb corresponds to the development of the frontal lobe of the neocortex, bringing with it the higher cognitive abilities related to creating beauty, precision, and art. The most refined human activities and aspirations have been made possible by the *precision grip* and the finely tuned nervous system that underlies it.

Now, the advent of TV, cell phones, computer games, and typing on a keyboard is causing young people to forego mastery of the physical art of writing. As a result, they're losing the opposable thumb and the skills that go with it.

As a reading teacher, I found reading to be an expressive activity requiring the development of language; therefore, the ability to write fluently is crucial to reading. At my reading centers we taught and encouraged writing, and the reading almost took care of itself. I see it as a disaster, then, that the opposable thumb—representing millions of years of evolution—appears likely to be lost in a single generation.

We must write, and encourage our children to follow our lead. Writing and the use of tools with the opposable thumb builds critical pathways in the brain that are necessary to the ability to read, as well as to the blending of attention and comprehension.

Becoming Conscious Learners

Before children in a school setting can enter into abstract learning with written codes and symbols, they need a foundation of concrete, three-dimensional experiences of moving spatially, in real time. Yet most school-age children haven't yet had enough foundational movement experiences to be able to coordinate their eyes and hands or even sit comfortably upright in the classroom. They're still struggling to organize their body in gravity. And though they may master academic skills, until their physical and sensory confusion is resolved, everything they learn will be associated—and remembered—with that same physical and sensory confusion.

Stress is an inescapable factor of modern life; depending how it's managed, it can either undermine or underscore the schooling experience. It is either a call to failure or a call to action. Children who are given permission to make mistakes, and to notice their own signs of stress and work through them with Brain Gym, soon demonstrate the wisdom to use stress to their benefit and direct their own learning.

These young people who have learned to master stress can mature their skills in reading, writing, and mathematics because they're able to develop to precision the physical movements involved in doing these activities—the movements of hands, eyes, head, and body—and integrate these movements into the functioning self.

Stress must be acknowledged, not swept under the carpet, so children can learn how to handle it. For there is no pleasure without stress; pleasure comes from working *through* stress until various skills are mastered. This is why a shallow experience of artificial fun, such as a field trip to an amusement park, can't give the same deep satisfaction as a classroom project in which the children achieve a learning goal and overcome their challenges in the process.

When I wanted to master a capital *O* so I could write the name of my hand puppet, Oscar, the *o* finally took on real meaning for me. It made me think of Oscar's round head and how it felt to shape it, and of his round, painted eyes and small round nose. Now that I could finally experience an *o* in my body by tracing a wooden *o*, drawing *o*'s in the air, and feeling my teacher write an *o* in my hand, I was easily able to inscribe on paper a small, beautiful circle in which I could take pride.

I was now joyfully becoming a conscious learner and a more active one—discovering how to pay attention to the state of my mind, body, and emotions. I was learning how to attend to the changes, both subtle and profound, that enabled me to be more comfortable, confident, and effective in making linear (over real time) the physical skills and abilities I had experienced spatially, with all my senses.

Noticing is a way to intentionally associate a kinesthetic experience—one involving muscles and movement—with a sense of mastery, by taking the time to do it well. As a teaching tool, it offers a sensory baseline for identifying changes and a body-based structure to provide feedback for the development of self-directed learning. I was now able to notice how I was thinking, feeling, or moving in terms of my brain stem (which governs automatic, learned, and spatially integrated functions) and my neocortex (which governs controlled, not-yet-learned, sequenced-in-time abilities).

The "Trying" and "Doing" Aspects of Learning

As a young man, I financed my studies by working as a driving instructor. When eighteen-year-old Ben, a new student, got behind the wheel for the first time, I must have had as many butterflies in my stomach as he did. Ben's quick and erratic movements sometimes scared me half to death. He'd make a quick swerve of the wheel or place a sudden heavy foot on the brake—mistaken actions that I thought would be obvious to him but that were sometimes hard for him, as a learner, to inhibit.

When I asked Ben to combine several actions, such as signaling, turning to look over his shoulder, and steering, disorganization and frustration were often the result.

Just like me attempting to draw a round *o* in my second grade classroom, Ben tried to speed up to do these separate tasks instead of slowing down. I refer to this as the "low-gear" or "trying" stage of learning. When we're overly stressed or overstimulated, we have a hard time moving into a spatially based aspect of the learning process. We've already withdrawn as active participants, and then must force ourselves to try to catch up. When we're able to relax back into our sense of space, things seem to slow down and we find that we have plenty of time to learn the new process.

In many ways, the vehicles we drive are like our lives. This is why I think of a learning stage involving new mental processes as being "low gear." When we first learn to drive, we're thinking too much and trying too hard. Each movement must be performed slowly and methodically, and carefully sequenced over time; there is little integration between various actions.

I would break down these low-gear processes into linear steps for Ben to repeat—with him just sitting comfortably behind the wheel at first, then shifting from "reader's vision" to "driver's vision," keeping his attention focused on the middle of the road ahead—the "big picture." Next, I'd direct him to start distinguishing between the movement of his arms and hands turning the steering wheel and the movement of his legs and feet as they worked the brake and clutch.

After sufficient practice to code the skills into memory, Ben began to do the distinct actions more fluently. He now had a better sense of the spatial relationships of his head, back, hands, and feet in the car, and he no longer appeared clumsy, awkward, and reactive as he drove. He soon began to sense the relationship of his car to the other vehicles on the road. Toward the end of his lessons, he was starting to make comfortable eye contact with other drivers and to sense their intentions as well as the overall flow of traffic.

Now Ben was able to combine all the details of this experience into that exquisite piece of choreography known as driving a car proficiently. When he had mastered this state of excellence, we celebrated that he was now in high gear for driving. He was doing it, and was he ever proud!

This celebration didn't mean that there was anything wrong with his linear, low-gear, "trying" state, for that's a natural part of the learning process. The purpose of language is to make novelty familiar. In driving, this low-gear, step-by-step process is absolutely necessary to achieve precision and accuracy when such are needed, and it always remains available to a driver at times when measured, thoughtful movements are required, such as when parking, backing up, or making a right turn.

Our best driving requires that the basic skills be automatic—freeing us to use our discriminating abilities for the conscious effort and decision making that will fine-tune the ride. Life's journey is similar: the more integrated and automatic our movement patterns, the more mindfully we attend to present experience, make associations with past learning, anticipate where our road is leading us, and apply our new learning appropriately.

This automatic, high-gear, "doing" state of mind provides a feeling of sureness, a "yes" quality in which no doubt exists. It's a state of ease and enthusiasm in which a safe, accustomed structure is created and new distinctions can easily be added to expand skills or knowledge within a subject area. As long as your "vehicle" is valued, maintained, and operated properly and you're in familiar territory, you can enjoy your ride in this pleasurable, relaxed, and more receptive state in which you're open to new experiences.

When our life is challenged by a new set of circumstances, we can reenter a more linear, low-gear learning state to achieve a new level of mastery. Perhaps there's a detour, or maybe a ball rolls out into the road. Our comfortable structure is temporarily threatened, and all of our resources must now focus on a novel situation. So we take control and analyze the existing data. We discriminate the known from the unknown and make an educated guess as to the best choice we can make, experiencing some indecision and hesitation as we focus in on a solution.

As we reduce our uncertainty, we regain structure and equilibrium both physically and mentally. This is the thrill of accomplishment and coherence as stability is restored. We may feel euphoric pleasure as our muscular tension fluctuates from contraction to relaxation.

Like learning to drive, conscious living, thinking, and learning provide a pleasurable experience of mastery. We use our low gear to control the vehicle around corners, or while driving in slow traffic. It's by slowing down that we become the master of our machine. When we're learning, we become proficient only to the extent that we stop to ask questions, make an effort, cry any necessary tears, and see a task through to the end—even at those times when the connections to our previous knowledge aren't immediately apparent.

Since human beings have different body types and a broad range of circumstances, not everyone associates high gear with the same types of life experience. And since so many of us learned early to be externally directed, we may well be learning about the relaxation of high gear for a long time. Reclaiming a sense of our internal choices may call for patience, but it's well worth the effort.

In our learning, just as it was for Ben, the key to fulfilling our own potential is acquiring automatic access to either the high-gear, "doing" state or the low-gear, "trying" state, as appropriate. A skilled learner explores new learning in a state of ease, motivated and challenged by goals, deadlines, and commitments. For this learner, tension seldom deteriorates into a fight-or-flight response, as comfortable, automatic moving and learning provides a context for stopping to think about any new task at hand. Ideally, the need to analyze, question, or doubt (low gear) will happen primarily within this familiar, relevant structure that I call high gear.

Let me share with you, as an example, one of my favorite Brain Gym activities, a movement known as Arm Activation.

Arm Activation

Take a moment to notice your neck and shoulders. Do you feel any tension there? Do your hands and arms feel relaxed? Is there any tension in your fingers? How warm or cool do they feel?

Reach up above your head with your left arm, feeling the arm lengthen from your rib cage. Hold your arm just below the elbow with your right hand. Now isometrically activate your left arm for a few seconds in each of four positions: away from your head, forward, backward, and toward your ear. Rest your left arm again at your side.

Now stand and let your arms hang comfortably by your sides. What differences do you notice in the arm and shoulder that you just activated? How do they compare to the other side in relaxation, flexibility, and warmth? How do your two arms compare? Does one feel longer? Your noticing of the activated arm gives you information about the learned-and-familiar high gear, while your noticing of the unactivated arm tells you about the not-yet-learned and unfamiliar low gear. If you were now to learn to write *o*'s with your activated arm (even if that's not the side you usually write with), the openness of your shoulder and arm would now be reflected in your *o*'s.

If you noticed a difference, what you've just experienced is how, when large-motor movements precede small-motor movements, the small-motor control will then be freer and less constricted.

Now repeat the Arm Activation movement with your other arm. Take the time to notice any additional changes that you now experience. Perhaps you're breathing more expansively or your thinking is clearer, or your vision may even be sharper. Are your shoulders more relaxed, and perhaps more level?

Teaching to Nurture Awareness
We all learned to think, read, and write by noticing what worked and what didn't. Unfortunately, though, many of us noticed what *other* people thought was working—not what was truly working for us in our own physiology. Yet we can still (whether quickly or more gradually) start to change our reference point to notice our own movement experience, providing a context for new learning.

In education, noticing for ourselves is called "having a central locus of control." This is an important skill of self-initiated or self-directed learning, and it means that you can tell for yourself whether you're truly learning something or just cramming information (and probably stressing yourself in such a way that you'll soon forget it again).

Noticing is a proficiency that everyone needs to learn. For some children, noticing skills need to be taught. When a child is under stress and tense from either overstimulation or withdrawal, she can't relax enough to feel how she's moving. And, without that awareness of how she moves her eyes, hands, and entire body, she can't learn to initiate her own learning.

Teachers and parents need to take occasional brief moments of time to help young learners (1) notice how they're learning; (2) recognize when they've learned something; (3) identify what that learning is; and (4) imagine what the next appropriate learning step might be. (These four kinds of noticing don't all happen at the same time, which would be overwhelming, but at different times, as appropriate.)

It's also important for teachers and parents to distinguish the difference between what a student has actually learned and what is unlearned or just a compensation. (For example, I knew I hadn't yet learned to make round *o*'s, and would have been relieved and grateful to hear a relaxed acknowledgment from my teacher that I was still in the learning stage.) At every stage of development, the more noticing, choice making, and active participation we invite our children to do, the more we're supporting the development of their mature decision making.

As we're about to see, all this noticing is in the province of the prefrontal lobes.

As you probably noticed when you did the Arm Activation exercise, noticing is easy when we're comparing two or more things. For example, *Is it more comfortable to hold the pen in my right hand or my left?* I use this example to make a further point about how all learning involves noticing: even toddlers choosing one hand over the other to hold a rattle are doing so because they've noticed a greater degree of comfort or ease of motor control on that side.

For some people, the realization that noticing is intrinsic to learning represents a profound advance toward freedom. As one participant in a Brain Gym class said, "I don't have to move through the same behaviors over and over. I can notice what I just did and then experiment with doing something else!"

Many of my students are astonished to discover that much of the stress and imbalance they feel as adults can be traced back to how they learned as children. With the appropriate Brain Gym movements, many can unlearn an ineffective coping strategy in one session, while for others it takes longer. I'm committed to seeing us all model for our children how to learn through play and movement. Let's teach them that they can learn without fight-or-flight activation!

The Prefrontal Cortex and the Noticing Bridge

The prefrontal cortex (the frontal lobes of the cerebrum) holds the essence of our humanness—our ability to be self-aware—and is essential to our learning and growing. When we can witness our own behavior and evaluate it, or witness the positive behavior of others and emulate it, we can make important personal choices and can remain relatively "in charge" of our life and learning.

This region located just above the eyes includes the front 30 percent of the neocortex. It's known by many names, such as the forebrain, the frontal lobes, and the prefrontals. Brain researcher Paul MacLean refers to this area as "the angel lobes," attributing to them the virtues of love, compassion, empathy, and understanding.

The prefrontal cortex controls working memory, allowing people and animals to keep several pieces of information in mind at the same time and regulating "executive" functions such as planning and the control of emotions and behavior. This "noticing" part of the brain allows us to learn something new and enter it into long-term memory, or to recall similar learning from long-term memory for comparison or conjoining with the new information.

In the Educational Kinesiology work, my wife and partner, Gail, first described the prefrontal cortex by its function of creating a neural bridge to the sensory elements of our experience, referring to it as "the Noticing Bridge."

The prefrontal cortex develops simultaneously with our movement and sensory skills. This means that our discovering of reaching, turning, scooting, crawling, and standing, and also of smelling, tasting, touching, seeing, and hearing, is integrally related to our emotions— our ability to connect with or disconnect from the world around us.

Some of our deepest conditioning at the level of the brain stem has to do with our patterns and sensations of movement. Since noticing is a frontal-lobe activity, the simple act of noticing our movement patterns is, in itself, a process that grows the frontal cortex and integrates it with the brain stem.

In other words, the prefrontal cortex develops, in response to movement, in an interplay with the innermost areas of the brain, and it develops as a result of our own noticing of all aspects of ourselves as we grow through childhood, through our teenage years, and on into adulthood.

Joseph Chilton Pearce remarks that these prefrontal lobes are fully in place by age three. Ideally, Pearce says, these structures continue to evolve by neural interaction, creating a "consciousness container" or matrix that always self-references previous states of awareness.

Pearce points out that we cannot overemphasize the importance of nurturing toddlers for optimal development of "rich neural connections . . . between the forward-most section of the prefrontal lobes (which have developed in the first year after birth) and the highest region of the emotional (old mammalian) brain, which was developed in utero."

We could say that movement grows the brain and the prefrontal cortex grows the mind. As we learn to sense, move, feel, and think for ourselves, we are able to notice and code our experience of these various personal aspects.

We humans share with some of the higher primates, such as the apes, the ability to notice things around us. We can hold something in the eye or the hand . . . a face, a flower, a hummingbird . . . and say "Wow!" This is the true gift of being alive: to be able to reflect on and appreciate our life.

And since the shadow side of noticing includes criticism, it can always benefit us to take a moment to notice our judgments and to shift into nonjudgmental noticing—in a light overview of our experience that notes its events, patterns, and sensations simply as information.

The following Brain Gym activity allows us to direct energy and awareness to the prefrontal "poles" at the forward-most neural area, where the brain is so connected to heart and play that the fight-or-flight response can be neutralized by a mere act of intention. These points were discovered by Dr. George Goodheart and are described in the Touch for Health work as the emotional stress-release points. Early research with these points demonstrated that, through their use, a fight/flight response could be changed into a more conscious, reasoning approach.

The Positive Points

Lightly touch the points above each eye, halfway between the eyebrows and the hairline, with the fingertips of each hand. Use just enough pressure to pull the skin taut, and hold the contact for about a minute.

Under stress, the frontalis muscle in the forehead is one of the first to contract, thus limiting easy neurovascular flow to the prefrontal areas of the frontal lobes. If we can relax the frontalis muscle by bringing gentle touch to it, the other facial muscles also relax and neurovascular flow is no longer constricted. The increased blood flow to the frontal lobes, where rational thought occurs, nourishes and grows the prefrontal fibers and helps prevent the fight-or-flight response so that a new response to any situation can be learned.

Recently, certain researchers have been stimulating the frontal lobes with drugs; this Brain Gym movement, though, brings support to the frontal lobes with touch alone.

The Source of True Pleasure

Until we develop our prefrontal cortex, our parents, teachers, and mentors must fulfill its role for us, modeling for us that self-reflection and appreciation of life that we call "attention," which translates into curiosity and learning.

I wonder what might have happened in second grade if Miss Murphy had known about kinesthetic learning and had mentored me as I struggled to guide the pencil to make round o's? Might I have learned some alternative pencil grips or a positioning of eye, hand, and paper more appropriate to a left-handed writer? Might I have been able to compare alternatives and taken charge instead of helplessly backsliding? Might I have learned to evaluate my writing against my own physical abilities, instead of comparing myself to Nathan, Sylvia, and others who were able to effortlessly please the teacher?

Paying attention to our own thoughts, feelings, muscular tension, or physiological processes is the first step in being able to do something differently. If I had known Brain Gym in second grade, I might have done Lazy 8s (the activity you learned in Chapter Two), so that I could *feel* the difference between a counter-clockwise circle I drew in my left visual field and a clockwise one that I drew in the right. Without this sensory aspect of noticing, one kind of circle feels the same as another, but when we do Lazy 8s we can easily feel the difference.

The ability to notice, to make decisions, and to have sufficient self-determination to create changes in our life is the source of what I call true pleasure. This pleasure comes from positive stress, when we feel actively engaged in a process—not from overexerting ourselves or withdrawing from participation.

Without this authentic pleasure, we may be finding amusement; we may be having fun. But when other people are taking care of us and making our decisions for us, we may also be wondering why we're not happy.

When we learn in a state of negative stress, we're only being trained and conditioned. In contrast, when our frontal lobes are operant, they enable us to set goals, move with intention, and participate in our own learning. This active commitment and involvement gives us the feeling of making and doing—one of the keys to satisfaction.

Chapter Four

How Movement Can Free Our Self-Expression

My home in Brookline, Massachusetts, was a world of art, imagination, and creativity. As my mother fashioned marionettes, often staying up all night to sew, paint, and dress the puppets and design the stage sets, I saw the power of storytelling and how stories begin in the imagination and are then communicated, both in words and from heart to heart.

I have always loved everything about live theater, from working as a stagehand to performing onstage to being a member of the audience. I especially love to see young people perform, giving it their all in the way that they do.

The Land of Ahhhs
I've enjoyed many children's productions through the years, and one of my favorites is *The Wizard of Oz*. Pamela Curlee, my good friend and fellow Brain Gym faculty member, once invited me to participate as Oz in a grown-up performance called "The Land of Ahhhs," and my on-stage encounter with Dorothy, the Scarecrow, the Tin Man, and the Cowardly Lion inspired in my mind the following metaphor.

To me, the Land of Ahhhs is the place we come home to when we reconnect with our marvelous sensory awareness and our joy in moving. In my work, this means understanding and integrating the head, heart, and body. The integration is accomplished through three primary dimensions and their corresponding neuropathways that bridge the front-to-back, side-to-side, and top-to-bottom fields in which we move and experience daily life. By "head," I mean our language centers in the neocortex; "heart" refers to our emotions, led by the biochemistry of the midbrain; and "body" denotes the physicality of the brain stem, which houses our sensorimotor survival systems.

Our brains evolved because we have a body, not the other way round. Learning that "sticks" is learning that has been recorded in our sensing body—with our eyes, ears, tactility, and movement. We make our memories in the cells of the body. For thousands of years our physical, concrete experiences superceded any theorizing or mental explorations involving language or information systems. Without movement, information that's too abstract or ephemeral may be difficult to access. When we're free to move, our sensory and spatial faculties have the opportunity to integrate around new information, and we truly "get" what we learn.

Understanding Brain Gym and its emphasis on movement may require you to make a paradigm shift. Therefore, I'd like to set the scene by creating a visual picture of the principles we'll be exploring in subsequent chapters. Prompted by Pamela's "Land of Ahhhs," I'm going to do this with the assistance of L. Frank Baum's classic children's story *The Wizard of Oz*.

This book happens to provide a wonderful and imaginative allegory for the human brain, in its states of both fragmentation and integration. And, like all good literature, *The Wizard of Oz* tells us much about life.

Our Challenges Provide a Catalyst for Change

Brain Gym is about wholeness and integration, so I hope that you'll enjoy the following combination of fable (inviting the right brain) and exposition (inviting the left).

Imagine a young girl, Dorothy, who lives with her aunt and uncle in the flat lands of Kansas. One fateful day a tornado blacks out the sky. The swirling wind lifts Dorothy's house, together with Dorothy and her dog, Toto, and transports them to a strange and mysterious place called the Land of Oz. The little people in those parts are called Munchkins. They dress in blue and wear tall, pointed hats. They are awestruck by Dorothy's sudden appearance, all the more so because her house has landed on and killed the Wicked Witch of the East. A Munchkin removes the Wicked Witch's silver shoes, dusts them off, and hands them to Dorothy.

"The Witch of the East was proud of those shoes," says one of the Munchkins, "and there is some charm connected with them; but what it is we never knew."

Dorothy begins to sob. Observing that she is grieving the loss of her family and her home state of Kansas, the Munchkins suggest that she follow the yellow brick road to the City of Emeralds. There she'll find the great Wizard of Oz, who may be able to help her.

Like Dorothy's tornado, our words and fears sometimes take us on a journey of stress. Adrenaline, cortisol, and other neurochemicals pour into our bloodstream as we mentally journey further and further from the heart and ground of our body—the living home of our aliveness.

Natural learning is a continuous cycle of balance and imbalance in which the status quo is upset by a goal that puts us into perturbation, reintegrated through movement into a new structure, and then challenged yet again. Ideally, our kinesthetic intelligence—how we move and sense—provides the home base for how we process all spatial, mental, emotional, and spiritual information. Because our movement patterns form the foundation for how we approach and integrate new learning, ease of learning and the creation of new structures can be happy by-products of our whole-brain activation.

We're always going to be presented with problems, because the overcoming of challenges is what life is all about. We live in a world full of troubles and change—both personal and societal. The tornados will come, and we get to choose which ones to meet head on. Nearly always, if we look beneath the surface of someone's apparently carefree life, we'll find some form of difficulty going on. There's nothing wrong with this: we live in an expanding and evolving universe, and the force that energizes our transformation is friction. If nothing opposed us, how would we learn and grow?

So we can choose to see life's challenges as catalysts. They cause us to live on the edge, where we can feel the tension of opposites. From pain and suffering to health and vitality, from fear and alienation to love and compassion, from poverty and failure to success and abundance, our experience of these oppositional forces allows us to learn from them. When we work with a difficulty and overcome it, we make a quantum leap in personal development and we taste the exquisite life that rests in the balance between these diverse elements.

In the course of several decades, I've worked with thousands of people. These individuals of all ages have represented the full spectrum of humanity . . . from delayed learners to gifted students . . . happy people to those in tragedy and despair . . . bookworms to athletes . . . househusbands to women who run corporations . . . and across the spectrum I find that people everywhere are more alike than different.

People come to me because they feel blocked in one or more areas of their life—education, career, relationship, and finances being the most common—and they hope I'll help them find the key to moving in a new way. Even when a session requires a translator, this work communicates itself. What I have to offer is simple: I do my best to create a context in which my clients' innate intelligence and body wisdom can function and their natural state of integration can be reestablished. When this happens, the client doesn't simply return to their previous automatic-pilot mode, but progresses to an entirely new level of functioning. This is because we are creative beings, designed to re-create ourselves constantly.

Julie's Story: From Struggle to a New Aliveness

I worked some time back with a client I'll call Julie, a single parent who owned a travel agency. For years, the airlines paid commissions to travel agencies for selling tickets to their customers. Then, with the advent of the Internet, airlines placed a cap on commissions. Julie told me that, whereas in the past she'd have earned one hundred fifty dollars selling a first-class ticket from Chicago to Los Angeles, she now earned only a third of that. She'd been struggling to adapt to this situation ever since, but her business was losing money.

The goal Julie brought to her session was to remedy this situation so her business could again thrive. I noticed that, as Julie talked emphatically about her situation, she began first to move her head slightly, as if saying no, then to sway her whole body in various directions as she gestured, as if she were searching for a central theme to her difficulty.

Our movement patterns can change, often in a moment. I see the Edu-K balance process as an opportunity to slow down in our daily lives and "stop a moment in time" to really observe our circumstances. We can then take a deeper look at the pattern of movement we're using for whatever current goal we've identified, and invite some new ways of moving toward that goal that will draw from a wider array of our resources.

It's been my experience as an educator that, until people are able to make their own choices or set goals from their own unique needs, no true learning takes place. When I observe a toddler learning to climb stairs, or coach an athlete to perfect her golf swing, I see the skill of noticing in action. Noticing is the ability to self-reflect around "How I do what I do" and "What I do or don't already know how to do" and to observe my own experience. For associations to be created, all learning must be felt in the body. Curious learners spontaneously review their experience to notice which elements of the learning have been truly integrated and which have not yet been absorbed.

Using one of the noticing techniques I've developed, I asked Julie to compare two movements: first, to bend her knees and move closer to the ground; next, to stand and reach up toward the sky. I suggested that she notice her experience as she did each one. Julie noticed what she felt with each movement, then conveyed to me that she felt numb to her senses and her movement and disconnected from her feelings. In this way, we used movement to check whether Julie's goal was aligned with her body wisdom, and discovered that it wasn't. In this situation, it seemed Julie was out of touch with her true desires and needs.

Julie had learned to override messages from her body so that she could force herself to keep going in spite of fatigue, pain, or discomfort. She hadn't had much experience actually listening to what her body was telling her. She decidedly preferred the latter movement of reaching upward, and seemed uncomfortable in the grounding, stabilizing part of the movement. Like Dorothy caught up in the tornado, Julie was stuck in a "higher altitude"—the analytical atmosphere of the left brain.

Analysis is a vital ingredient of our functioning. We need our powers of discrimination to make sense of our experience and to bring together and use new skills as we develop them. Unfortunately, though, the analytical mind has come to dominate our modern world, and in doing so it has brought a plethora of problems. Overanalysis is actually a form of worry—one that spins us away from the balance and clarity of our body wisdom.

With a little coaching, Julie discovered a goal that had more aliveness for her: what she really wanted was to earn her living with more joy and greater ease. She felt burned out and disgusted by her current situation, yet was unable to take action in a creative way. Julie felt she was frantically try to push the grindstone harder so that a little more corn would be ground at the end of each day.

When we use the cerebral, thinking part of the brain to the exclusion of our feelings, we often bounce from the analysis of the left brain to a state of judgment that can derive from the right frontal lobes, and we then feel stuck and unable to make decisions. This cycle often leads to frustration, anger, and depression.

Yet, when we honor our feelings, the right frontal lobes access associated memories and movement experiences that provide neural connections to the left frontal lobes and our sense of possibility, giving us that euphoric "Aha," not just of making a choice, but of having a choice choose us.

After her balance, Julie told me how good it felt to walk around my office feeling the soles of her bare feet make contact with the floor. She now expressed an entirely new perspective on her situation. Her agency was located in the center of the city—where it had to be, if it was going to survive. It had suddenly become clear to her that she no longer wanted to struggle. She'd had more than enough of stressed travelers placing unrealistic demands on her. She now reconnected with a long-time dream to live in a more rural area of the state, several hours to the north.

The next time I spoke with Julie, she had a beautiful story to tell. She'd found a job in the human resources department of a prestigious hotel and spa located in the coastal mountains. She loved her job, and she and her daughter couldn't have been happier with their new life in a quaint little town that Julie had previously only visited as a tourist. Many of the skills that Julie had acquired as a travel agency owner—hiring and managing people, familiarity with the travel industry, and so on—were being put to use in a new, life-affirming environment. Once she had accessed her freedom of movement, she was no longer stuck in the old rut. She was able to conserve the useable threads from her past and weave them into a wonderful new pattern of living.

Julie's story reminds me that when the tornado lifts us up and deposits us in unfamiliar territory—when we can no longer rely on our old paradigms and assumptions—that's the time when we can make a real breakthrough. But we can't do it if we're fragmented and unable to access our sensory resources.

The Scarecrow: How We Communicate

When the left and right sides of the brain and the rest of the body work together, communication—whether through oral or written language—becomes clearer and more vibrant. In our work, Gail and I refer to this left-right interaction as the Laterality Dimension.

The midfield is Laterality's common area, where our two hands coordinate and our two visual fields and two auditory fields overlap for ease of pen-and-paper skills and other creative tasks involving hand-eye coordination. Full use of this midfield area depends on a sense of postural awareness at the center or core of our physical being.

When there is improved integration of the left and right sides, the communication between the two cerebral hemispheres becomes more automatic and spontaneous and we're able to do centralized work more easily. As a result, the expressive, analytic part of the brain (usually the left hemisphere) works synergistically with the receptive, gestalt side (usually the right), which means that we're able to think from the whole to the parts and vice versa. And that fulfilling integration takes us to the Land of Ahhhs.

Going back to Dorothy, on her way to the Emerald City she comes across a scarecrow who winks at her and then speaks. Surprised, Dorothy asks the Scarecrow if he knows the way to the Emerald City. He answers, "No, indeed; I don't know anything. You see, I am stuffed, so I have no brains at all." Dorothy invites him to accompany her to see the Great Oz, who can perhaps give the Scarecrow some brains.

The arms, legs, and head of Dorothy's scarecrow move in all directions as he thinks and speaks. In a live production I once saw of *The Wizard of Oz*, put on by children, I was especially delighted with the Scarecrow's antics. The young actor who played the part—an accomplished gymnast—brought the Scarecrow to life as he flopped, danced, whirled, and gyrated, always somehow avoiding his body's midfield and core postural muscles, where his two sides might coordinate.

Our movements and posture speak volumes. We've all sometimes had difficulty holding ourselves upright, or known children or adults who tilted their heads, stood on one foot, leaned on their elbows, or otherwise avoided the body's midfield in an unknowing avoidance of centralization.

The Scarecrow appears to be seeking a reasoning brain, but we quickly see that he already has one. When Dorothy's yellow brick road enters a thick, dark forest, it's the Scarecrow who uses admirable logic to figure out that they should carry on. So all he really needs is to learn to use his whole brain in an integrated way.

"If this road goes in, it must come out," says the Scarecrow, "and as the Emerald City is at the other end of the road, we must go wherever it leads us."

"Anyone would know that," says Dorothy.

"Certainly, that is why I know it," responds the Scarecrow. "If it required brains to figure it out, I never should have said it."

During the rest of their journey, the Scarecrow reasons out all manner of things, often thinking of the best course of action before Dorothy does.

The Tin Man: How We Participate

In addition to the left-right Laterality Dimension, the body houses a back-front system that Gail and I have termed the Focus Dimension. This system coordinates the brain stem in the back of the brain with the prefrontal lobes at the forehead. It represents the relationship between the front and the back of the body, together with our ability to both hold back when a situation is perceived as unsafe or to read an unfamiliar situation and then take risks for new learning. When the front and back areas of the brain and the rest of the body work together, we're able to express ourselves as active participants in life.

Focus is the key to sustained attention—to concentration, anticipation, and comprehension. In its balanced state, the front-to-back system provides us with the focus, attention, and muscular awareness we need for flexibility and ease of functioning. We can then be full participants in life, and the more actively we participate, the more rich with meaning our life will be.

The more we withdraw from life, the harder it is to find meaning. One part of this withdrawal system is aptly called the tendon-guard reflex. This is a reflex that, in times of perceived danger, automatically tightens all the tendons in the back of the body to protect the muscles from tearing or overextension. This "guard" or "warrior" within us shows great sensitivity to our boundaries, and is able to bring us to attention to defend them or to withdraw and hide, as needed, for our safety. When overstimulated, this same system can leave us hypervigilant—in a state of postural rigidity, unable to relax and restore equilibrium or to soften and feel the pleasure of physical sensation, including the sense of spatial awareness provided by our movement.

In her journey, Dorothy next comes across the Tin Man, who tells her he is looking for a heart. The Tin Man's tendency to cry and rust his joints shows us the operation of the tendon-guard reflex, which tenses the back of the body in order to keep us rigid and strong in a time of danger. This useful reflex is important for our survival, but too often becomes a habituated response.

In consequence, we become inflexible and unable to flow with changing circumstances. We may then find it hard to make choices and to think outside the box. The tendon-guard reflex is linked to fear, which blocks access to the heart's emotion, our source of creativity and inspiration. Brain Gym can help us to release this reflex behavior, let go of the fear, and get back in touch with our true nature, as revealed by the heart.

It's the organizing capability of the rhythmic heart that coordinates the front and back areas of the brain and rest of the body, softening the tendon-guard reflex so that we can respond to our environment, rather than defend or react.

The Tin Man tells the Scarecrow that he misses his heart more than his brain. "All the same," says the Scarecrow, "I shall ask for brains instead of a heart; for a fool would not know what to do with a heart if he had one."

"I shall take the heart," replies the Tin Woodman, "for brains do not make one happy, and happiness is the best thing in the world."

The Cowardly Lion: How We Stabilize

Our third dimension, the top-bottom system, integrates head and heart for access to body wisdom and innate intelligence.

Corresponding to this dimension, Dorothy and her companions next encounter the Cowardly Lion, a loveable character who joins the group in hopes that the Wizard of Oz will give him courage. The friends come to a gulf that's much too wide for them to traverse. Only the Lion has a chance at making it across, so he decides to try an experimental jump. In doing this, the Lion takes a great risk and demonstrates undeniable bravery. He is then able to carry his friends across, one at a time.

Unlike the Scarecrow, the Lion is unable to dance around all his possible options by avoiding the midline; unlike the Tin Man, he's unable to lock his knees and hold his boundaries for a sense of safety. The Lion also lacks vestibular balance, the innate sense of where we are in space. What the Lion does have is a wonderful emotional vulnerability; he is "in his heart." He's also gifted with a strong kinesthetic intelligence (the muscular aliveness in his body), for knowing the map of the forest and surrounding territory in minute detail. The Cowardly Lion shows us how to stay centered in our feeling energy, to protect and champion our heartful dreams.

Our own kinesthetic wisdom keeps us breathing and healing, when we let it. It allows our organs to function with amazing body wisdom and is the basis for how we organize all of our learning. It is our kinesthetic intelligence that allows us to feel our feet on the ground, so as to reach for our dreams. The motivation of our feelings is a central component of courage. We can feel what to do, know how to do it, and have the physical capacity for it; but if we lack motivation, nothing comes of even the boldest plans. If the Lion's caring had not been stronger than his fear, his traveling companions would still have been waiting on the wrong side of the gulf. The Cowardly Lion shows us how our voice expresses our feelings and courage.

The Cooperation of Mind, Heart, and Body

Dorothy, Toto, the Scarecrow, the Tin Man, and the Cowardly Lion pursue their journey to the Emerald City, encountering many obstacles along the way. At one point a river cuts off the road, and the friends must work together to find a way to cross it. It's the Scarecrow who thinks of a rational plan that Dorothy's three heroes cooperatively carry out. The Tin Man steps forward to cut down trees and build a raft, putting his whole heart and soul into the project. As the companions are crossing the river on the raft, the strong current begins to carry them away. The Cowardly Lion jumps courageously into the water and, with the Tin Man holding on to his tail, pulls the raft to safety.

The mind, heart, and body must work together in this way, with reason, focus, and feeling, if we are to overcome the obstacles life presents. Indeed, obstacles are placed along our path precisely so that we'll learn how to develop and integrate our God-given faculties. Life flows for us when we learn how to activate and coordinate these different aspects of our being. And this is where Brain Gym comes in: it offers practical tools for achieving integration that, although quite simple, are truly effective.

Through the Brain Gym balance process, we can each explore and bring together our unique combinations of these three movement dimensions— Laterality for communication, Focus for comprehension and meaning, and Centering for heart and passion, and in that way discover the fuller, richer life awaiting us.

An indispensable element in the mixture is intention, which glues all the other elements together. The traveling companions in *The Wizard of Oz* have a common goal: to find the Great Oz and be healed. The Scarecrow wants brains, the Tin Man wants a heart, the Cowardly Lion seeks courage, and Dorothy is after the greatest healing of all: to return home. It's the power of their intention that binds these individuals together into a team.

And intention does even more than this. When we orient ourselves toward a goal, we set into motion the forces that will bring our intention into manifestation. Though they don't realize it, each of the companions already has what he or she seeks. The Scarecrow is quite a philosopher, the Tin Man is a paragon of compassion, the Lion is valiant, and Dorothy already has in her possession the very thing that can take her home. Like a magnet, intention has the power to draw out of us the qualities we need to reach our goal. We need only to take the first step; then all manner of assistance comes to us.

Intention comes from the frontal lobe, which connects the back of the brain to the front and helps us see where we want to go. I advise my students to organize their whole life around the setting of intentions. After all, if you don't know your destination, how are you going to get there?

Our organization for thought, speech, or action depends upon the balance of these reflexes through the heart. Neural organization is associated with the Centering Dimension, which has to do with the way the top and bottom areas of the body interrelate. Our centering reflexes depend upon the midbrain, the area of the brain that invites a sense of relationship between the "thinking" cerebral cortex and the "reacting" brain stem.

There is partial truth in the Scarecrow's opinion that a person with too little brain wouldn't know what to do with a heart. You may know people who have a strong emotional response to poverty or injustice, but are never able to take effective action. When our heart is without direction, our compassion and sympathy may be of little help, even to those closest to us.

On the other hand, contemporary science is going beyond the idea that the heart, in its functioning, is limited to being the center of emotion. As we shall see in Chapter Seven, the heart is actually the center of intelligence. It is tuned into a realm that, though invisible to the conscious mind, is real and vast. When we follow the subtle promptings of this intelligence, we're taken in a direction that the mind may consider but can never be sure about. Therefore, in a very concrete way, the heart is actually also a kind of brain.

My travel agent client, Julie, was following heart intelligence when she uprooted her life and embarked on an entirely new adventure. She used her mental intellect as well, of course, and it confirmed what her heart knew: that the plan was feasible and had a good chance of working out well. Julie's mind also planned and executed the whole process of selling her home and business and relocating. But it was the emotionally propelled motivation of the heart that gave her a deep knowing that she was making the right move.

Analytical thinking, in itself, is a valuable, indispensable human faculty that constructs houses, runs governments, explores the universe, and has made possible the age of technology. The difficulty occurs only when it dominates us and ceases to be used in the way it was intended: namely, in a balanced manner in which it cooperates with the rest of the mind-body system. When this analysis takes us over as individuals and societies, it can become mechanical and heartless. However, once analytical thinking is brought back into balance with our wisdom, it's a wonderful tool.

To sum this up, we do need a brain in order to execute the plans of the heart and confirm the validity of its suggestions. With only a heart, we would feel what we needed to do but wouldn't know how to do it. At the same time, a brain without a heart makes for an empty, directionless existence.

Since heart-directed purpose brings joy to our lives, there is also truth in the Tin Man's opinion that the heart makes one happy. It's the source of enthusiasm; if the heart is left out of the equation, life becomes dull and uninspired.

Summoning Personal Power

The companions finally reach the Emerald City and meet the Great Oz, who summons each of the travelers individually. Each of them sees him in a different disguise—as, variously, an enormous head, a lovely lady, a terrible beast, and a ball of fire. The Wizard refuses to grant any wishes, however, until the companions have accomplished a nearly impossible task: destroying the Wicked Witch of the West.

They set out in the direction of her land, but the Witch spots them and makes short work of them: the Scarecrow and the Tin Man are scattered over the countryside, the Lion is hitched to the witch's chariot, and Dorothy becomes the witch's slave. What Dorothy doesn't know is that actually the witch can't harm her. To the contrary, the Witch herself is extremely vulnerable, since water melts her. Dorothy discovers this by accident, and the witch dies.

Dorothy is now able to use the witch's most powerful allies—the winged monkeys—for her own purposes. So she has them transport her and her companions back to the Emerald City.

Life asks us to confront our darkest fear. When we do, we discover that this fear has no power of its own; it has usurped the power that rightly belongs to us. When Dorothy faces up to the Witch, the Witch melts, unable to resist goodness and innocence.

The Return Home

The Great Oz is revealed to be a little man who lost his way many years ago and ended up in this strange land. He's unable to assist the travelers, but realizes he doesn't need to, since they already possess the attributes they're asking for. So he pretends to grant their wishes. He fills the Scarecrow's head with pins and needles and packs them down with straw; he gives the Tin Man a silk heart stuffed with sawdust; and he has the Lion drink a green liquid that will give him courage.

Dorothy's three companions can now believe in the gifts that were already theirs. Dorothy, however is a different matter: Oz has no idea how she can return to Kansas. But he tells her that Glinda, the Good Witch of the West who lives on the edge of the desert, may know the answer.

The four companions, together with Toto, find Glinda, and the Good Witch does indeed help them. She asks the winged monkeys to carry the Scarecrow back to the Emerald City, where he becomes the ruler. The monkeys take the Tin Man to the land of the Winkies (fine craftsmen and goldsmiths), who want him as their leader. And the Lion takes his rightful place as king of the jungle.

This leaves only Dorothy, who's still trying to get back to Kansas. The Good Witch tells her the secret she's been needing to know.

"The silver shoes," says the Good Witch, "have wonderful powers. And one of the most curious things about them is that they can carry you to anyplace in the world in three steps, and each step will be made in the wink of an eye."

And that's how the story ends: the mind, the heart, and the body each have a kingdom to rule. The mind governs the capital city; the heart reigns over the land where gold is wrought; and the body has dominion over the wild, untamed regions. The result of each faculty regaining its power and its kingdom and working in harmony in the Land of Oz is that Dorothy, the now fully integrated human being, gets to click her heels and go home.

The story of Brain Gym has the same happy ending. We activate the brain and connect it to the heart, we fortify intention and purpose, and we anchor new learning in the body. The result is that we become more fully what we have always been: curious learners freely actualizing our potential.

When we're in that place in our body—back home—we have a life with purpose, and can simply click our heels to bring the magic of the Land of Ahhhs, the heart and the sensory delight of learning, into the home of our body.

Chapter Five

Physical Access to Brain Function

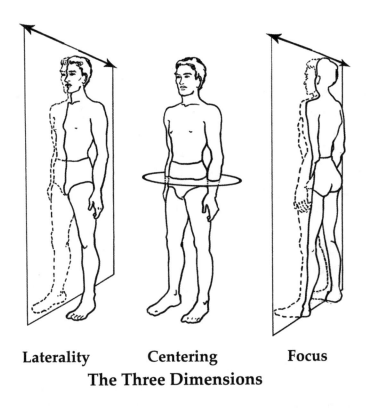

Laterality   Centering   Focus
The Three Dimensions

Like the Scarecrow, the Tin Man, and the Cowardly Lion, all humans
need a brain, a heart, and courage. We all need the ability to access and
function within three dimensions of movement: side-to-side to access
the brain (Laterality); top-to-bottom to access the heart (Centering);
and back-to-front to access courage (Focus). These simple movement
patterns help us to maintain our balance in space and provide the
neurological foundation for all our higher functions. In this chapter,
we'll be exploring these three dimensions in depth.

Laterality

Over millennia, we humans have developed a remarkable skill—the ability to focus our attention and center our body in space as a stable base for thought, using our two hands and two eyes in the midfield as we also coordinate our two auditory channels. Our laterality refers to our left-to-right and right-to-left movements and the ability to cross the body's vertical midline with ease and comfort. When our left and right cerebral hemispheres work together, we have the ability to communicate and use tools—to record our thoughts or designs through writing or drawing and to explore the thoughts or images of others through reading.

Our lateral midfield is the space where the left and right visual, auditory, and kinesthetic fields overlap, allowing us to use contralateral and bilateral movements and to bring images and language together for listening, thinking, and speaking. As our left and right visual fields meet, they provide us the beauty and immediacy of depth perception and the visual world; as our left and right auditory fields converge, we receive linguistic communication and all the rich information of sound; and as we coordinate our two hands in the midfield we can touch, create with tools, and otherwise interact within our environment.

The Laterality Dimension is where we make experiences familiar and create meaning for our life. It enables an inner verbal dialogue, an ability to encode and communicate in linear, temporal fashion our sensory and spatial experiences so that we can later reexperience them. Our coded words "bring it all back" to us for recall. The ease with which we think, read, speak, listen, and write—in fact, use any skill of communication—provides a clue as to how well we are accessing this Laterality Dimension for receiving and expressing information.

Paradoxically, these subtle, fine-motor, higher brain functions of communication are understood and developed by means of the left and right hemispheres, which in earlier humans governed gross-motor laterality. For thousands of years, as nomads, hunters, and farmers, our contralateral movement—especially our walking or running—was the primary movement pattern that trained us in the simultaneous use of both cerebral hemispheres and both sides of the body.

Our simultaneous accessing of the rational, linear, language-mediated qualities of the logic brain (usually the left) and the symbolic, spatial, and intuitive processes of the gestalt brain (commonly the right) is a complex ability. What matters most to us in Educational Kinesiology is that this accessing depends on our creating, through movement, a strong and active lateral bridge of neuropathways between the two cerebral hemispheres and their corresponding sides of the body.

The Cross Crawl is perhaps humankind's ideal movement for experiencing this bilateral integration, as it requires coordination of dual brain hemispheres and left and right arms and legs, all working in rhythmic sequence.

The Cross Crawl movement, done consistently over a period of weeks or months, helps to restore or develop the three key elements of human movement patterns: core postural awareness, muscle proprioception, and vestibular balance. Like the Scarecrow, we need postural awareness (a sense of our core postural muscles) so we can stand upright. Like the Tin Man, we need muscle proprioception for fluid, flexible, and coordinated movement. And like the Cowardly Lion, we need vestibular balance to give us equilibrium. Whole-brain learning—the kind that came more readily in the world of our grandparents—depends on these three elements to provide a context of whole-body movement. This context in turn supports the fine-motor skills required for such areas of higher learning as reading and writing.

The Seated Cross Crawl

Would you like to experience the relaxing and invigorating qualities of the Cross Crawl for yourself? Let's do a seated version. Simultaneously lift your right hand and left leg, lightly tapping the hand just above your left knee. Then return the hand and leg to a resting position as you lift your left hand and right leg, touching your left hand to the place above its opposite knee. Continue this back-and-forth pattern for a minute or so, as though walking rhythmically.

89

Now rest for a moment with your feet flat on the floor. What are you experiencing, now that you've activated both your cerebral hemispheres at the same time?

Dennison Laterality Repatterning

| **The Cross Crawl** | **The Homolateral Crawl** |

The Cross Crawl, which helps people coordinate their thoughts and actions, is learned and performed by the motor cortex, and can become automatic through continued practice. One of the better-known processes in my work is Dennison Laterality Repatterning (DLR), through the use of which people can more readily enjoy the benefits of the Cross Crawl—often in a single experience. In DLR, within the context of a five-step balance process we perform a specific pattern of Cross Crawl and one-sided (Homolateral Crawl) movements.

The Homolateral Crawl involves lifting the arm and leg on the same side of the body, rather than on opposite sides as in the Cross

Crawl. Controlled by the cerebellum, the movement modulator of our brain stem, it's a more primitive movement. The reflexive Homolateral Crawl is a parallel, one side-at-a time movement and, as such, doesn't access whole-brain integration as the Cross Crawl does. Once the Cross Crawl is learned and automatic (integrated), however, I find that the Homolateral Crawl elicits a more integrated state of parallel processing that helps people stop and think for split seconds in the flowing, bilateral context of simultaneous movement and thought.

Ideally, cross-lateral (side-to-side) integration develops naturally at around nine months of age, when babies bring together several previously learned infant reflexes, such as lifting the head and looking with both eyes together, as they coordinate opposite arms and legs for crawling.

Yet too often today's children miss the opportunity to integrate their infant reflexes. They are not as free as infants once were to turn over, scoot on their stomachs, crawl, play, and eventually run around— normal movement experiences biologically designed for a specific purpose: to grow the brain.

One problem is that they are confined too much in playpens and walkers. Also, many children aren't breastfed. Breastfeeding is a natural process that stimulates key one-sided reflexes in the child, as well as bilateral coordination. The confines of baby swings and carriers, the flickering sedation of television (now found in the bedrooms of many children age two or less), and the movement-deprived environments of pre-schools and schools all contribute to a weakening of the cross-lateral reflex.

Dennison Laterality Repatterning can greatly benefit one's life. When the first reaction of our nervous system is to run from stress, we go into a survival regression known as the homolateral or parallel-processing state. The Homolateral Crawl then becomes our automatic response; we might do this one-sided movement all day long without giving it any thought, yet wonder why we feel so rushed, fragmented, and scattered.

When DLR has enabled us to default to the Cross Crawl as our preferred movement pattern, our response to perceived stress is different. The Cross Crawl engages both sides of the whole body, including the brain's cerebral cortex, integrating them into the form of a moving X. The left arm and right foot form one line of the X; the right arm and left foot form the other.

The pioneering brain surgeon Wilder Penfield discovered that his patients would involuntarily move their eyes when he used electrodes to stimulate different areas of their brain. The eyes would move away from the stimulated area; when the motor cortex was activated, the eyes would look down, and when the brain stem was activated they would look up.

In confirmation of Dr. Penfield's finding, I can tell immediately when a person is challenged for doing the Cross Crawl, as he or she must look down when moving and has to guide the Cross Crawl visually and self-consciously. This indicates a stress state, one in which the Cross Crawl is not learned and automatic and the sense of the X is not anchored in the core of the body. Whole-brain learning is integrated only when it is learned at the brain-stem level and therefore automatic. A key concept in Brain Gym is that we can only begin to access our full potential when we move in this whole-brain way.

DLR in Action

Paula has come to see me all the way from Perth, Australia. She read about the Cross Crawl in my first book, *Switching On*, and wants to finally learn the movement, one that she's never been able to do. (I'm telling you about Paula because hers was such an extreme case of developmental delay that it serves as a good example of the potential benefits of Dennison Laterality Repatterning.)

I notice that Paula looks perpetually startled; she seems to have forgotten how to assume a normal state of relaxation. She says that the Homolateral Crawl (simultaneously lifting one leg and one arm on the same side of the body, then switching to the other side) is a delight to her because she doesn't need to plan and think about the movement. This activity mimics the Moro startle reflex (the reflex to fling the arms outward when startled), which infants ideally integrate in the first few months of life, and evidently Paula's neural development had been arrested at this stage.

When Paula attempts the Cross Crawl, though, she can't even begin to do the movement. Crossing the midline is still unfamiliar to her, and she appears lost and confused. She looks down at her knees, starting again and again to lift the same arm and leg instead of opposite limbs, struggling to figure it out. When Paula does the Homolateral Crawl, she looks up and appears to be in a state of infantile bliss, accessing her cerebellum but without the added benefit of conscious thought, which must be provided by the motor cortex in the prefrontal lobes.

I ask Paula to read a paragraph from a book, and find that she has a hard time reading the words in the center of the page. She has no sense of the midfield, and has to point with her finger even to read the words on the sides of the page. Paula, her father, and her children have all carried the label and stigma of dyslexia.

Left Field	Midfield	Right Field
Right-Brain Learning	Integrated Learning	Left-Brain Learning
	Midline →	

In 1984, I coined the term "midfield" to describe the area where a person's two perceptual fields overlap. We can imagine an X in the middle of this convergence area. This is the place where the whole is more than the sum of its parts. It's where centralized vision takes place, where we develop the ability to learn with one eye without inhibiting the other. If we don't learn this, we will always avoid the midfield and midline in favor of working on one side or the other, and our usual experience will be the stress and dysfunction of parallel processing.

When we're under stress, our eyes move laterally, searching for danger in the periphery. If someone asks us to read when we're distressed, we'll use only our nondominant eye, for the primary human function is survival. Our dominant eye is searching for danger, which makes central eye focus or eye teaming impossible, thus diminishing our ease of reading and comprehension.

To teach Paula to do the Cross Crawl, I move one of her arms and its opposite leg toward each other along the diagonal, saying, "Why don't you look up instead of down, as you do for the Homolateral Crawl, while I guide you like this?" I assist her in moving through the pattern three or four times, alternating her arms and opposite legs. When I can feel that she's doing the Cross Crawl by herself, I let go of her limbs and let her do it unaided.

"Look, Paula," I exclaim, "You're doing it!'

Paula looks down and cries out, 'I am! I'm doing it!' Paula is cross crawling for perhaps the first time in her life.

"Now let's see what happens," I suggest, "with the homolateral crawl that was so automatic and blissful for you a moment ago."

This time, instead of doing the crawl like a reflex, Paula is looking down mindfully and with intention. I can tell she's paying attention and is able to stop and think about what she's doing. She is now able to do the movement thoughtfully, with conscious control. She can still do the Homolateral Crawl, but is no longer doing it mechanically. Her motor cortex is reorganizing around the movement, and she's clearly beginning to be aware of her body moving in space.

Before her repatterning, Paula did the Homolateral Crawl reflexively—an indication that her brain stem (where the startle reflex is located) was in control. When she did the crawl, activating her brain stem, she instinctively looked up— a further indication that she was searching her primal memory for survival information. When trying to do the Cross Crawl, Paula was using her motor cortex to reinvent the pattern, and had to look down to take control of her postural awareness, muscle proprioception, and vestibular balance.

The eye movements I asked Paula to do allowed her to learn the Cross Crawl movement in her brain stem as a pattern. She now knew how to perform the movement automatically, while still being able to bring consciousness into it as needed—meaning that she could move and think at the same time, or stop and think when necessary. In this way, the repatterning process provided a metaphor for experiencing parallel processing (the Homolateral Crawl) in the context of bilateral processing (the Cross Crawl).

When we take people through this ten-minute process in the context of a Brain Gym balance, it results in deep learning that is usually permanent. In some instances a person needs more than one repatterning for the Cross Crawl to become automatic. Yet, once someone actually "gets it," it seems they've connected with a lasting template of what ideally should have happened at that critical moment at nine months when an infant gets up on hands and knees and starts crawling toward an object of desire.

I don't believe we can reproduce this experience for an adult by simply having him crawl on his hand and knees. An infant's brain is more holographic than an adult's, meaning that a child can generalize learning more easily. It's been my experience that when adults crawl without repatterning, the needed integration doesn't occur.

Cerebral Dominance

Our discussion of laterality and left-right integration leads us to the topic of cerebral dominance—assumptions about the left and right brains. The popularity of this topic and resulting conjecture about the qualities of the left and right brains have caused the validity of brain dominance to fall into disrepute among scientists. Some complain that they'll do research, for example, on a very small sample of people who are musical and left-handed, and suddenly newspaper headlines are proclaiming: "Scientists Say Right Brain Is in Charge of Music."

The pop-culture idea of left brain/right brain carries the concept way beyond what science has actually demonstrated. A common notion, for instance, is that language is initiated from the left hemisphere, but this isn't strictly true. Language, albeit language of a different kind, is also initiated from the right hemisphere.

The whole human physiology (brain, eyes, ears, arms, etc.) reorganizes itself moment by moment to perform specific tasks. Performance perceived to be successful and therefore reinforced, whether actually beneficial or not, establishes patterns that are repeated and that become behavioral habits. Healthy, whole-brain learning comes from the ability to balance these previously learned strategies with new, more flexible patterns as they become available. Whole-brain neural organization is a dynamic, continuously changing process involving the three dimensions, not the static, one-sided state suggested by the concept of "cerebral dominance."

Dominance Is a Misnomer

I'd like to say at this point how unfortunate I find it that the word "dominance" is so prevalent in the literature on brain function. I would prefer the term "hemispheric lead." Dominance implies a suppression of the nondominant, as happens during the survival reflex of parallel processing. But any time an attempt is made to accomplish learning in an environment of fear, hemispheric inhibition will result. When fear isn't a factor, neural processing is more balanced: one side leads and the other supports and collaborates. This is whole-brain processing or integration.

The brain-dominance principles espoused by Brain Gym are different from those held by past specialists, who adhered to the paradigm in which "dominant hemisphere" meant the left brain—the side in control of language and expression. Using handedness as a determining factor, these earlier experts believed that most people were left-brained and speech-center-dominant. Since right-handedness prevails in 80 percent of the population, the mistaken idea that the language brain is dominant seemed logical. Fortunately, this thinking is changing as the new science provides more information about brain function.

Granted, in the case of a stroke or accident, the loss of speech seems more disruptive than the loss of movement. However, there is no "better" dominance for healthy people, nor has nature selected one side of the brain to lead the other.

To the contrary, considerable research proves that analytic-brain personalities and gestalt-brain personalities occur in equal numbers in the population. That is to say, half of all humans are left-brained and the other half are right-brained.

Scientists now recognize that, in the animal kingdom, half the creatures in the world are right-pawed and half are left-pawed. These same scientists must reconcile this finding with the ratio of right and left "paws" in the human population: 90 percent of us are righties, and only 10 percent lefties.

The explanation for this discrepancy is obvious when we consider how humans differ from animals. Humans are uniquely blessed with a sense of time and a conscious mind that learns to use new tools and do new things with intention, control, and fine-motor skills. This motoric control and near-point focus is done over time, with a beginning, a middle, and an end. It originates in the same hemisphere where speech and language also originate: for most of us, the left hemisphere. And so, as we activate our left brain, most of us will feel a greater sense of control when we use our right hand.

Thus it is survival in the human environment and the need for manual dexterity that create right-handedness. Therefore, handedness isn't a good indicator of hemispheric lead. Foot and leg dominance may be much more reliable, as how we move our legs suggests metaphorically how we move in the world: spontaneously (with a right-brain lead) or (when the left brain is dominant) according to the control of step-by-step rules, over time.

Valid Brain-Area Distinctions
I can offer a useful distinction between the left and right brains that resolves most of the previous speculation. The right brain, more connected to sensory experience, is open to new learning and experiences, processing novelty in a spontaneous, kinesthetic, and imaginative way, whereas the left brain, more involved in performance, codes new information as a blueprint for future use, going step by step in a linear, logical, timely fashion. The integration of the two allows a learned experience to be registered in the whole body in the form of a pattern. No real learning can take place unless this happens, and once this pattern has been established in the body, the new behavior is remembered forever.

Another valid distinction is that the left hemisphere operates from the head down, whereas the right hemisphere processes information from the body up. What this means is that the left brain can only be aware of and analyze information coming from the direct experience provided by the right brain. It can't know anything new without the body informing it, being confined to the task of creating strategies and language that can then be stored for later use. The right brain, on the other hand, is aware of what comes up from the body and all the lower parts of the brain, including the emotionally charged limbic system.

Without the body and the right brain, we stay confined in the old structure and can't do anything new. We're on automatic pilot and eventually get bored and depressed. Conversely, without the left hemisphere the new input experienced in the right brain can't be utilized again in the future. We need a fully functioning left brain in order to organize novel information and make it meaningful, and we need it for pleasure, too, since pleasure arises chemically in the left brain when we learn and do something well.

When our left hemisphere is teaching us how to do something new out of our right-brain sensory and play experiences, we feel like successful learners and are rewarded with increased dopamine levels and the endorphins that give us that euphoria of mastery, of a job well done. We need to be learning and growing every day to feel alive and in love with life. When we can't learn, especially if we're feeling helpless and overwhelmed, a stressed or frustrated right frontal lobe comes under the influence of lowered serotonin levels.

Also involved is melatonin, a depressant (produced by the pineal gland) that is the chemical equivalent of darkness, depressing the reticular activating system so the brain can sleep. So an unbalanced right hemisphere puts us in the loop for depression. Yet, when our left brain is able to code new learning and express itself, our right brain knows everything is going to work out after all; serotonin levels rise, while melatonin is inhibited. In other words, the whole brain and body need always to be creative—learning and doing something new in order to avoid frustration and depression. Pleasure comes from mastery. It's like repeatedly baking a certain kind of cake, making the recipe better and better until finally we get it perfect or create something new. That's what it's like when the whole brain and body are in action.

Unity, Not Uniformity

Patterns of brain dominance have individual differences: some people are right-handed and left-eyed; some are right-handed and right-eyed; and so on. A person's exact version of sidedness indicates his or her dominance pattern. As Carla Hannaford proposes, this may be connected to the first survival-reflex development in utero.

I first began to suspect a relationship between dominance patterns and learning profiles in 1969, while testing the students who attended my Southern California learning centers. (My intent for these centers was to provide a place in which children and adults could improve their academic skills, and especially reading, using the most advanced techniques available.) I noted the dominance patterns of the students and correlated the findings with their educational profiles. This procedure revealed compelling evidence that learning challenges are directly related to a person's dominance pattern.

The understanding that we each have our own preferred circuitry can contribute greatly to the development of tolerance and more enlightened teaching methods, not just in schools but in all the other places where learning takes place. The many different dominance profiles are useful for educators and parents to know because they supply important information about an individual's learning style. This empowers us to design learning situations that work *with* the person's inclinations, not against them.

It's not possible here to give a complete account of this vast subject. Whole books have been written about it, and you may wish to refer to one of them. I recommend *The Dominance Factor: How Knowing Your Dominant Eye, Ear, Brain, Hand & Foot Can improve Your Learning* by Carla Hannaford, because Carla has been a colleague through the years and knows Brain Gym well.

It takes some time and persistence to become familiar with dominance profiles, but it's worth the effort. Not only is it good for people to be recognized and respected for their individual circuitry but awareness of brain organization is good for all of society. We all benefit when we learn to value each person's unique style.

In the course of my career, I have found that understanding brain-dominance patterns assists me enormously in identifying an individual's learning style, and thus provides the most successful tools and educational context for that individual.

I was not the first researcher to take note of a student's dominant hand, eye, and ear: psychologists and educational therapists had made this a routine part of their practice. However, to my knowledge nothing constructive in the way of effective educational intervention was ever done with the information. In fact, most authorities in education, psychology, and medicine ignored brain-organization findings, and absolutely no allowance for these dominance patterns was made in the way teachers presented their subjects.

In accordance with educational convention, each student, even in schools where the profile was known, received much the same curriculum. Remedial teachers would therefore break down the material to be learned and present it in small, manageable pieces, with emphasis on rote memorization, long study hours, and great effort on the part of the student. Caring, patience, and one-on-one instruction often helped the student reach mastery, but while many succeeded in this way, others fell by the wayside.

Teaching doesn't have to go on in this haphazard manner. New discoveries about learning continue to be made, yet the many studies completed in the areas of education and the mind have already unearthed all the information we need to create academic programs that respond to each student's individual learning style.

Instead of measuring performance against an unrealistic standard, it's possible to appreciate an individual's unique abilities, as identified by his dominance profile. Moreover, with the development of Brain Gym it's possible for parallel processors to more easily access a natural state of unified thinking, one in which both hemispheres function synergistically.

If one looks at PET scans and EEGs during stress, the nondominant hemisphere shuts down by 75-85 percent. In such times of limbic-brain survival response, the whole brain isn't needed. With the brain adopting an efficiency pattern for survival that doesn't allow for whole-brain functioning, a person need only react by reflex. The Brain Gym program is profound because it provides a context for the two hemispheres to work together, stimulates the frontal lobes via the motor cortex (as well as the sensory cortex in the parietal lobes), and activates the entire motor mechanism throughout the brain, including the vestibular (balance) and reticular activating systems.

Certain brain-dominance patterns have been shown by researchers to be associated with particular traits. In Brain Gym we honor the inherent brain organization of each individual, as manifested through personal behavior as well as through the preferred eye, ear, hand, and so forth. We also recognize that mainstream educators have traditionally ignored many of the learning styles represented by these dominance patterns. Not only can we inspire educators to help children reach their full and unique potential, as is beginning to happen all over the world, but, since these patterns are often familial, we can also counsel parents about the gifts and needs that they share with their children.

How to Determine Your Own Brain-Dominance Profile

To find out your own dominance profile, check yourself in the following ways. Before you start, I should mention that it's preferable to check without thinking about it, since spontaneous action reveals dominance more accurately than trying to figure it out. Since it's hard to read instructions and be spontaneous, I suggest you ask someone to read the following to you.

Eye dominance: Focus on an object in the distance, looking through a small opening in your joined hands as you hold them at arm's length. Alternately close one eye and then the other. Which eye is focusing through the opening?

Ear dominance: Pick up the telephone and listen to the dial tone. Which ear are you using?

Hand dominance: With which hand do you write?

Leg dominance: Stand with your feet together and let yourself start to fall forward. Which foot steps out to keep you from falling?

Hemispheric dominance: Everyone has one hemisphere that leads; the other one follows. Ask yourself, *When I'm under stress, do I need to talk about it and figure it out before I'm willing to take action?* If you do, this indicates that you're most likely left-hemisphere dominant. If you tend to act spontaneously, you're probably more right-brain-dominant in your orientation to life.

Uniform Dominance

For ease of learning the basic skills of reading, writing, and spelling, ideally the student's analytic (left) hemisphere will be dominant, as well as her right eye, ear, hand, and foot. An individual with this profile will tend to excel academically without a great deal of apparent effort. She will always be ready in class, will follow directions well, will be highly verbal, and will understand linear and logical concepts more readily than do most students. This student will be prime "teacher's pet" material!

When this student's left brain is firing, she's activating the right side of her body, with no neurological conflict between language activation, on the one hand, and vision, hearing, and fine-motor control, on the other. (The writing function is controlled via the motor cortex of the brain's left hemisphere.) By the age of six, if this child has been in a safe, nurturing environment, she has developed her gestalt,

101

global, open-to-new-information right hemisphere to be in synchrony with her analytical left hemisphere, and is able to cross the midline competently, without "switching off" or inhibiting either side of her brain.

She is thus able to see the whole and the parts together, and to anticipate, remember, and visualize. Her dominance pattern will tend to have few, if any, learning complications.

However, uniform left-brain, right-sided dominance doesn't guarantee an effortless academic experience. There may be a marked tendency to exclude the gestalt hemisphere when the language brain is activated. If the child is denied positive, enjoyable movement and life experiences, she may not learn to interact, to use her imagination and creativity, or to relax and let go. She may have stress from her language brain, related to time, goals, or self-criticism. She may try too hard and be paralyzed by a need for perfection.

Sometimes children who have uniform dominance are so well rewarded for switching off the gestalt brain in school that, by the time they are in third grade, they lose the advantage they had in the earlier grades. They often know the answers but can't write them down because they're trying too hard; that is, they allow the analytic/language brain to control the writing hand so that movement becomes awkward as they vacillate between thought and action.

In this one-sided state, they can't express what they know because their language brain, which can do only one thing at a time, is involved in the mechanics of writing instead of thinking and expressing. They can't access their long-term memory to retrieve the information that they thought they knew.

If children who are uniform-dominant try too hard (and thus become stressed), they may read with the right eye only, becoming easily fatigued. They can't always infer the meanings of words from the context—a gestalt function—and may rely excessively on their superior decoding abilities. They may read with a high, shrill voice, which shows the stress of the language brain analyzing the text. These children can think much faster than they can read. Reading usually bores them, since the joy it can bring depends on an integrated state in which both eyes and hemispheres work together.

Children with uniform dominance also tend to make spelling errors that reveal their tendency to sound out words rather than visualize them. They have difficulty recognizing that a word looks wrong, and it's a challenge for them to sense the similarities between the roots of new words and familiar words. They may repeat the same spelling errors, since they're unable to associate the word they're writing with the same word in long-term memory. They may not be able to make use of rhythm clues such as rhymes or syllabication.

Still, uniform-dominant learners tend to compensate well in school; they can achieve academic success with relatively little stress. They are usually good workers, although they may lack imagination. They sometimes have difficulty expressing their feelings, and may be unable to associate creativity and feeling with work or success. They may not see the connection between life and school or, later, life and work.

Mixed Dominance

Mixed dominance occurs when the dominant eye, ear, hand, and leg are not on the same side of the body. More than 50 percent of the learning-disabled population is mixed-dominant, for this pattern invites confusion and disorganization, especially in the parallel-processing state.

The problem is particularly acute when a child is left-eye-dominant and right-handed. The compensation for (from this student's point of view) the unnatural process of reading from left to right is to switch off the dominant eye in order to lead with the right eye. Visual memory and other gestalt skills then become minimally available.

One-Sided Dominance

Many people with learning challenges are completely right-sided as well as right-hemisphere-dominant. So under stress they become overwhelmed and stuck, unable to simultaneously think and access hand, eye, ear, and foot.

Jim's Story

Jim is a thirty-three-year-old executive who wants to improve his poor reading skills, which he has self-diagnosed as dyslexia. He feels that his problem is holding him back in his career, and confesses that he does everything he can to hide his difficulties. When his secretary asks him to review a letter, he tells her he's busy and will take care of it later. In reality, he wants to avoid perusing it while she's standing over him. If he is expected to review documents in a meeting, he says he has forgotten his glasses and asks a colleague to give him an account of the salient points. His job has become a nightmare.

Jim has never enjoyed reading, since it has always been such a struggle for him. His brain-dominance profile is mixed: right/gestalt-brain-dominant, right-handed, left-eyed, and right-eared. He sits nervously in my office, holding a book I've given him and looking as if his life depends on reading a paragraph from the book perfectly.

I try to put him at ease by telling him that the "before" reading isn't supposed to be a punishment. "It allows a before-and-after comparison," I explain, "so that both of us can have the satisfaction of observing any change. This reinforces the new behaviors you'll be learning." Jim looks unimpressed, and clearly has no intention of relaxing.

As he reads across the page, Jim's eyes jump uncontrollably instead of flowing back and forth from line to line. He stops every few lines to think, or to reread something he has already forgotten. His reading voice doesn't sound like his natural speaking voice, a well-modulated tenor, but is strained and high-pitched. He sometimes stumbles over punctuation or gasps for air in the middle of a phrase.

When I ask him to say in his own words what he's just read, he's unable to paraphrase, instead searching his short-term memory to echo the author's exact words. This behavior would typically lead to Jim's being labeled as having dyslexia or ADD. He's switching off his dominant gestalt style and far-sighted left eye in order to read. While avoiding the midfield, he has survived the educational system by parallel processing, alternating from one hemisphere to the other and memorizing and cramming his way through printed material.

I ask Jim to do several Brain Gym movements to learn bilateral processing in the midfield. This involves performing movements selected specifically for his profile, to help integrate the two sides of the brain. For example, Jim does a series of Lazy 8s, tracing infinity signs in the air. To activate his nondominant gestalt ear, I ask him to do another series, this time with his right ear pressed against his right arm. We call this movement (which is unique to Brain Gym) "The Elephant," because the outstretched arm looks like an elephant's trunk.

When we've finished the selected movements, we return to the book. Jim still looks nervous. He begins reading a paragraph and immediately starts to relax; he can tell there's been a change. He now reads fluently, and can picture the overall meaning effortlessly. When I ask him to give a summary of what he's read, he no longer needs to repeat key sentences verbatim, but is able to paraphrase the information in his own words. Jim is delighted, and asks me if that's all there is to it. I tell him that he ought to practice the movements for a month, in order to reinforce the new behaviors, and that once he's done the anchoring he should have no more problems.

"Can it really be so simple?" he asks.

"Imagine that you're in the habit of driving a car with crossed legs," I reply. "You're accelerating with your left foot and braking with your right. It's not a natural arrangement for your body, and it results in discomfort—not to mention awkward driving. You've done this all your life; this is what driving means to you, so you keep trying to make it work. Every time you go on a car trip, you feel miserable.

"How hard would it be for me to guide you into uncrossing your legs? It would be simple! Yet the results—in terms of increased driving skill and pleasure—would be astonishing."

"Why doesn't everyone do Brain Gym?" Jim exclaims with boyish enthusiasm.

I laugh. "That's a question I'd love to be able to answer!"

The Laterality Dimension, then, has to do with left-to-right and side-to-side and how these join effectively in the midfield, but optimal performance requires that there also be integration with the dimensions of top to bottom—coordination—and back to front—participation, or the balance between holding back and moving forward. We need a "sweet spot" between the back and the front to keep us focused and on task without losing perspective. We need the ability to be rational and under self-control while remaining in touch with our feelings. To reach our full potential, then, the Centering and Focus Dimensions must be available and supportive of the lateral system.

Centering

Our ability to achieve centering is the source of our emotional intelligence and the basis for our joys, passions, playfulness, social bonding, memory and associations, and sense of self and personality. The Centering Dimension depends upon the relationship between the rational cerebral cortex, at the top of the brain, and the emotional limbic system at the bottom, through which all incoming sensory information is processed. This relationship juxtaposes the more logical and verbal abilities of the cortex with the more instinctual, intuitive, and sometimes irrational needs of the lower parts of the brain.

When Centering is balanced with Focus and Laterality, we feel more present in the moment, alive in our feelings, grounded in a sense of self, and organized for effective action. We can relate to others and can explore the world through play. Perceived distress blocks the ability to access this state and reduces the efficiency of all cortical function, resulting in the limbic response of fight or flight. "Fight" may show itself as aggression or merely nonconformity, whereas "flight" may reveal itself as running away or just being off-task or unable to get started.

Such Brain Gym activities as Hook-ups and Positive Points support us in restoring organization and emotional intelligence to our system. We can then manage stress more effectively, thereby keeping our cerebral hemispheres engaged.

Focus

The Focus Dimension provides for our attentional intelligence. As human beings, we have evolved with the unique ability to plan, accomplish goals, experience intention, and find meaning in life. The brain organizes itself to focus our attention for efficient, directed performance. Its frontal lobes house our sense of self as a social being with a purpose in the world. The Focus Dimension depends upon the interrelationship of the frontal lobes, where the vision of our goals resides unencumbered by fear, and the brain stem. The latter holds our most primitive survival instincts to freeze, be invisible, or hold ourselves back to avoid taking risks that challenge our sense of self.

As soon as we feel overwhelmed, the capacity to focus becomes unavailable to us. In the modern world, our inability to move and to trust our body is probably both the cause and the result of any inability to comprehend, to express ourselves, to interact with the environment, and to lead conscious lives. The Footflex activity from Brain Gym enables us to release the tendons that hold us back and allows us the freedom to receive and express with more comprehension.

The Footflex

Sitting with one ankle resting on the other knee, place your fingertips at the beginning and end of the calf muscle on your lifted leg and gently pull and hold the ends of the muscle apart. Slowly point and flex your foot until any tight spots soften and "melt." Repeat the movement with the other calf and foot.

When these three dimensions of intelligence—Laterality, Centering, and Focus—are available to us, we have a sense of purpose and a feeling of comfort in moving toward objectives. We feel our emotions deeply, are organized, and are relaxed in our bodies so that we can think rationally in the present moment. We're able to process information laterally with ease, from left to right, right to left, or beginning to end, in a temporal, linear fashion. The full integration of these three aspects creates whole-brain organization and integration of the body and heart.

Chapter Six
Movement and the Dynamic Brain

For human civilization, the arrival of the railroad and the telegraph, with their schedules and coded demands, made time, speed, and long-distance communication major factors in our awareness. It was the age of machines; for the first time in history, information traveled freely and quickly.

In the United States and Europe, that latter half of the 1800s was an exciting era of theorizing, invention, and investigation. The Industrial Revolution was in full swing, and the excitement was palpable. People's lives were impacted by such innovations as the sewing machine, the phonograph, and, soon after, the telephone and the incandescent lightbulb—as well as by the rhythms of soulful blues and buoyant, staccato ragtime.

It was in this intellectual climate that we saw the development of modern medicine, including such diverse fields as psychiatry, psychology, pharmacology, chiropractic, and brain surgery. People wanted to know how things worked. Scientists, conceptualizing the human body as a machine, saw analogies, many of which (we realize today) were only partially true.

The Human Brain: Machine or Mystery?
The modern study of the brain began in the Paris of 1861, where lively Strauss waltzes, gay and emotive musical revues, and outdoor café concerts were part of everyday life. The soft colors of such impressionist painters as Edgar Degas and Claude Monet were redefining the human form with light, rather than with linear accuracy.

Here, the pathologist, neurosurgeon, and physiological anthropologist Pierre Paul Broca, the founder of modern brain surgery, first discovered that lesions in the left hemisphere inhibited the expressive use of speech. This was the beginning of cerebral neurology, which initially involved mapping functions of the brain by studying the effects of brain injury on performance. Broca's discovery was hailed as a breakthrough in our understanding of the brain's vast mystery.

Yet at least three erroneous popular beliefs about the human brain stemmed from Broca's work, and these misperceptions persist even though research has proven them false. First, Broca believed that the brain housed specific human functions—such as memory, musical ability, hand-eye coordination, or visual and auditory skills—only in specific locations, and that these areas could be readily mapped. His work thus incited a scientific search for these elusive functional locations.

Today's theorists in neuroscience tell us that, although certain functions of the brain may originate in specific locations, the brain is best understood as a hologram—meaning that all functions depend upon extensive neural interconnections. With its great plasticity, the brain is able to lay down new pathways in order to learn and adapt, and that earlier static and mechanistic view of the brain is slowly giving way to a more dynamic and multidimensional one.

Broca's second assumption was the concept of cerebral dominance— that the human brain exists primarily for the development of articulated speech and language. This concept argued that the development of language is the main function that makes humankind a unique species. Accordingly, the left hemisphere, where the speech mechanisms are located (now known as Broca's area), was seen as the dominant cerebral hemisphere, while the other, "minor" hemisphere was considered to have no significant function.

Thirdly, Broca believed that the function of speech came from a special faculty, independent of motor skills, and was a purely intellectual function. Broca's prestige as a medical doctor and anthropologist helped perpetuate this bias in favor of language, even though the bias was invalidated by his colleagues before the turn of the nineteenth century.

The brain research begun by Broca and his associates—in that historic time that so vividly juxtaposed mechanism and artistry—has continued into the age of cyberspace. Almost daily, new understandings are being reached that either build upon or refute older ones.

As more people populated the cities, a natural renaissance of the arts took place. Municipalities funded museums, architecture, ballet companies, and symphony orchestras, and a civic pride in beauty and the fine arts flourished. Yet Broca's linguistic emphasis belied the reality of the artistic, visual, and musical world in which he lived.

The Persistence of the Linguistic Bias

Parents everywhere agree that art, music, dance, and social play would enrich their children's educational experience and inspire them to excel. Yet our schools persist in emphasizing rote education at the expense of creativity. And, even though ample evidence has demonstrated that the right hemisphere holds qualities just as important as those of the left hemisphere, the idea of the right hemisphere being a lesser brain has persisted.

Research shows that language has evolved so that we can talk about our experiences, not replace them. Yet Western society has a left-brain bias that favors the three R's over experiential education. This emphasis continues to do more harm than good—especially in today's educational practices. As our culture comes to understand more about balance, we will come to see that excellence in education is not an either/or situation.

With its emphasis on academics, this one-sided view of learning continues to distort and mechanize our educational system. The truth is, the eye is more than a camera; the heart is more than a pump; the brain is more than a computer. In fact, modern brain research is telling us that the language brain is simply a tool for our alive, exploring, passionate bodies. The more we move in new, conscious ways, the more we learn.

The brain is experience made flesh, and its plasticity is limited only by our immobility. A child diagnosed as brain-injured can grow new neural pathways as his brain recruits other parts of itself to take over the work of the damaged area. So adaptable is the brain that, even if one hemisphere must be removed in a hemospherectomy, often the other side can take over the tasks of the missing area.

Until this understanding filters into our awareness, we parents and educators will continue to repeat old mistakes with our children, attempting to teach and evaluate them through language when we could be engaging the diversity of resources within them from which true learning is possible.

So we see that, in reality, the human brain is a dynamic system, composed of interconnected areas designed by nature to work together and help us learn and grow as we search for structure and order. Intrinsically, no brain area is more important than another. Mind, heart, and body will keep changing and developing in a dynamic interplay for each individual, as he or she meets a diversity of life experiences.

An Artistic Heritage

My maternal grandparents, "Papa Henry" and "Mama Rebecca" Ehrlich, fled Germany for America, the land of political freedom and of cultural and educational opportunities. They arrived in New York with one son and six daughters. Their eighth child, my mother, was born in New York City in 1910.

Papa Henry and Mama Rebecca were committed to excellence and beauty; the arts were their consuming passion, their very life's breath. They raised a talented family, but understood that their children would excel only through strict discipline and hours of practice. The children grew up to become professional artists: a painter, a sculptress, a pianist, an opera singer, a ballet dancer, an interior designer, and a Hollywood choreographer.

For most of my own school years, from the time I was six until I was about sixteen, I had the great good fortune of growing up within a milieu of art, music, and dance. This was because my parents were the producers, directors, and puppeteers of the Dennison Marionettes, performing in concerts for young people. My brother, Peter, and I got

111

to be part of it all. We may not have had Brain Gym, yet we learned to design, play, and move within the context of art.

Our modest home was continually transformed by art. Stage sets changed before my eyes from bare wood to the painted images of Peter Pan's Neverland or the Northwest majesty of Paul Bunyan's forest. These wonderful scenes came to life through my father's deft carpentry and my mother's evocative murals.

Under my mother's skilled craftsmanship, wood blocks, papier-mâché, and stuffed socks could become a three-foot-high marionette such as Captain Hook, Babe the Blue Ox, a Spanish dancer with her red shoes, or a little blonde-haired ballerina. Many times after I had gone to bed, I could hear Mama's sewing machine running late into the night. By morning, imaginatively clothed personalities would have appeared like guests in our home, bringing their stories to life in our living room as my parents practiced their lines and made the new puppets dance and move.

Although I had no idea of this at the time, we Dennisons were living the dynamic whole brain in action, and movement was at the center of everything. We were the brain's prefrontal cortex—envisioning, designing, planning, and directing the production. The story, the music, and the art, as well as the personalities Mama put into each marionette, were the midbrain. This emotional context is what brought the story to life and captivated the children in our audiences. The stage, scenery, choreography, and marionette strings were the brain stem, which held the show's context and was the place from where movement was monitored and mastered. The script and stage directions, infused as they were by our family commitment to excellence, demonstrated the integrated frontal lobes at work.

For us, nothing stood in the way of creating art. No hours of sewing, painting, and rehearsal were spared until we got it right. There was no question about the reward: we felt guided through every step of the process, and, when it came time for a performance, the rapt astonishment and delight on the faces of the children in the front rows made it all worthwhile.

Above: Paul Ehrlich Dennison
as an infant in Boston. *Right*:
Paul in the first grade, a shy
six-year-old.

*Photos from the Dennison
family archives.*

Above: Paul's parents, Joseph and Helen Dennison, created the Brookline Dennison Marionettes in the Boston area. *Below:* These handcrafted marionettes represented Peter Pan and Mrs. Darling in the Dennison production of *Peter Pan*. *Photos from the Dennison family archives.*

Above: Paul 's mother, Helen
Ehrlich Dennison, holds the
Giant's Wife, a marionette
she made for the Dennison
production of *Jack and the
Beanstalk*. *Right*: By the sixth
grade, Paul, age 12, was
wearing glasses and beginning
to find success as a scholar.

*Photos from the Dennison family
archives.*

Above: When not traveling the world to teach, Paul lives in California's Ventura County. *Below:* Paul and his wife, artist and movement educator Gail E. Dennison, shown here in 2002, have collaborated and co-written since the 1980s. *Photo above by Sonia Nordenson; below, by Koleen Murray.*

Seeing the Brain's Structure through Story and Music

The principal systems in the brain include a left and a right cerebral cortex, a midbrain (also known as the limbic system), and a brain stem. As we saw in Chapter Three, the front area of the cortex is identified as the prefrontal cortex or frontal lobes—that part of the cortex that gives us the ability to notice, move in new ways, make decisions, and, most important, be self-aware.

These frontal lobes are the newest development in the evolution of the brain, providing us with a sense of an "observer self" that can self-reflect, anticipate outcomes, defer gratification, read moods and social interactions, and recognize the large patterns behind cultural or global events.

How does all this play out in real life?

In his book *Tell Me a Story: Narrative and Intelligence*, the research scientist Roger C. Schank makes a strong case for the value of storytelling. I, too, see much value in the absorbing stories that, from childhood onward, enrich our imagination and enhance our intelligence.

When I was a child, one of my favorite marionette productions was the well-known story of *Peter and the Wolf*, with its wonderful music written in 1936 by Sergei Prokofiev for the Moscow Children's Theater.

We might imagine Peter, and the string instruments that represent him, as the right cerebral hemisphere in action. As you may recall, the narrator (let's see him as the verbal left brain) begins by telling us that "Early one morning, Peter opened the gate and went out into the big, green meadow."

The lilting, picturesque melody invites us to imagine Peter playing and dancing, enjoying his senses and open to new experience. The narrator continues and (again, like the left brain) puts the experience into words, giving it form, structure, and a sequence of events. The bird, with his warbling flute song, gaily chirps and twitters as he represents the frontal lobes, always providing feedback with his quick perception, keen vision, and ability to anticipate what will happen next.

The image of the duck, with her low oboe sound, is painted in a fluid, slow-moving, watery way. This image reminds me of the slower, more grounded rhythm of the heart. The bird and the duck argue about who can fly and who can swim—again, the duck plays the part of the midbrain that "swims" in the watery depths of our emotions. We see the age-old dichotomy between head and heart: the heady bird can fly but doesn't understand a bird that swims.

This abstract argument that questions their physical abilities leaves the "forebrain" bird and "midbrain" duck unprotected from the cat—heard as the stealthy sound of the clarinet. The cat, very much in his body, offers an image of instinctual movement, and can perhaps represent for us the developmental reflexes stored in the brain stem.

The very slow, plodding, and syncopated bassoons now announce Grandfather's arrival. Of course, our grandfathers must always carry for us the traditions and boundaries of the old brain stem—all that we need to know about restraints for the sake of safety and survival, and on which we can build the new.

The Amygdala Responds to Danger

Uh oh; what was that? The amygdala and the sympathetic nervous system take over as the wolf, announced by the French horns, appears and chases the duck, who (like the midbrain in its fight-or-flight reflex) jumps out of the calm water and becomes disorganized in her attempt to escape.

The wolf reminds us of the dangers of the unintegrated brain stem, which confiscates all other brain areas for the immediate reflex needs of survival. It is the internal predator that preys upon the heart and the slow pleasures of life.

The wolf catches his prey and swallows the duck—the heart—in one gulp. As the presence of the wolf predominates, fear and grief overshadow the theater audience.

Now the narrator matter-of-factly locates each remaining character for us, helping us to reestablish a structure in order to continue. Then he tells us in step-by-step detail how Peter uses his lasso to catch the wolf by the tail, giving us the sense that we, too, could defeat the predator of our aliveness if we needed to.

Now what do we hear? It's the hunters (announced by the kettledrums), coming to the rescue with their rifles. As we listen, the cerebellum that modulates our movements is activated by the even gait and stately Cross Crawl marching rhythm.

"Stop!" says Peter (now moving into the frontal lobe and overriding the response of the amygdala and the sympathetic nervous system to want to shoot). "Stop! Don't shoot! Birdie and I have caught the wolf."

Our hero's action (with the help of the bird's noticing skills) returns us to the big picture and to normalcy. The parasympathetic nervous system (all the instruments together) responds by slowing our rhythm and breathing and restoring equilibrium.

In the Dennison version, the duck is regurgitated whole and joy returns to the valley. Balance has been restored, and all characters cross the stage together in a triumphant procession, with Peter in the lead. Peter, through his calm observation, equanimity, and heartful response to the situation, has matured in his decision-making ability.

The Brain Stem Asks: *Where Am I?*

The brain stem is the "old brain"; it governs the physical body and is the first neural area to develop *in utero* and during infancy. It is the locus of all our sensory awareness, autonomic reflexes, and functions such as breathing, heartbeat, and movement. I see the brain stem as developing in response to the question *Where am I?*—a question being asked of the senses as they make their vast and perpetual contribution to human consciousness.

This query characterizes the infant's first search for structure, as he notices the environment of the womb and, later, the mother's heartbeat and body. This is his spatial question, as his infant reflex movements keep him alive—grasping, turning, sucking, and knowing how to be safe in his vulnerability. The brain stem evolves according to our senses and sensory responses to our environment. Answering the question *Where am I?* with our proprioceptive senses tells us our shape, our size, and our patterns of movement, as well as our location, as defined by where our boundaries lie.

We all revisit the brain stem's *Where am I?* question whenever we're in new situations. At these times, our sensory awareness is heightened and we are bombarded with sound, light, color, and movement from all around us. Until we're relatively comfortable within our surroundings, we continue trying to locate ourselves and cannot take the next step toward growth. For example, if we enter a new classroom, we might choose a seat that will enable us to see, hear, and participate without distractions or difficulties. Conversely, we might gravitate toward the safety of the back row, where we can feel less visible but will not be able to fully participate. While Peter isn't afraid of wolves and goes out into the meadow of new experiences, Grandfather is quick to withdraw behind his safe boundary, locking the gate and retreating from the reality of danger.

With constant vigilance, the brain stem takes in sensory information. It gives us our ability to be safe and present in the "now" moment. The brain stem holds our reflexive capacity to either engage and participate or withdraw, freeze, and hide until the system perceives that all danger has passed. Our ability to interact or participate is always inhibited until this system can determine where we are; until its search for "whereness" has been satisfied at least minimally, no higher brain function can be brought into play.

The Midbrain Asks: *Where Is It?*
I use the term "midbrain" to refer to the brain's emotional-cognitive limbic system. The midbrain asks, *Where is it? Where is the other?* Whatever the subject, this brain asks how to locate it in relation to the self. Its intent is to identify the feeling sense within and beyond our personal boundaries. When in balance, it searches, through the heart resonance, for the rhythm of the other—for a sense of connectedness and belonging.

This center, with its associative abilities, is where we feel our feelings—our joy, fear, frustration, and anger, as well as our grief. Because of its associative process, the midbrain is fundamental to memory. Even abstract or associative thinking depends upon emotion and feelings at the midbrain level, for this is the core of our heart resonance.

116

The midbrain, then, closely connected as it is to neural pathways to the heart, holds our emotional center. The vitality of this center is essential to our ability to reach out in relationship. Our ability to live in community as social beings is developed by our heart rhythms, which incline us toward others in the joy of play and cooperation. As we touch and connect to people and objects while manipulating our world—building, exploring, and creating, we answer the midbrain's question: *Where is it?* While the brain stem is keeping us safe and able to hold back, the midbrain is ready to reach out, interact, and join in. It's a risk taker if it feels safe. Like Peter and the duck, it's ready for physical and emotional experiences if the gate is open.

If our space is threatened by danger, the limbic system of the midbrain, closely wired to the amygdala, will activate a fight-or-flight response of the sympathetic nervous system. When this happens, our ability to connect with others will be interrupted by an emotional response to engage our fists in battle or our words in argument. Or we might engage our legs in escape or fly to another time or place through a book or in fantasies. Thus we return to the brain stem until it is once again safe to come out and play.

Responses to Negative Stress
Nearly all the people who enter my office, even little children, speak of stress, worry, or fear. In our modern world of thinking and hurrying, negative stress has become a chronic difficulty. Since it makes us regress to more primitive brain states, such stress is making our society regress, too.

Stress has a profound effect on the brain. As I often tell my students, no true learning can occur under duress. Negative stress triggers the flight-or-fight syndrome, flooding the body with hormones to ready it for instantaneous reaction. In earlier periods of our evolutionary history, when we had less protection from surrounding dangers, fight-or-flight was a necessary lifesaving response, but today it's merely debilitating. I see many individuals (again, including children) who are in a nearly permanent state of stress and rarely able to shift out of fight-or-flight.

The stress response is supposed to be a reaction to true danger, but for most of us danger is created in our imagination only, and not in reality. Unless we're in some unusual situation such as fighting a war, we're seldom in imminent danger of death. Our bodies were not built to deal with chronic trauma. Science tells us that intense stress actually produces hormones that destroy neurons responsible for learning and memory. These hormones may stay at high levels for a long time after the original triggering of the response. For example, the stress hormone cortisol is broken down in the liver, but it can take up to eight hours after an argument for it to be completed processed.

When we're stressed, we tend to regress to the areas of the brain developed earlier in life. If we retreat to the unintegrated midbrain, we get into a state of emotionally charged fight-or-flight; if we go to the brain stem, we're in an emotionless state of fight-or-freeze. The kind of fighting that originates in the midbrain is different than that of the brain stem. When fighting derives from the midbrain, it's passionate, like the argument between the bird and the duck. There are intense feelings involved, whereas a fight from the brain stem is more cold-blooded, merciless, and calculating, like the chase of the duck by the wolf.

So negative stress sends us back into the midbrain and then further back into the brain stem, which switches us to automatic pilot. Then we're are no longer fully connected to the frontal lobes of the neocortex, the seat of consciousness, observation, and choice.

Hooking Up the Brain Stem and Midbrain

Without these survival responses to danger, humankind might not have survived through the ages. Yet nowadays it's more appropriate for us to learn how to use the midbrain and brain stem more positively, for growth. The elements that facilitate positive brain-stem activity are our noticing abilities, working in concert with heart qualities such as love, kindness, and compassion. When these elements cooperate, the fight/flight and fight/freeze reflexes are activated only when they're appropriate.

When true danger threatens, we need our fight-or-flight response to survive. If we step into the path of an oncoming bus and then jump back onto the sidewalk, propelled by a rush of adrenaline, that's an appropriate use of our defensive system. The problem is that, in today's world, we may be in a near-permanent state of fight/flight stress, even with no legitimate stimulus.

When we're stuck in traffic on the freeway and late for an appointment, frustration and anxiety may push us into the same state of heated emergency, even though our physical survival is not at stake. In the fight-or-flight reflex, our energy goes away from the body's vital organs to the extremities, preparing us to fight or run. But in today's sedentary lifestyles this energy usually has no place to go, and the human body wasn't designed to cope with perpetual stress.

Habitual, inappropriate brain-stem reactions are extremely difficult to change. This is because patterns of behavior directed from the brain stem may be due to any number of reasons such as injury, poor nutrition, chemical poisoning, or incompletely learned movements. Part of the benefit of Brain Gym is that these patterns can be affected by movement education. That is, the Brain Gym activities can reach automatic behaviors located in this deep part the brain. If we can make a real shift there, then we can change behavior at the most profound level of our behavior.

When behavior doesn't change, it is often because we haven't connected mental and emotional experience to the physical body, but have only calmed the superficial areas of the mind. Unless we get into the body, we can't modify automatic behaviors operating at the deepest levels. In our Brain Gym classes, we teach that "Learning is changed behavior." Until new behavior is available in the impressionable and ever-growing brain, there will be no new learning; only words, feelings, and information.

In the Brain Gym community, the single most effective, best known, and most loved remedy for such a situation is Hook-ups, the movement I introduced in Chapter Two. When we do Hook-ups, we gather our attention at the center of the body, site of the core postural muscles and vital organs. The tongue on the roof of the mouth connects the midbrain and the brain stem, and deep breathing

119

activates the vestibular system via the hyoid ligaments, which allows the brain to come into a state of coherence so that we can think, notice what's going on, and make use of our frontal lobes.

Doing Hook-ups is like giving oneself a loving hug. It pulls everything together, connects all the circuits, lowers the blood pressure, and slows everything (such as the heartbeat) down. When this happens, we begin to move out of the brain-stem fight-or-freeze state and feel safe again. The crossover of arms, hands, and feet engages the vestibular system in a search for balance and engages both motor cortexes in the frontal lobe, to integrate them and counter the action of the sympathetic nervous system. "Don't shoot," Peter is saying to us. We know that everything is under control and it's all going to work out okay.

The brain, being a chemical soup of emotion-creating hormones, takes in this new information from the senses, scans it, and restores us to balance and equilibrium.

This, in turn, creates the opportunity for us to engage in new life experiences that build on the structure and familiarity of what we've done before. For example, whether we're learning to write our name or catch a wolf, each time we're able to notice—to make the frontal-lobe connection as we take pen in hand or lower the lasso—we develop greater mastery. And if we feel secure enough at the level of the midbrain, this center of play and relationship will allow heart-driven emotions to come through.

Through the right frontal lobe of the cortex, we notice what's happening. The information is sent over to the left brain for encoding, which that hemisphere accomplishes using language, systems, and rules. As soon as we've encoded the information in the cortex, it becomes conscious. Now, instead of having a blind spot, we can feel the movement pattern or see an image of this process in our mind's eye.

By the time we reach adulthood, many of the actions that we once struggled over have become automatic. Our learned patterns of movement have been stored in the brain stem, which operates by habit, and the resources of the left and right hemispheres have been freed to tackle the next levels of mastery. The brain stem, then, is involved in integrating and deepening new learning as well as providing survival responses. I'm gratified to see that researchers are finally recognizing the important contributions of the cerebellum (the part of the brain stem where our movement patterns derive) to learning and behavior.

Character Building and the Brain Stem

Through the years, my mentors have been people I admired for their passion, for their courage to live a life that honored who they were. I call that quality—the ability to stand up for what one believes and who one is—character. I used to think such people of character were born that way. From personal experience and from having helped many students discover their life purpose, I now see that, although we can't give people character, we can teach them how to develop it through successful movement experiences.

Much of what we call character emerges in just this way—from life experiences of testing our limits, making the inevitable mistakes, seeing what we can and cannot do. Physically, good character first arises from the simple ability to bend the knees in preparation for pushing off and stepping forward. This basic movement is the jumping-off place for taking risks. Peter, the little Russian boy, showed character in going after the wolf without hesitation. With sure, measured steps, he put himself at risk for what he knew needed to be done.

We develop character each time we take a necessary risk without consideration of the cost involved. The integrated brain-stem state that allows us to move forward becomes available only when we relax the fight-or-freeze survival reflex of the tendon guard. This holding-back reflex has first call on the nervous system, for which survival is paramount. The Brain Gym program seeks to reeducate this straight-legged, locked-knee stance, this holding back through the tendon guard. When we're stuck in its grip, we're frozen—we cower and want to remain invisible. When we courageously take a stand, our feet are firmly on the ground and our knees are relaxed enough for us to push forward with strength and take risks from a place of resilience.

Character, then, can be likened to a positive form of self-control . . . a quality of self-discipline that makes us dependable. When we follow our truth, operating from our own internal compass regardless of what the world might think of us, that's character displayed at its best.

When we're regressing, feeling swayed by outside influences, and unsure where we stand, we can always remember to do Hook-ups. This simple Brain Gym movement (introduced in Chapter Two) is like entering a cocoon: it settles scattered energy into the center of the body and gives us a sense of consolidation. The breathing deepens; the brain waves slow down (which takes us out of fight-or-freeze); the heart rate and blood pressure drop, and the blood leaves the muscles to return to the vital organs. We can feel the weight of the body—our substance— and any subtle movements that we make.

Now we can easily answer the question *Where am I?* The feeling is one of *I have located myself. I know that my feet are on the ground. I'm sitting (or standing) in the room, and I can feel secure.* In this state, we become more present with what our mind, feelings, and senses tell us is happening right now. This presence is a dimension of character.

The Cerebellum and the Sense of Balance

Crucial to all learning and behavior is the development of multiple neural connections throughout the brain and the rest of the body. These connections depend upon movement and balance. The cerebellum, our motor-performance modulator in the brain stem, plays a vital role in the functioning of these pathways. A foundation for development during the first year of life and for all later learning, the cerebellum is involved in all automatic behavior. It stores our memories of the patterns—from infant reflexes to higher cognitive patterns—on which we depend to respond appropriately, moment to moment, in new yet reminiscent situations.

The cerebellum works in conjunction with our vestibular balancing system to coordinate incoming and outgoing signals from the brain and the rest of the body, ensuring that motor output is accurate and under control. It operates at the unconscious level to monitor muscular proprioception as we sit up, find balance, maintain posture, walk, and run. These basic functions profoundly affect later brain development and how we learn, or fail to learn. Ideally, we develop a sense of stability and balance as a reference point for directional movement, which will provide a foundation for all of our reading-and-writing activities.

Through the remarkable technology of computer imaging, new information about the brain is daily being revealed. Through this imaging, neuroscientists are able to see that the brains of successful learners show activity in the cerebellum, while those of children who struggle in school do not. A truth that my students have demonstrated to me for the last thirty years is now being validated by science: the fundamental movements first learned in infancy are a prerequisite of mature cognitive processing.

The cerebellum, in addition to conducting motor activity, is intricately involved in all metacognitive activities such as mental imagery, judgment of time and speed, the shifting of attention among sensory modalities, and all metaphoric thinking. The cerebellum organizes the brain and influences its full development by making learned, repetitive, and practiced physical activities automatic, so that the higher centers of the cortex can depend upon them, feel safe, and be free to build new learning upon the old.

Communication and Behavior: A Case Study

When Mark and Gloria came to see me, they wanted to do a balance together to improve their communication skills and their relationship. It soon became clear that Mark was struggling with emotional volatility, and that this was affecting the marriage. Small things would make him angry, both at home and at work.

Mark was an intelligent man who saw clearly that his behavior was unacceptable. He also realized that he hadn't yet discovered how to apply the cognitive tools provided in the anger-management class he'd been attending. Those tools are especially useful when a person is operating from the cortex—specifically the frontal lobes, which are the seat of conscience and self-awareness—but they're not as useful if a person is functioning from brain-stem reflex behavior, as Mark was, and unable to reflect on or anticipate his own actions. In such a case these skills simply become inaccessible, just as a map is of no use if you're in the woods at night with no flashlight.

When we're unable to feel safe because of a real or imaginary threat, we may, if provoked, take a direct elevator down to the brain stem and suddenly exhibit old habits or "adolescent" behavior that's uncharacteristic of us when we're calm. For most of us, there's no predicting one kind of behavior by the other. Often we allow the good we do in life to be sabotaged by a "predatory wolf"—an internal reflex to freeze or fight, and the resultant fighting can be of a vicious and destructive kind. If we're feeling safe and making positive associations with our experiences, then we're less likely to be triggered by irrational survival patterns.

In Mark's case, when stress overwhelmed him, before he could bring his reactions under conscious control he was already functioning from the limited territory of survival. From this brain-stem reflex, his habit was first to freeze and then to lash out cold-bloodedly.

In our culture, freezing—the inaction and paralysis that happens when we experience fear—is considered an unattractive behavior for a man. Mark, like many men, wanted to appear as the independent male who is able to take action without help. So he would try to defend himself, soon resorting to hostility, anger, and even verbal abuse while rationalizing that he was expressing his feelings, as Gloria so often asked him to do.

Using the Brain Gym techniques, Mark made significant headway with his condition. Through the balance process, he learned to become more alert to the early warning signs that he was moving out of a conscious response and into his survival reflex. He learned to then immediately go into Hook-ups. He also discovered that he could stay more relaxed by doing Positive Points (see Chapter Three) regularly throughout the day, whether or not he noticed obvious indicators that he was becoming distressed.

I suggested to Mark and Gloria that they take turns holding each other's Positive Points for a few minutes before spending quality time together. Since we're unable to feel loving and loveable when in a survival reflex (either withdrawn into a frozen or defensive mode or acting on a fight-or-flight reflex), this quiet preliminary activity is one way I encourage couples to grow their mutual receptivity to love.

In that way, Mark could feel Gloria's loving touch at the same time that his neurovascular system was becoming more balanced. Using the Positive Points release, we can keep the frontal lobes active even in stressful situations and can learn to stay present without going into the fight-or-flight response unless it's truly needed for survival. Since love is the opposite of fear, over time Gloria's and Mark's Positive Point balance began to support them both in identifying brain-stem behavior and moving more easily from withdrawal to loving frontal-lobe behavior. It also added to their ability to make their conversations more enjoyable and more expressive of their needs and feelings.

Now let's move on to some of the brain's other functions.

The Cerebral Cortex Asks: *What Is It?*

The cortex asks the question *What is it?* The cerebral cortex is the "new brain" — the one we associate with our logical, rational, and linguistic human abilities. It's how we think, decide, wonder, and imagine, based upon the input and experiences provided to it by the emotional midbrain and the sensory brain stem. Within the cortex, the right hemisphere has the overview of a situation; it's spatial and spontaneous. The left hemisphere, for all primates, sequences information over time. The ability to perform activities temporally leads to the dexterity and fine-motor skills needed for the control and manipulation of tools, the use of the opposable thumb, and, in humans, the development of speech.

As neuroscientist Elkonen Goldberg explains in his book, *The Executive Brain*, the human brain is designed to search continuously for order, rules, patterns, structure, and frames of reference. "When the organism is exposed to a new pattern of signals from the outside world," he writes, "the strengths of synaptic contacts gradually change in complex distributed constellations. This represents learning, as we understand it today."

At different ages of our lives, and in differing cultures, this search for structure and stability may take different forms. We need some type of dependable context in which to function or we can't exist. Goldberg hypothesizes that, in our search for a frame of reference, two basic subsystems are continuously at work: a coding system and a receptive system. The left cerebral hemisphere makes experience familiar by arranging it in a linear and sequential form, so that we can replicate it step-by-step and learn patterns of language and behavior. The right cerebral hemisphere scans for new information, first through the senses (opening us up to novelty), then through play and interaction with the physical world.

If it is safe to move, the system opens to the new in an expansive embracing of fresh experiences. To the extent that we move and master our movements through learning, creating new neural pathways, we will also be constantly open to rebuilding our brains and, ultimately, recreating our lives.

Once we have an experience in the body, the brain encodes it into a structured, orderly code. In this way, we create a new structure from which we perform and perceive the world. What we can see as a pattern becomes visible and part of the context, so that we can better scan and recognize new information in a safe, engaging, and exploratory manner.

The Prefrontal Cortex

The frontal lobes, constituting 30 percent of the neocortex, comprise the structure that notices, makes decisions, and is aware. In evolutionary terms, this part of the brain came late. The brain researcher Elkhonon Goldberg has made it his life's work to study the prefrontal cortex in primates, and he describes it as the neural area that is conscious of surroundings, of the connection to nature, and of social context.

Some of the decisions we make here, involving expediency and practicality, are personal and related to the self; others, involving values and principles, affect other people or even the entire planet. When fully developed and accessed, the prefrontals give us our civilized mind. When they're made inaccessible through fear and activation of the survival instinct, we can become violent or depressed.

The frontal lobes are wired to all the other parts of the brain and develop with them at each stage of our growth; hence the profusion of neural pathways from them to every other part of the brain. The prefrontal cortex is instrumental in integrating the whole brain. When our brain is organized around the prefrontals with intention and

126

purpose, we can then engage in heart-directed action. (For more on the prefrontal cortex, see Chapter Three.)

The Analytic Hemisphere
The vocabulary that associates certain brain functions with the left and right hemispheres has now become universal. You might hear a woman complain that her husband is "too left-brained," meaning that he tends to be excessively rational and literal. I don't find this kind of labeling useful. On the other hand, understanding the function of the hemispheres as a part of a dynamic brain is extremely helpful. So I prefer to name the hemispheres "expressive/analytic" and "receptive/gestalt."

The word "analysis" comes from the Greek word for "dissolve," and this is exactly what analytic thinking does: it breaks down the whole into fundamental elements just as water, when it dissolves a substance, breaks that substance down into its constituent molecules. Analytic thinking moves in a line from one building block to another, as when we plot a course on a map or balance a checkbook. It looks first at the details and then creates a general picture from the specifics; once we have plotted our course, or balanced our checkbook, we then have an overview of our route or our finances.

In other words, analytic thinking examines each tree, and only then steps back to register the whole forest. Such thinking is critical, judgmental, and aware of time. It works in terms of goals, language, and self-expression. Like a computer, it works with information in bite-size pieces that it can sequence and order, one at a time. It forms the language center, where the ability to speak and understand verbal information is generated and stored.

The Gestalt Hemisphere
Gestalt thinking, on the other hand, starts with "wholism," meaning that it grasps the whole picture and then moves into the details. The word "wholism" refers to the theory that the determining factors in nature are wholes and that these wholes are greater than the sum of their parts. According to this theory, no amount of analysis (examination of the trees) fully explains the principles governing the whole (the forest).

Gestalt thinking, therefore, is wholistic thinking. It registers context and feelings, and it is intuitive. It senses, for instance, that the finances are in a shambles and are putting a strain on the marriage; it first registers the whole situation, and only then considers specific actions such as balancing the checkbook. It looks at the entire forest first, and only then notices the trees.

The gestalt brain is responsible for the recognition of faces and other long-term visual memories. It is involved in spatial orientation, rhythm and tone, and body awareness. The gestalt brain is in its element when we need to process information in recognizable "chunks," when no analysis or linear, sequential operation is necessary. This hemisphere is open to new experiences and receives information passively. It contains our connection with our body, with nature, and with our surroundings.

The Benefits of Hemispheric Integration

Chess players can easily understand the differences between analytical and gestalt functioning, because both forms of thinking are used in the game. Calculating the next move can be a solely analytical process. Like a computer, the player looks at each move and its consequences—not to mention the consequences of the consequences—in a sequential fashion, until he figures out which one leads to the most advantageous outcome. This is the analytical brain at work. Sometimes, though, an experienced player can look at the chessboard and instantly see the best move, which means the entire situation is present in his mind as one whole image. This is the gestalt brain at work.

We all know the type of mental functioning our society favors. The analytical mind builds malls, writes legal briefs, defends our borders, manufactures cars, engages in politics, manages the stock market, and develops the telecommunications upon which all the rest depend.

It's not surprising, therefore, that our schools mirror this. Math, science, and an analytical approach to language predominate, at the expense of gestalt activities such as music, dance, and the creative use of language. In times of budgetary shortfalls, gestalt activities such as the arts may be eliminated altogether.

When a pendulum swings in one direction, there is a tendency for it to swing back to the opposite extreme. We can observe this phenomenon at work in hemisphere preferences. A growing number of people speak disparagingly of "left-brain" thinking because it is slow, boring, old-fashioned, and male, and is also the stuff of which wars are made. The "right brain"—heartfelt, big-picture, intuitive, female thinking—has received much better press recently. However, an imbalance in either direction is a problem.

Too much linear thinking makes us unfeeling and impersonal, but a dominant gestalt mind is impractical and impulsive. The two minds are designed to work together; they function best in synergistic collaboration.

Integration through Movement

It has been said that the brain is experience made flesh. The brain is always engaged in a dance of moving into the new, storing it deeply, and taking its new structure into the next unexplored territory. Integrated learning grows from the bottom up; it explores the world with curiosity and capability, first activating the brain stem and midbrain by engaging in play and concrete operations—a process that's coded into mental patterns in the cortex only later, if at all.

This dance can also move in the opposite direction—toward disintegration, rather than integration. This is a result of stress, competition, and fear; the fight/flight or fight/freeze response keeps us safe but excludes the possibility of new learning.

Movement, then, is truly crucial to learning. We first find structure with respect to moving in space. The vestibular system (the semicircular canals within our ears that are like vestibules or doorways) gives us our sense of balance and is always the foundation of our search for new structure, just as it helped us, as infants, to move within the context of the earth's gravitational pull. Once we achieve this initial balance in gravity, we discover that we are in the body. We can now run, jump, and play, preparing our mental acuity to translate physical reality into useful codes and symbols for our ultimate safety, growth, and development.

If our goal is the accumulation of information and data, we can be conditioned, drilled, and forced into memorizing information from the head down. But the forgetting curve will be high. This development of the left brain without benefit of the right, although possible, is of limited use. It amounts to bypassing the feeling center and the kinesthetic intelligence, and can lead only to reflexive behaviors based on fight, flight, or survival. Such experience is never truly integrated into a functioning self.

The Corpus Callosum Is a Bridge, Not a Barrier

The laterally unified person uses the two hemispheres together, as a whole system. The fragmented person has not yet accessed his innate ability to use more than one small part of his consciousness at any given time. As infants, we're programmed for integration; crawling, for example, stimulates whole-brain activity. But unfortunately our society's preference for linear brain functioning means that our natural state of hemispheric balance is often lost.

Most of us fail to realize the level of integration that's actually available to us. Instead of experiencing the spontaneous and joyous lives that we are capable of living, we have a tendency to function in controlled and rigid patterns, like machines. Many intellectual and emotional dysfunctions are just symptoms of the failure to achieve an integrated state. They disappear when a person learns to use his or her whole brain.

The left and right hemispheres have always been designed to work together. They are connected by a bundle of two hundred million nerves called the corpus callosum, which transmits a staggering four billion messages per second. The corpus callosum is a bridge, not a barrier, one whose optimal function is to link—not separate—the two sides of the human brain. In fact, our neural anatomy makes it quite clear that integration is the brain's intended state.

In infancy, we develop a complex system of switches during the first few months of life. As we learn to crawl and perform other, similar actions that tend to synchronize information in the two hemispheres, we use the corpus callosum to establish patterns of cooperation that are designed to continue throughout our adult lives.

The Parallel Processor

The right brain controls the left side of the body and the consciousness of the left eye and ear. Conversely, the left brain controls the right side of the body and the right eye and ear. As we've been discussing, the nerves to the muscles and sense organs cross over from the controlling hemisphere through the corpus callosum to the other side. When one side of the brain is in control, the other side may cooperate or it may switch off and block integration. Stress tends to trigger this switched-off, one-sided functioning. When near-point skills are taught under stress or before our developmental stages have prepared us to do them, the corpus callosum is unable to link the two sides as nature intended.

I call this one-sided functioning "parallel processing," because the one-sided person can move from one hemisphere to the other and back again, but cannot easily use both sides of the brain together. The integrated person, on the other hand, has both pictures in mind at the same time.

In the forest metaphor, there is a person in a helicopter and another person on the ground, and both are sending information to a control center that integrates the two perspectives. For the parallel processor, however, this unification of perspectives is limited: he can receive information either from the helicopter or from the ground, but not from both places at the same time. He may be adept at switching rapidly from one perspective to the other, but to some extent he will always experience a coordination problem. Whether it affects his eyes, ears, or body as a whole, there will always be some level of fragmentation—a failure to use the two sides of the brain together, through the corpus callosum, as nature intended.

For example, a child might switch off the analytic/language ear in school and become so absorbed in the intonation of the teacher's voice, which is a gestalt perception, that he loses all sense of the meaning of the words. As a reader, he might switch off his gestalt eye, thereby breaking down the words into sounds but failing to blend them into whole units or to register them in his long-term visual memory.

The parallel processor is confused by bilateral activity. Walking,

131

swimming, running, or jogging all may require increased conscious effort and conscious control, which may cause him to switch off the gestalt brain. Instead of relaxing and energizing him, these activities seem to bring him further frustration, and may even lead to injury. His tendency may be to avoid large-muscle activity or, conversely, to place high demands on his body in order to gain a sense of achievement from competition or goal setting, as opposed to the pure, intrinsic reward of joyful movement.

When the parallel processor moves in space, the spine, cranial bones, and sacrum don't move together, which results in a blockage of the cerebrospinal fluid that should be nourishing and cooling the whole brain from back to front. The parallel processor moves in more rigid, blocked, or controlled patterns—often with minimal breathing, which further inhibits the integration process.

The parallel thinker functions mostly from the brain stem. This is where incoming sensations are processed, where motor activity generated by these sensations is initiated and reflexive survival patterns originate. The parallel processor can learn material by rote, and often does so quite skillfully. In fact, this person thrives on the familiarity of automatic or conditioned behavior. However, the parallel thinker is often denied the true learning experience that occurs when something becomes uniquely his own creation and expression.

Lateral Integration

Parallel thinking is dysfunctional, no matter which side of the brain is used. The qualities attributed to the now popularly favored "right brain" are not actually manifested when it functions on its own. Alone, the gestalt mind is more passive and receptive, with little ability to encode behavior. It expresses itself physically, not verbally. By itself, it is very limited. The analytic mind, alone, can do little more than compare, criticize, and regurgitate information.

What most people attribute to the right brain is really the result of the integration of brain stem and forebrain, which takes place in the common integrative area. The integrated person expresses himself from a context, through this language area. He knows who he is, believes what he's saying or doing, and expresses himself fluently. No performance, be it painting, dancing, reading comprehension, or any other activity, can belong to the performer until this level of integration is achieved.

The laterally integrated person is able to process information simultaneously, with both hemispheres switched on at the same time. She can move and think at the same time, read with the writer's hand, speak with the listener's ear, and commit to any task by bringing her whole person to it. In fact, the integrated person thrives on the new, the spontaneous, and the creative. Even the simplest undertaking becomes a joyful opportunity for self-expression.

This is the power of creativity . . . the frontal lobes in action—a life of living on the edge of our dreams. Letting go of needing to know why, we harness the passion to create. We give it all we have. We study, we learn, we ask, we grow, until out of the euphoria of mastery we achieve excellence.

Chapter Seven

The Ardent Heart, Our Organizing Intelligence

Teaching is my life, and I consider it a gift to be able to contribute to the education of others. When I'm in communication with a student or in tune with a class, I know the joy of heart resonance.

I remember little Miroslava, a Hispanic child in my third grade class who worked hard to understand the rudiments of reading and spelling in English, her second language. I taught the two subjects to her as separate lessons, knowing that she would integrate these elements when she was ready to, at her own pace.

The day came when Miroslava said, "Don't tell me the words, Mr. Dennison. I can figure them out all by myself." A thrill such as I have seldom known ran up and down my spine as I listened to that little girl proudly reading on her own for the first time. My joy came from seeing her drop down out of her mental striving and awaken to that sense of knowing that is central to the heart.

The heart is our harmonic, organizing, playful intelligence. It knows where things are, where they go, and where they belong. When we can feel safe enough to let the heart take over, it will know what to do. No learning can take place without risk taking and mistakes. In fact, the heart thrives on the explorations of "mistakes."

The heart has an intuitive grasp of relationships; when we heed its promptings, it lets partners know how to move together like dancers. I've facilitated Edu-K sessions in which an aloof husband and wife have begun to learn how to move together and rediscover their sense of connectedness.

I've listened as a father, ready to give up, has told me with a strained voice that his child has a disability and cannot learn, and I've watched that same child, less than an hour later, move in synchrony with his mother and father—the whole family learning kinesthetically from one another.

I've had the good fortune to attend Edu-K Gatherings in North America, Australia, and Europe where some three hundred people, as if dancing together, seemed to be of one mind. I've also joined in board and faculty meetings where people from different cultures—sometimes with polarized needs—were willing to set aside intellectual differences long enough to move together toward shared goals, and were able to move into a place of resolution and even harmony.

The Site of Our Emotional Intelligence

It's said that more than 90 percent of every human communication is nonverbal—exchanged in the form of facial and body language, voice intonation, rate of breathing, and rhythm of movement. This nonverbal language, colored and enhanced by our spoken communication, is the most powerful language we have.

Yet this rhythmic language can't be accessed through the mind. The heart is the organizing principle of our movement and harmonics—the site of our emotional intelligence. When we inhabit this place of the heart, we have a sense of belonging and can connect with others who are standing on similar ground.

I see the phenomenon of heart-mind connection and disconnection everywhere—in teachers, politicians, office workers, and corporate managers. I can remember a high school graduation ceremony at which a student spoke, and her talk had a profound effect on me. What she said wasn't especially erudite or clever, but somehow it captivated me. I laughed, cried, and joined her in every word, feeling as though she spoke directly to me. What a difference the heart can make! Words, with their power to make distinctions, may tend to separate us, but words that carry the feeling of our common, shared experiences connect us all in our humanness.

Science of the Heart

What is the reality behind this phenomenon of heartfelt communication? It's partly that the heart brings live, passionate feelings into a situation, and feelings bring us closer together in our humanness. Emotions are like the underlying rhythm in an evocative piece of music. They provide a vital beat—a pulse—for our dance of connectedness. And feelings involve us in the story.

The rise of American movie making to its preeminent economic position is due to many factors, an important one being that American filmmakers have perfected the art of stirring their audiences emotionally. They know how to use image, music, and experiences that are universally human to appeal to our basic longings for love and connection, or even to appeal to our less refined emotions such as fear, anger, or the desire for revenge. Invariably, they bring feelings into the story and give us a means to access our own emotions.

Beyond our personal experience that the heart is important, we now have the beginnings of a scientific understanding of the role of the heart. The first breakthrough in the scientific view of the heart occurred in the 1970s, when John and Beatrice Lacey, two physiologists at the Fels Research Institute in Pennsylvania, conducted research that challenged the most cherished assumption about the brain: namely, that it is the sole decision maker in the body.

The Laceys found that, when the brain sends a command to the heart, the heart doesn't respond by reflex, like a machine. Rather, the heart's response to arousal signals from the brain seems to vary according to the situation. In the Laceys' studies, sometimes the heartbeat speeded up, but on other occasions it slowed down, even though other organs responded with arousal. The Laceys discovered that the heart *actually sends its own commands to the brain*, as well as receiving them, and that the brain responds accordingly.

Since the Laceys' research, neuroscientists have made the amazing discovery that the heart includes a physiologically tangible brain in the form of forty thousand nerve cells, equal in number to certain subcortical areas of the brain. Every neurotransmitter (the various chemicals responsible for relaying neural information) found in the brain is also found in the heart. From a neurological point of view, the heart is intelligent, and it has an ongoing dialogue with the brain—though they're not always in agreement. It's as if, speeding to work in your car one day, while thinking of the demanding schedule ahead of you, you pressed the accelerator and the engine spoke to you, gently suggesting that you head south for a meandering walk along the beach instead.

The heart appears to interact with the whole body system in multiple ways. The HeartMath Institute, established by Doc Childre, has provided more than thirty years of scientific research on the power of the heart, completed by cardiologists working alongside physicists. In their book *The HeartMath Solution: How to Unlock the Hidden Intelligence of Your Heart*, Childre and his collaborator and coauthor, Howard Martin, describe this research and their approach to connecting head to heart with techniques of biofeedback.

In their research, Childre and Martin discovered scientific evidence that the heart speaks with the brain and the rest of the body through at least three biological languages: the neurological (via transmission of nerve impulses), the biochemical (via hormones and neurotransmitters), the biophysical (via pressure waves), and possibly the energetic (via electromagnetic field interactions). Through reading their work, we come to understand that no other organ has a greater influence on the function of our intellect and all our bodily systems—our entire state of health and sense of well-being—than the heart.

The heart, we discover, is more than an organ of the circulatory system, helping to move blood through the body. It's a self-governing organ that communicates with the rest of the body, affecting not only our emotions—our responses to people and situations—but our physical health, including our immune and nervous systems.

Of special interest in our high-pressure world is the fact that the heart exchanges signals with the amygdala, the body's alarm system and a key structure in the brain's limbic system. The amygdala is responsible for all reactive emotional processing, triggering our blood sugar and adrenaline as well as the stress hormone cortisol. It compares incoming information with stored emotional memories, and so evaluates the meaning of an event, particularly with regard to sending us into a fight-or-flight response.

The heart actually mediates this system, sometimes telling us (when we're listening) that something we were experiencing as a threat doesn't actually amount to a life-threatening emergency after all.

Suppose you're walking alone down a silent street at dusk when you see what appears to be a gang of teenage boys coming toward you. You might feel the urge to run. This urge is a result of a complex series of interactions between the heart and the amygdala, which the heart appears to direct, since more signals flow from the heart to the brain than vice versa.

As the teenagers come closer, you see that they're not a gang but a team: they're wearing soccer uniforms and are evidently on their way to a match. Now you feel friendly toward them . . . even energized by their laughter and youthful camaraderie. Your heart has sent an "all is well" message to your amygdala, the fight/flight response has subsided, and you feel safe again.

The Heart and the Temperament

Recent studies with heart-transplant recipients have revealed another dimension of the heart that scientists never previously imagined: it may be the actual seat of our temperament. Some recipients have related astonishing stories about acquiring the tastes, drives, and personalities of their donors.

The internationally renowned author and psychologist Paul Pearsall gives examples of this in his fascinating book *The Heart's Code: Tapping the Wisdom and Power of Our Heart Energy*.

An especially exciting opportunity to study this phenomenon occurs in those rare situations in which both the donor and the recipient of the heart are still living. How can this happen, you ask? When an individual with failing lungs receives both new lungs and a new heart (to improve the chances of a successful transplant) from someone who has died, and donates his own healthy heart to another person. Pearsall relates how the wives of two men involved in such a so-called "domino transplantation" experienced changes in their husbands.

138

These studies suggest that the heart is a self-contained organizing organ, since it can apparently retain its characteristics after transplantation so as to strongly influence the behavior of a new host.

The Coherence Factor

In the 1990s, Dr Carla Hannaford became interested in the idea of "coherence," which was at that time beginning to be used with reference to an electromagnetic reading of the heart called a heart rate variability (HRV) pattern. In her wonderful book *Awakening the Child Heart: Handbook for Global Parenting,* Dr. Hannaford wrote this about heart rate variability:

> Researchers observed a coherent HRV when a person experienced feelings of appreciation or a playful, harmonious environment, was engrossed in joyful work or learning, or meditated. These findings further showed that a coherent heart pattern determined the brain's ability to optimally receive sensory information from the environment. This coherent pattern affected the brain's ability to assimilate and construct understandable patterns from that sensory information, remember them, learn from them, and act on them in appropriate, effective, and creative ways.[5]

Coherence refers to the energy-efficient, coordinated state that occurs when the elements of a system are synchronized. If you play basketball or watch professional basketball, you know this phenomenon. There's a "zone" or a "flow" that a team sometimes enters. When the team is in the zone, everything unfolds like a choreographed ballet. The individual players appear to dance together, separate in their individuality, connected in their collective purpose.

I remember the first time Gail and I traveled to Denmark to teach. We had just arrived in Copenhagen, and were jetlagged and exhausted after a long journey. Disembarking at the train station, we happened upon a concert at Tivoli Gardens, right next door. We felt invited by the gardens, with their lively music, lush greenery, twinkling lights, and laughing and strolling people.

We were just in time to get the last two standing-room-only tickets to a concert with Zubin Mehta conducting, and Itzak Perlman playing the violin. Leaning against the back wall, we rested in that wonderful sound. As we listened with rapt attention, the music rose and fell, washing over us in waves of full, vital sound that energized us and kept us enthralled. Throughout the concert we were entranced, our eyes often shining with tears.

At the end, when the maestro and the virtuoso stood together, hands clasped as they bowed, the audience responded as a single being, clapping in rhythmic unison—something we'd never experienced before. My heart leapt with the joy of this coherent moment. Gail and I knew we had experienced something extraordinary, and, tired though we were, we both felt invigorated and refreshed by that wonderful, healing experience.

While discordant rhythms such as a bumpy train ride, a day of thinking too hard, or erratic conversation can leave us feeling stressed, disorganized, and out of sync, coherent rhythms such as a beautiful piece of music, the sounds or sights of a natural environment, or people expressing joy together can bring us back to a more heartful, energized place.

Basic to the Brain Gym work is the idea that the natural rhythms evoked by simple and specific movements provide one of our most reliable ways to return to this natural state of coherence. To put it in simple language, when the heart is harmonic, the brain functions optimally. And balanced movement can help us release the stress response and reconnect with the heart. When the whole system of mind and body is balanced, a person learns, creates, and works optimally. The natural genius is free to unfold.

The Mind-Heart Tug of War
A challenge goes on, however, between the rational, intellectual brain and the intuitive, intelligent heart, one that often stops us from functioning in the most integrated manner. This imbalance is well known. It manifests outwardly in such various battles as the ones we face daily—battles between the pull of tension or that of ease,

between strategy and flow, or between the urge to create and the need for scheduled time. This is the tension we must hold as our ambition and rationality contend with feeling and intuition. This is the age-old tension between power and love.

In close relationships, many of us experience this as a stereotypical characterization of the sexes. Most often we project those assertive, domineering qualities or receptive, meandering qualities onto our partners, who remind us of our parents. Then we play out our polarization against them. This battle also manifests ecologically, as control and exploitation are pitted against the nurturing, abundant, but ultimately fragile Mother Earth.

How did the intellect ever preempt the body wisdom of the heart? The child in each and every one of us wants to follow the heart. Yet, because society honors the mind, the signals from the heart have become fainter than those from the intellect, and that's a challenge for us, since it means we have to learn to hear more subtle signals. The brain, governed by habit and survival strategies, makes itself heard more strongly, and if we're accustomed to following its dictates, it's hard for us to hear the softer tones of the heart. And yet it is urgent that we begin to hear the heart's signals, because they can guide us out of the chaos, violence, and stress of the world we live in today.

Whether we heed it or not, the heart can't be silenced. If it's not heard directly, then it will find some indirect means of expression. Even though men have governed autocratically throughout recorded history while women have mostly taken a submissive, obedient role, it would be wrong to conclude that women have been powerless—just as it's wrong to imagine that love is powerless. It is not. Love is the most powerful force in the world.

When I was ten, my parents produced a puppet show about the biblical character Esther. Queen Esther was married to King Ahaseuras, whose vast kingdom stretched across Persia and Medea, spanning one hundred twenty-seven provinces. Such was the power of the king that a law stipulated that no one—not even the queen—could enter his presence without being summoned; violation of this law was punishable by death.

In my parents' play, I was fascinated by the large and colorful hand puppets that would appear on stage, their movements and bold voices dramatizing the event. When Esther's cousin, Mordecai, asks her to intercede with the king to stop a genocide that's about to take place against her people, Esther risks her life to approach her husband. Yet her grace and courage, together with beauty and some sweet cunning, preserve her, and she is able to convince the king of the treachery of his viceroy, Haman, and persuade him to countermand the decree. Goodness, then, triumphs over evil.

During the puppet performance, Esther's passion to save her people kept the children rooting and cheering for her, while they would boo and hiss at the wicked and controlling Haman. If we become sensitive to the interactions of our heart and mind, we can see this story as accurately representing an inner war that we must all sometimes face.

The Value of Coherence

We can see, then, that it's important to bring the movements of our mind-body system into harmonic coherence with the heart, as the heart will guide us in ways that the mind alone cannot. As our body's patterns of movement and rhythm become more integrated, we feel more caring and appreciative of life, we have a greater sense of well-being, and we're better able to focus and concentrate with calm. Our ability to learn, create, and understand improves, and—whether we're at home, at school, or in the workplace—we experience greater pleasure in whatever we do.

The reason for this greater ease is that coherent heart frequencies induce coherent brain waves, which optimize the brain's ability to be receptive to external stimuli and to take in, code, and integrate new information. Returning to the basketball analogy, it's as though the players can see and hear better and the information they receive is better coordinated.

The heart helps us to *be*, whereas the brain—at least the left hemisphere—urges us to *do*. The head tries hard, but it's limited in its range of responses. Yet when we're connected to our heart's intelligence, we can see infinite possibilities. When we're disconnected, a solution may be right in front of us yet we can't see it, because the very effort we're making to find it is inhibiting our vision. When we regain our connection with the self-organizing heart, solutions often come to us effortlessly.

Elkonon Goldberg tells us that the left brain evolved to code and record and make familiar our experience, which the right brain can then use in creative ways. The left brain has built-in "how to" and "how not to" mechanisms, which means its function is all about making distinctions and separating, in a linear fashion.

Yet life isn't linear and life isn't organized. It's wild and confused—full of paradox and mystery. We need the abstraction of our cerebral, left-brained language to recreate things, to think in a sequential way, and to develop symbols and cues to remind us what to do. Yet it's the poetry and song and dance of the right, novelty-seeking brain that brings things back together, helping us to express qualities of joy, play, beauty, harmonics, and cooperation.

Learning and the Language of the Heart

How can we reclaim that voice that speaks the language of the ardent heart?

When we memorize a poem, its deep rhythm speaks to us of how to move in new ways. We speak of "learning it by heart," meaning that we have internalized the movement patterns connected with the words. In its purest form, the language of the heart speaks through a poetic voice. This voice has a rhythm and a meter that come directly out of the body's natural movement. Poetry brings us back into our hearts and our passion, back to the patterns of nature, and back to the mystery of life. This integrating language (whether in verse or prose form) can move us right into our heart and even touch the brain stem.

When I write poetry, the process of letting those words flow is amazing for me. In a manner similar to what happens when I do the Brain Gym movements, poetry brings me into my senses and my body, and then into my heart. Something happens, and my relationship with the room changes.

Whether we read or write poetry, we can experience these special qualities of poetic language that bring together our noticing and linguistic skills (the front and left brain) with our awareness of senses, feelings, and movement patterns (the brain stem and right brain).

Poetry invites us to listen to our inner and outer rhythms and sounds—of heartbeat, breathing, voice intonation and modulation, and rhythms of walking or moving about—and to observe any images that hold these particular patterns of movement in our awareness. For me, writing poetry can only happen when I'm feeling safe enough to notice my inner experience.

When students are invited to read or write poetry, it's important that they feel safe to explore this art form, with its opportunities for noticing and heart connection. This is one reason why, in my own teaching with adults, I do my best to create an experiential setting where people learn from one another and competition isn't rewarded.

In a classroom, reward or punishment of behavior tends to create a harsh, competitive atmosphere. This stress reduces heart/brain coherence and makes people feel as if they're under threat, leading to a fight/flight response.

Student reactions vary, yet often include aggressive behavior in the form of an overfocus on learning information to please the teacher, or oppositional debating with the group—sometimes with angry or disruptive behavior. The flight syndrome shows up as withdrawal: these students do their best to disappear, so as not to have to participate.

In any case, in a classroom atmosphere of reward or punishment an individual's ability to stay connected to his and her heart and to the marvelous, poetic world of infinite possibility is severely curtailed.

In contrast, the classroom inclusion of music, learning games, and lots of Brain Gym movement activities sets a relaxed, exploratory tone that helps students release stress and stay connected with their feelings and senses.

Invisible Connections

Stress and competition are contagious, because heart and brain coherence between people is communicated through many invisible connections. This is made possible in part by the fact that the electro-magnetic field of the heart, as described by Pearsall, extends, on average, sixteen feet beyond the body.

We tend to learn patterns of stress—that is, incoherent heart/brain rhythms—at home, at school, and at work. It's easy to become locked into these patterns, which severely limit our ability to learn, create, and cooperate. Effort, discipline, and willpower can counteract these effects to some extent, but such strivings go against the grain of the underlying structure, so that expanded and integrated functioning is further inhibited. I have found that the single most powerful way to shift into heart coherence is through movement and play.

Also, Wayne Muller in his *The Sabbath: Finding Rest, Renewal and Delight in our Busy Lives*—a beautiful little book about setting aside one day a week in order to rest and celebrate life—emphasizes that we can't make good decisions when we're exhausted. Muller's work inspires me to walk in my garden for five minutes each day and simply notice what I see there, and I often invite students in my workshops to do the same. I sometimes see panic in people's eyes when I suggest this. Perhaps, as a culture, we have so completely lost the art of rest and relaxation that the mere thought of it can make us anxious. It's easy to become habituated to stress-based patterns of movement, and useful to remember that even a few minutes of calm and beauty can help us resume our more restorative patterns.

Play and Aggression

Play brings the heart into the picture. Children whose hearts are closed begin to open up. There's a beautiful video that shows a polar bear cub that's closed down and traumatized. Another cub in the cage keeps on playing with him, never giving up. Finally the traumatized polar bear opens up his heart and is able to start participating in the games. This is how education, in humans as well as in polar bears, is supposed to happen.

When children are relaxed and in a truly playful mode, there is no aggression or competition. If there's fighting, or winning and losing, it's all part of the game; there is no venom in it. Harmful aggression arises when stress and social conditioning propel a child back into the brain stem. From that place, the options become severely limited. There is no time for learning or creativity, as physical survival is at stake and all other considerations take second place. As we have seen, this is entirely appropriate when there's a real danger. But how often does a bear wander onto a playground?

Until recently, girls fitted into school better than boys, from the Brain Gym perspective. They apparently enjoyed easier access to love and other feelings associated with integrated functioning, and their language skills were superior. They were able to release emotional stress by talking about it to girlfriends or a special adult, and this made them less susceptible to lower-animal reactions. Today the lines are becoming blurred between boys and girls. Both sexes are failing to receive the necessary heart stimulation. Brain stem competition is beginning to rule the girls' world, too.

Fun, play, games, touch—all these nurturing interactions within the peer group are fading from the developmental landscape. Play is turning into something digital, sterile, and cold-blooded.

In the past, boys were ten times more likely than girls to settle a dispute by fighting. Now, the ratio has dropped, and 25 percent of fights involve girls. The age of the combatants is dropping too. The front-page story in my newspaper this morning was about a pre-teen girl who was beaten almost to death. She is now in a coma and probably has permanent brain damage. The children witnessing the attack, together with the mother of one of the children, egged on the assailant, encouraging her to defend her honor because the other girl had kissed her boyfriend.

Well-intentioned adults often blame TV and video games for this rise in violence, but from the Brain Gym perspective we know that children are not getting their heart developed, which means they increasingly resort to brain stem behavior, including cold-blooded aggression.

When a parent, teacher, or co-worker is able to bring a more coherent heart/brain rhythm into the home, school, or work environment, this can also be felt. I've many times experienced how, when a relatively small number of people learn to bring themselves mentally and physically into synergistic balance, a wave of change is set into motion that can shift what's happening in a room. Such a shift, happening on a larger scale, could transform our entire society.

Regaining Coherence

In response to hearing the information I've shared above, many people wonder *How do I get back into a state of coherence once I've lost it? How do I nurture balance and openness? How do I reconnect my mind and heart to increase my learning capacity and enjoyment of life?*

In answer to these questions, I make the following two recommendations. First, we have to notice that we're out of coherence, which means seeing the necessity for coherence in the first place. Life never thrusts itself upon us; it waits patiently until we see what we need and ask for it. As soon as we set a clear intention in the direction of greater mind/heart coherence, life will help us in response to our sincere desire. This happens in many ways, but my own focus is on the easy-to-understand manner in which it occurs through the body.

The body responds to our thoughts, which is why it's vital to cultivate positive, healing thoughts. When we silently express a desire for some form of change—whether it's a wish for emotional stability, more love in our life (greater internal coherence), or anything else—the body begins to mobilize its resources in the direction of our desire.

Secondly (and this arises naturally out of a sincere wish for greater coherence), we can regain a state of coherence by continuing to practice the Brain Gym activities described in this book.

The PACE activities that you will learn in Chapter Twelve are especially helpful for moving us out of the stress reflex and helping us settle into the more relaxed state of heart coherence. In this chapter, I'm inviting you to experience two more Brain Gym movements that can help reestablish a coordinated heart response. These two movements are especially helpful in supporting our feeling of "grounding" in the body.

These movements are also valuable for supporting the health of the whole body, as they help to release the tendon-guard reflex and the withdrawal or "freeze" response, diminishing the stress response and any stress hormones (such as adrenalin and cortisol), so that we can come back more quickly to the calm of heart coherence. As the cortisol levels diminish, DHEA, the "fountain of youth" hormone, increases. With its antiaging effects, DHEA moisturizes the body's systems, improving immune function, releasing feelings of confusion or frustration, and increasing the clarity of thought and attention.

Just in the minute or so that it takes to complete these two movements, notice any changes that you may experience in the activity pattern of your nervous system.

The Gravity Glider

The Gravity Glider is a key movement for helping to relax the tendon-guard reflex—the stress response for "freezing" or withdrawal. The release of this reflex prepares us to reconnect with heart coherence.

Sit comfortably in a chair and cross one foot over the other at the ankles. Keeping your knees relaxed and your head dropped forward, bend comfortably forward from the waist. Let your arms reach out comfortably in front of you. The idea is to relax and "glide" on gravity—as though resting on a pillow of air—so it's important to lean forward only enough to feel relaxed.

As you exhale, allow your arms and upper body to glide slightly down; then allow yourself to glide upward, being lifted by your inhalation. Do this to the left, right, and center, gliding back up before each new direction. Then cross your feet the other way and do it again.

This movement is particularly helpful if you need extra confidence in public—for example, when giving a speech. You'll be more likely to express yourself with heart, and you'll feel more self-assured.

The Grounder

Exercises that balance your mind and open your heart are especially helpful, as are ones that give you focus. The next movement, "The Grounder," has a similar effect to that of the Gravity Glider. It will also help you to feel more grounded and relaxed.

Keeping the left foot pointing straight ahead, point your right foot toward the right so that it forms a right angle with your left foot. Now bend your right knee as you exhale, and then straighten your right leg again as you inhale. Keep your hips tucked under, and make sure that your torso and pelvis are sitting squarely, facing the front, while your head, your bending knee, and the foot of your bending leg face to the side. Notice the relaxation in the muscles along the inner hip and thigh of your straight leg.

Heart Knowledge

In our busy modern world with all its daily input of information, we tend to dwell excessively in our head, where we have access to a limited form of analytical information. In our body, on the other hand, we have access to body wisdom—a more personal and internal kind of knowledge that is limitless.

Each of us is connected to every other person at the heart level, and everything that's knowable is potentially available to us through heart coherence, in the form of insight and intuition.

When I see how science and technology advance in leaps, I get the impression that an Intelligence in the universe decides, "Okay, now it's time to transmit this piece of information into the human growth story; they're ready for the next step."

Once we have received the new piece of information, however, we still need to have the body integrate it into a structure. Indeed, it's that particular combination of experiences—inspiration and integration—that gives us a sense of euphoria when we learn.

The Brain Gym movements activate the two brain hemispheres and connect them with the heart, thus opening us to an influx of creativity and enabling us to process and internalize these new experiences.

When we ask ourselves *What are the true miracles of the world?* we might respond by going into our mind—remembering remarkable places we've seen, people we've known or heard of, and events we've read about. But if we respond to the same question by moving and going into heart coherence, we can immediately reconnect with the miracle of having our own hands with which to touch, ears with which to listen and receive, eyes with which to see and enjoy, and a heart with which we can feel, laugh, and love.

Chapter Eight

Movement and Memory

It's 1963. John F. Kennedy is president, and the cost of a first-class stamp is four cents. I'm seated in a Boston University classroom, taking a final exam in American History on an economic interpretation of events from the Civil war to the present. I need to write an essay, remembering critical dates and important names and places to compare and contrast past political events with contemporary issues.

Dr. Hill, the head of the history department and proctor of this four-hour exam, happens to be standing behind my desk. Feeling her presence, I'm frozen in fear, unable to turn my head either left or right. My mind has gone blank. All it can do is repeat, *Please move away. Please move away.* Until Dr. Hill decides to stand somewhere else, I can't think, can't remember, and can't write a single word.

What was causing my mental block so that I couldn't think or move my pencil until the proctor moved on? How does fear affect mental recall?

It would be another twenty years before I'd understand the physical component that prevented me from thinking during those long moments back in college. What I'd been in the grip of—what had caused the inhibition of my mental acuity—was the tendon-guard reflex exemplified by Dorothy's Tin Man. When we can't relax our neck to turn our head, we're unable to access certain neural pathways of the temporal lobe that are critical to the functions of memory and speech.

The phenomenon of memory is a complex function, involving such senses as touch and movement. It also involves our feelings, such as those evoked during play. Memory is the ability to relate the present moment to a past experience through an emotional association that enables us to relive the event as if it were happening again. In brief, memories are states of mind or conditioned associations activated by sensations within the body.

The olfactory sense is a memory trigger most people understand because they've experienced it. Whenever I walk into a bakery and smell hot apple pie, I remember visiting my grandmother's house on a nippy New England afternoon. The brisk winter day and the rosy warmth of Nana's hands are immediate and real again.

Without memory, have we learned? If we're unable to relive an event or relate it to our lives, did it really happen?

Learning by Heart

Good memory is more than successfully memorizing information for a test, as the forgetting curve for such "cramming" is at least 80 percent. To memorize "by heart," as in learning a song or a poem by heart, means more than a flawless recitation from memory. It means to resonate with the meaning of the words and feel them in the body, so that the poem or song becomes an expression of our own experience.

The creation of new memories is the core of learning. Each experience we enjoy lays down rich new growth upon existing neural pathways. Our first learning is physical and body -related. When we first learn to walk, that kinesthetic learning is stored in the brain as a memory, available whenever we go to take a step, so that—unless we have a serious injury—we don't ever again have to think about how to walk. Those neural pathways established during our first movements, our first explorations of the world, later provide the basis for the abstract thought processes of adulthood.

To resonate with something means to relate to it harmoniously. When we resonate with the world around us, we can learn with a relaxed heart, from a sense of joy, exploration, and cooperation rather than stress, fear, or competition. Our brain is vibrating with the slow alpha waves of relaxation and a sense of being in the flow, rather than with the faster beta waves of stress. This is true alpha and beta learning, and has its roots in our sense of an interior connection with the world.

The alphabet, so easily learned through movement, has stood the test of time. The Phoenicians who invented those letters knew something about what integrated the brain—what constituted a balance of left and right hemispheric attributes—and movement was part of that. The movement of my writing hand can bring me balance, just as any movement can induce in me a state balanced state.

The moving body is involved in every experience; every thought we entertain involves the movement neurons of the brain, although physical movement is sometimes subtle, as when we move our eyes. The cerebellum modulates movement patterns mastered in infancy, enabling us to function in time and space and to reach out to our environment and explore new experiences. Our memories build upon one another to create a matrix of interconnections that we know as the fullness of our lives.

Short-Term Memory

In today's world, memory loss has become an obsession; each day the proliferation of dementia and Alzheimer's disease is serving to intensify interest in the subject. When a friend or loved one confesses to us that he thinks he's losing his memory, usually his real concern isn't long-term memory but short-term. When we can't remember what we just said, what we just read, or what we came into the room for, we have become so disconnected from our movement patterns that we're using only the passive, receptive pathways of the brain. Expression, planning, and intention, the executive functions of the frontal lobe, have become inaccessible.

Our short-term memory is our "working" or conscious memory, which involves our feelings, connecting us to a past event; our senses, connecting us to the present moment; and our thoughts, which help us plan for the anticipated future.

If I'm packing for a trip, I scan a memory of my last trip to recall what I wore and what I needed to have with me for my lectures, reliving the prior trip's events as I do this. As I look, right now, at the objects I've assembled, checking off items on a mental list, I'm also anticipating the future, imagining what I will or won't need at my next destination.

We must create new neural pathways: literally create our future mentally, before we live it. Short-term memory is the awareness responsible for the active collation of incoming data with long-term patterns so that we can move into the unknown future. It's a restructuring process whereby we recreate ourselves and initiate contexts for new learning yet to come. Without the activity and involvement of the expressive frontal lobe, we can't process new information or experiences in this way.

In contrast, long-term memory depends on our body-based learning experiences. This is why elderly people often revert to memories of their younger days, when they were more active—when they walked, worked, cooked, played sports, and carried their children. That is to say, when they moved and worked their muscles.

I remember reading books on memory improvement—about memory "pegs" and the need to activate the right brain to make mental pictures and associations that can, with imagination, be linked to new information. In those student days, I was disconnected from my body and from real experiences, and these tricks enabled me to store and retrieve impressively long lists of data with ease.

Despite their techniques and gimmicks, these programs were limited, though useful for certain types of learning and to impress friends. They did make me think about the brain and how important it is to create conscious emotional associations. Many of these techniques are still taught. Yet how about the importance of drawing out meaningful, true memories without gimmicks—memories made from genuine experiences with concrete reality and with people I love, people with whom I play?

"Senior Moments"

Whenever I discuss memory in my classes, students ask why they can easily remember a face yet not as easily recall the names of the persons they recognize. When I'm telling a story, I often block an important word or can't recall the name of a city. This is a well-known phenomenon shared by people of all ages and identified as a "tip of the tongue" experience: we know what we want to say and can see and feel the associations, but the word won't quite come. So we use another word, or wait until the needed word appears sometime later, after we've stopped trying to remember and have moved on to something else.

How can we be more present, inclusive, and sensory in our learning, so that we can listen actively and engage the expressive frontal lobe and the auditory temporal lobe, building our love for and use of the sounds of language to improve our verbal recall?

Equally fascinating are those memory phenomena known as the primacy and recency effects—the predisposition of the right brain (where we experience things) to process novelty for retention in longer-term storage and record recent events for a shorter term. As I was writing this book and wanting to provide examples regarding my work, I could best recall some of the earliest sessions I shared with students, and of course the most recent ones. We tend to remember best the first time we did something—our early experiences—and also those events lived through more recently. It's the days, months, or years in the middle that are harder to bring to mind.

The early research on left-brain and right-brain qualities suggested that memory was more strongly associated with the right brain. This is corroborated by the current neuroscientific understanding of the brain, which emphasizes the right hemisphere's involvement in processing novel experiences through the senses and emotions, evoking the joy of curiosity and discovery.

So we see that we build more memories when we playfully engage the mind in what is new to it. When routine becomes *too* routine, it also becomes less memorable. This should naturally lead us to ask how we can lead our lives and teach our children with more novelty, movement, and adventure, so that we will have more to remember!

Memory isn't located in any one place in the brain. Certain organs, such as the hippocampus, are essential to memory, which fails on their injury or removal. Yet the brain is holographic. Whole-brain memory depends upon the interfacing of those various modules of the brain that give us speech, vision, hearing, and tactility when the brain is organized around a purpose or goal. New learning has no meaning until it's measured against past experience, and until it can help us imagine something yet to come. We have a well-functioning memory when we can live fully in the present, with the past available to us as necessary for anticipating our needs in the future.

Memory's Biochemical Component

We have come to accept memory loss as biological—an inevitable feature of the aging process. But in reality this problem is vastly exacerbated by environmental factors. The brain and its memories are electrically and biochemically based, as neurotransmitters convey electrical impulses across the synapses between nerves. Because of this biochemical component of memory, anything we can do to promote the brain's chemical balance is beneficial to the long-term health of our memory.

Brain Gym can play an important role in memory by bringing the body back into the equation, using conscious movement experiences as the door to learning. Our physical activity helps oxygenate the brain and assists in countless bodily processes in the various organs, including the manufacture of any needed chemical elements. All this results in clearer thinking. In Educational Kinesiology we observe that mature adults who follow a daily Brain Gym movement program perform better in their mental activities than do sedentary people, and new medical research on the value of daily exercise is corroborating this.

Play and Memory

I've had the good fortune to work with play specialist O. Fred Donaldson, who is internationally recognized for his research into play with children and wild animals. Fred is the author of the Pulitzer-nominated book *Playing by Heart* and has written more than thirty articles on what he terms original play. He describes play as "belonging to and being in touch with a world that is in touch with us." Fred goes on to say that "Original play is a practice of kindness, which permeates all of one's relationships. It cultivates an ever-renewing sense of enchantment and engagement with the world." Fred has identified specific characteristics of play that are common to both humans and animals, and offers us the understanding that the intrinsic intelligence of play is universal, across all life forms.

When we're ready to learn, we're relaxed and ready for whatever's next—ready to play. Brain Gym frees us to play; it helps us leave the competitive fight-or-flight state and return to a sense of connectedness and homeostasis. Children love to do the movements, especially in pairs and groups. Once Brain Gym has become a part of their daily routine, they'll ask for it if the movements are inadvertently omitted from the schedule.

What do you remember best about play? In the play mode, we experience a sense of ease, well-being, and joy. We're able to sustain our efforts toward self-improvement, and are delighted as new challenges are added. When we're not afraid to make mistakes, learning is natural, and never perceived as hard work. When we engage with the world from this creative space, we make cognitive leaps. We're more in the moment, yet not unduly aware of time. At play, we're more aware of our interactions with others than focused on ourselves, moving from a sense of mutuality and equal acknowledgment. We laugh easily and interact in a state of equanimity.

Movement stimulates the growth of neurons in the brain. The best kind of physical activity is that which engages the body's midfield, crossing the visual/auditory/kinesthetic midline, which is either a line that divides the body into mirror images or a bridge that joins two sides. In such physical activities, the whole is more than the sum of the two parts. A baby makes this kind of motion when crawling, rolling over, and, later, when learning to walk. Research shows that these universally common patterns of movement are critical to the development of a child's neural pathways, and are also crucial for optimal mental functioning in the adult.

Crossing the Midline for Yourself
The Cross Crawl (see Chapter Twelve) and Lazy 8s (see Chapter Two), two of the Brain Gym activities described in this book, are beneficial movements that involve crossing the midline and thus integrating the brain hemispheres for enhanced recall and mental clarity. When these two activities are done slowly, they stimulate the vestibular system, which assists balance and equilibrium as well as vision, hearing, and mental integration.

Neck Rolls

If you notice that you need to move a bit and are at work or in some other environment where doing the Cross Crawl or Lazy 8s isn't an option, I suggest that you do some Neck Rolls.

Breathe deeply, relax your shoulders, and drop your head forward. Allow your head to roll slowly from side to side as you breathe out any tightness. As you relax your neck, your chin draws a smooth semicircle across your chest.

Think of an X

In everyday life, many sports—golf, tennis, and ping-pong, for example—can help you engage the right and the left brain simultaneously if you play them with that conscious intention. Even sweeping the floor can be done with a contralateral crossing of the midline! And of course nearly everyone walks every day. To do the Brain Gym activity known as "Think of an X," all you need do is actually think of an X and swing your arms from side to side across the midline in front of you as you walk. In this simple way, you'll be giving your neural networks a good boost.

Finding Lost Keys

Stress is antithetical to memory. A major stressor at our house is lost papers or other objects. Have you ever had the experience of losing your car keys when you were late for an appointment? Even though we know where we last saw the keys, we rush around the house looking for them everywhere, certain that they've vanished from the face of the Earth. This happens because stress has shut down our integrated brain functioning and we've gone into fight-or-flight state. Our only hope of finding our keys is if we happen to see them as we rush about—and even then we may not notice them!

Next time you find yourself in this predicament, if you can quiet yourself long enough to do Hook-ups (even though every cell of your being wants to get out of the house), this will restore your physiology to normal, overriding the fight-or-flight reaction, and you'll experience a surprising result. More often than not, the exact location of the keys (or any other object you're searching for) will pop into your mind.

This Brain Gym exercise serves to bring us back into our calm mid-brain and rational cortex, where we have ready access to the relevant memory. Our confidence helps alleviate our stress, allowing the brain to shift out of the state of emergency that restricts our ability to remember and into a more integrated, whole-brain state.

Memory Needs a Sense of Safety

One way to see life is as the creation of memories. The pleasure of learning is the knowledge that we have lived and are alive. The game of life is one of living together, connected by the music of heart rhythms that enable us to know who we are as we take our turn and give others theirs. We know who we are as we tell stories, sing together, dance together, and truly see each other.

Unbeknownst to her, Dr. Hill helped teach me that testing and the demand for recall of information has little to do with real learning. When I'm afraid, I tend to block my ability to perform until I feel safe again. If I need to "perform," to access memory on cue, and to relate to others, I must be able to connect with the safety I know as play.

A Quick Way to Notice Your Sense of Balance

The standing version of Hook-ups, with one ankle crossed over the other and arms intertwined over the chest, is especially effective for activating the balance-related muscles in the body. I invite you to take a moment right now to explore this movement, for which you learned the seated version in Chapter Two.

In the standing position, the muscle systems related to balance are in a state of dynamic relaxation—engaged but not fully contracted. We can use this posture for noticing our structural balance. Standing in Part One of Hook-ups, simply allow your body to sway left and right as you notice your sidedness (your laterality). Do your eyes, your head, or your whole body pull to the right or the left, or do they gravitate to the center? Do you notice any tension, pain, or discomfort?

Now allow your body to lift and relax in an up-and-down motion, noticing your centering. Is this posture naturally more comfortable in the rising or in the grounding position? Or perhaps you're able to access both extremes while simultaneously finding the comfortable middle ground.

Again, allow yourself to sway to the front and back, noticing your body's focus. Does your posture pull forward or hold back? Can you readily access both movements, and can you rest in the center of the two?

Now close your eyes and simply relax into the posture for a good thirty seconds (about three to five relaxed breaths). Open your eyes, stand with feet shoulder width apart, and place your fingertips together for another thirty seconds. Check those three movements again: side-to-side, up and down, and back and front. Notice how it feels to move into the center of each space. Is there any shift in postural tension? Any difference in your level of comfort, relaxation, or ease?

We can use this activity to support ourselves in shifting from the fight-or-flight reflex, in which our muscles tense and our adrenaline level soars, or from the fight-or-freeze reflex, in which we withdraw and find it hard to participate, to start to return our system to heart coherence and normalcy. A simple shift in the posture, providing more support from the back and torso, also provides more room for the movement and workings of our vital organs.

We can thus make a shift toward greater health and ease in our life, and away from many daily stresses and dis-eases, just by doing this simple one-minute activity on a daily basis.

Gail and I developed the following guidelines for our Optimal Brain Organization course manual, to help students notice the congruity between thoughts, feelings, and sensations.

What Am I Thinking?

Noticing the thought patterns—whether they're calm or stressful—is one way to pay attention to the learning process. The eyes and ears are another good indicator of such balance. When we take information from one eye or ear only, inhibiting information from the other side, it is usually a compensation for too much "noise." This noise might manifest as, for example, a blur, distortion, or disorientation, resulting from the unintegrated bilateral input. Ultimately the "noise" becomes a background that interferes with my thought process. When the two sides lack cooperation, it is actually easier to do a task that requires lateral skill (like reading or writing) in a one-sided rather than two-sided way, but this inhibition requires the shutting down of whole-body movement.

In another instance, the inhibition may be due to lack of integration between the visual and the auditory channels, between the visual and the tactile channels, or some other combination of unintegrated factors that, again, create physiological discomfort.

What Am I Feeling?

Noticing emotional expressiveness or the level of stress is one way
to focus on the feelings. The hands, arms, and breathing pattern are
other good indicators of emotional stress. When we're under stress,
our instinct is to run or fight. The ability to use the sides together to
organize the workspace or physical environment is lost as emotions
direct irrational behaviors outward toward the environment. Only
when we restore equilibrium, allow feelings to surface, and at the same
time allow ourself to think more rationally about the situation, are we
able to feel the easy up-and-down motion of the breath directly at the
body's midline. Then we can "settle in" with our emotions and feel our
ground center, our experience. Only when we reach out from the heart,
with compassion for the self and others concerning the matter at hand,
do our organizational abilities return.

What Am I Sensing in My Body?

Noticing the ease of access to sensory experience is one way to
experience the level of physical awareness. Noticing the function
of the brain and posture as a whole is another good indicator. Our
attention toward a goal provides the energy to move forward into the
experience rather than hold back from that goal. The physical energy
follows the specific intention from which whole-brain behavior derives
its strength and also its connection to soul or life purpose. When the
brain and posture are unintegrated, there is a lack of focus, an inability
to understand or find meaning in the situation, and a sense of being
blocked or unable to participate in the community.

When the thoughts, feelings, and sensory awareness are available—
as demonstrated by noticing—we're often able to experience a state
of balance and of whole-brain integration. When one or more of the
these areas is unavailable for integration, there is stress, tension,
confusion, chronic pain or general discomfort, and less-than-optimal
performance.

Accessing the Gifted Space

We all have certain life activities for which we're able to perform
in a more whole-brain manner. It's important to discover and

acknowledge that we have these integrated spaces in our life for which the movement of the brain and the rest of the body is not static, and for which we're continuously reorganizing ourselves for creative interaction with the challenge of the task.

When the brain and its corresponding movement patterns are organized for optimal performance, we function at our best. We experience feelings of "flow," synergy, or a sense that everything is right. Learning environments that inspire us to such aliveness are often found in art, sports, nature, music, invention, and other potentially creative endeavors.

People with learning challenges often find this sense of integration in an activity, like running or swimming, that doesn't require focus at near-point the way reading and writing do. I encourage you to take time now and then to stop and remember times in your own life when you had a sense of aliveness, of being in the flow. Whenever you do, step completely into that experience for a moment. By reliving the fullness of whole-brain integration in this way, you can build upon it for the future.

The Three Dimensions of Whole-Brain Learning

As you may recall from Chapter Two, balance can affect our three dimensions of laterality (communication), centering (organization), and focus (comprehension). Notice, now, if you experience any difference in these three functions after doing the Hook-ups. How could such a simple movement affect our "mental abilities"?

Communication through both spoken and written language becomes clearer and more alive when the left and right sides of the body and brain work together. As we saw in Chapter Two, we refer to this two-sided system as the Laterality Dimension. When the integration of our two sides is improved, communication between the two cerebral hemispheres becomes more spontaneous. As a result, the analytic part of the system (usually the left brain hemisphere of the cerebral cortex) works synergistically with the gestalt side. Like the Scarecrow in Chapter Four, we're than able to process information by thinking from the whole to the parts as well as from the separate, analytic parts to the whole.

Organization is the Centering Dimension: top to bottom. Our centering or core reflexes depend upon the relationship between the cerebral cortex and the emotional midbrain—our ability to organize our thinking around reception as well as expression. We're like the Lion in that our organization for thought, speech, or action depends upon the balance and sense of stabilization of these reflexes around a central locus—our heart coherence.

Comprehension is related to the Focus Dimension—the relationship between the expressive frontal lobes and the receptive parietal, temporal, and occipital lobes. Comprehension ultimately depends upon being able to integrate and talk about what we've experienced, making it truly our own. Like the Tin Man, when we're able to release the tendon-guard reflex and relax forward in our body, we participate more fully and are better able to anticipate, pay attention, and concentrate as we read, write, speak, and interact in the world.

These Brain Gym movements to stimulate integration of the laterality, centering, and focus dimensions were originally developed to support slower learners, but they have evolved into an effective learning tool for everybody—athletes to schoolchildren to corporate executives. Anybody can use them and be on the way to the exquisite life.

Chapter Nine

Natural Learning in the Classroom

Learning problems are not diseases. They are "crossed wires" in
the communication network that connects a child to his world.
—Paul Dennison
Switching On: The Whole-Brain
Answer to Dyslexia

Less than six hundred years ago, a revolutionary idea about
learning took hold in the Western world, changing humanity's social
structure along with the whole idea of education. The new idea was
this: that a physical experience could be encoded into words and
then "downloaded" by a reader, who would gain that experience
vicariously. In the centuries since, the idea has only gained in
influence.

Prior to 1450, educated people were those who knew how to use
their hands in the mastery of a craft. They were versed in the art of a
particular trade for which they had been mentored or apprenticed—
e.g., as a baker, tailor, shoemaker, silversmith, or fresco painter.

A young man usually spent the days of his youth working closely
with a teacher who modeled for him the concrete, kinesthetic skills
of a profession that he would keep for a lifetime. Unless he was a
monk, this young person would have no reason to ever read or write.
Books didn't yet exist except as rare, handscripted volumes, vigilantly
protected and handed down within an elite group. Most information
was passed on orally, which meant that storytelling and listening were
valued skills.

In 1450 a German inventor named Johannes Gutenberg converted a wooden olive oil press into a device for printing words on paper. With Gutenberg's invention of moveable metal type, a new way learning was born. Soon an educated person was one who could read the Gutenberg Bible. With the invention of the printing press, the mark of a person's intelligence shifted from the mastery of physical skills to the ability to read a printed code. That profound shift continues to influence us today.

The Tyranny of Literacy

Over the centuries, literacy and the ability to read, write, and spell the "code" progressed from a specialized art form mastered by a few to a requirement imposed upon the average person. Schools were created as formal institutions to teach the young, and with them came the dunce cap, standardized testing, learning disabilities, hyperactivity, and attention deficit disorder.

The ability to read was considered to be a natural one, like walking. Children who didn't learn to read in pace with their peers were judged by parents and educators to be lazy, uncooperative, or mentally challenged, and teaching theory devolved to a system of helping educators cope with students' failure to learn.

Despite humankind's history of movement and of using the body— of dance and song and communal cooperation in work and play—we came to a new isolationism . . . and, with it, a disengagement from the body. Educators came to perceive learning as a mental act involving only the intellect. The goal of education became (and remains today) the achievement of the ability to acquire and use information. In cultures on every continent, school is now a place to learn how to survive in a world of competition, hierarchy, and shaming.

The Reembodiment of Learning

Imagine a world where learning is recognized as a natural, physical ability . . . one involving the innate intelligence of the heart and the rest of the body.

Our present-day academic skills of reading, writing, spelling, and arithmetic originally grew out of our interactions with real people and concrete objects in the physical world. People once counted on their ten fingers; they experienced weight, distance, density, and mass in their own body in real-life situations. Education has come too far away from this foundational grounding in the physical.

Very literally, it was living that created the brain—not the other way around. Science, arithmetic, and the very way we think have their roots in the physical. Thanks to the body, we have a number sense, we can organize our thoughts, and we see or "get" it when we finally understand something.

True learning is a lifelong process that equally involves the hands, heart, mind, and entire body; it's not a product to be assembled or a destination to be reached. A child readily learns to understand quantification when she can start by relating numbers to her own fingers. For the sake of all our children, who are struggling and too often failing to learn, modern education needs to go back to the roots of learning.

The body at play offers an ideal context for reinventing the physical codes handed down within our culture through the centuries. Play enables the learner to notice the shape, texture, tactility, sensations, and interrelationships of his own movement patterns as he interacts with the world. Through play, he is able to recapitulate the movement experiences of his ancestors and, in effect, rediscover his culture.

In this more natural view of education, the emphasis is on the development of wisdom rather than the mastery of information. The teacher asks questions rather than giving answers. Learners' playful interactions with their concrete physical world bring them a sense of immediacy regarding the properties of that world—size, weight, mass, distance, gravity, and so forth—and their place within it.

In this ideal school, teachers emphasize cooperation, "us," teamwork, holding space, wholeness, and mutual honoring. They model natural education, since they understand how to let children learn for the sheer pleasure of it by following their own interests and creative curiosity.

This school will never be associated with trying or with hard work. When we're in touch with our purpose and joyfully expressing our true potential, the word "work" doesn't begin to describe what we're doing. The more accurate word is "play."

Playful vs. Coercive Learning

The traditional school of today grew out of the industrial revolution. Just as we had the schedules, mass production, and standardization of the factory system, children began to be age-grouped, ability-grouped, tested, and graded as if the production of look-alike, think-alike graduates were the primary business of society.

Some children like to play games; others like music. Some like to learn by themselves in a quiet nook; others would rather learn by climbing trees and observing nature. Some want to sit quietly and read, while others prefer to move and dance. Some like to tell stories, while others prefer to have stories told to them.

What happens to children when we treat them as if they were all the same? Unless they're the "type" of children who happen to fit the prescribed mold—and no student really fits it—they become shut down and bored with school. Walk into any middle school or high school classroom in the United States and you'll see a preponderance of disengaged students in various states of frustration and anger.

Having placed children in contexts that don't awaken their innate love of learning, by what means do we motivate them to perform? We use the age-old carrot-and-stick technique. We get them onto that treadmill—we herd them toward success—by dangling before them the rewards of good grades, college acceptance, and career opportunities and threatening them with the specter of failure. If they complain, we assure them that all this is not only absolutely necessary but for their own good.

In my own life, I was driven to succeed "for my own good." When I became a young adult, I looked back on my experiences in public education and realized that I'd been cheated by the system. Lured into the pursuit of that elusive carrot and seeking to avoid the punishing stick, I had been denied the pleasure of learning that is our human birthright.

Way back then I formed a new intention: to avoid the outer-directed approach to life. I was eventually able to free myself from the system of punishment and reward and return to a more honest and immediate approach that reflects my true nature. That is, I've regained some of the genuineness I had as a child, when I was full of curiosity to learn and explore and not sidetracked by a need for "carrots."

I didn't come easily to this place. I had to learn to be suspicious of carrots, and ask myself frequently toward what end I was moving: whether the end justified the means and whether I was being honest with myself. When I say that I found a more honest approach, I'm defining honesty as the emotional and intellectual authenticity that characterizes any individual committed to living life to its fullest.

A life worth living is a process, a highly individual endeavor—a self-selected curriculum, we might say. We came here to experience, learn, and grow. Honest, authentic behavior is committed to this purpose; inauthentic behavior denies it. To behave honestly, a person must know who he is, take responsibility for his own life, be able to evaluate his own behavior, and respect the right of others to do the same. The currently prevailing educational system brings about the opposite: it convinces our young people that the denial of their true nature is necessary for survival.

Children Know What They Need to Learn

In the 1960s I read everything I could find by the educator John Holt, who addressed many of the above educational issues in such books as *How Children Learn*, which was about preschool children not yet exposed to learning institutions.

In that book Holt described children in natural situations where their curiosity has free rein. Such children have no adult concept of failure, knowing instinctively that "mistakes" are actually stepping-stones to new possibilities and have no meaning outside the context of learning. Unhampered by the fear of failure, they assess the total situation before them, decide on a course of action, and teach themselves methodically. They trust insight as well as logic to help them figure things out. They know their own limitations. They grasp the structure of a learning task and, when they're sufficiently motivated, have long attention spans.

The learning Holt described is anchored to dynamic movement, as compared to the stress-anchored learning now predominant in our schools. Holt's work started a wave of reform in public schools, and Holt carried his work into the home schooling movement. He well understood how classroom teaching to elicit informational responses, teaching in which the sole motivator is the pressure to perform, amounts to an education devoid of intellectual honesty.

The psychologist Barbara Clark, writing on these same subjects in *Optimizing Learning*: *The Integrative Education Model in the Classroom*, states: "The use of external rewards is another practice resulting in different effects than those desired. Research has shown that external rewards (any reward that is not the natural consequence of an activity) often become goals in and of themselves."

Providing children with opportunities to experience the intrinsic rewards of discovery and problem solving is the most sacred responsibility of the educator. Children learn by touching their environment, manipulating it, and moving within it. The accomplishment of physical mastery is far more important to the child's self-concept or sense of identity than the teacher's approval. As psychologist William Glasser points out, "Regardless of his background, his culture, his color, or his economic level, (a person) will not succeed in general until he can in some way first experience success in one important part of his life."

The experience of safety and consistency creates a sense of trust within a child. Further, a child's authenticity is reinforced through a parent's or teacher's trust in that child's ability to learn. Ideally, a young student will be able to sense that her teacher's goal is to educate learners so that they may become more "themselves." Such a teacher treats the subject matter in a sensitive way so that a pupil can incorporate it into herself, drawing from it what will be important and useful in her own life.

Such a teacher wants the pupil to be able to develop her own thoughts, opinions, and beliefs based on genuine interest and individual research. The teacher doesn't want to just hear his own words being mouthed back at him. He wants the pupil to realize that she is capable of making her own learning choices, free to make those choices, and responsible for whatever results the choices may bring about. Without the benefit of such a teacher, a child's decision-making skills may never be developed.

Far too often, educational authorities don't trust children or teachers. Teachers are not given credit for being professionals. The community rigorously certifies them, then turns around and offers them its lowest level of trust. Physicians are considered to know what they know, and are trusted, but a teacher has to follow state-mandated lesson plans and an assembly-line curriculum.

Children know what they need to learn. They want to move, play, sing, invent, and laugh. They delight in expanding their boundaries. They love to dress up and pretend they are other people. You don't need to be a "professional" to know that true learning is taking place when children imitate the adult roles they observe around them: mother, father, nurse, firefighter. Yet when was the last time you saw "dress up and pretend" on your child's school schedule?

The problem goes all the way up into universities. On the first day of my freshman year, one of my professors explained to his class the school's weeding-out process. "Everyone look to your left and look to your right," he said. "Statistically, neither of those two students you see will be here next semester." Since the professors graded their classes on a bell curve, the accuracy of that prediction was ensured, regardless of the actual levels of competency among that year's new students.

Getting through the four university years, then, was the same as getting through the earlier levels. It felt as if you had to sell your soul for a grade.

When I entered graduate school, one professor declared to the class, "You're all *A* material. You've survived the academic filtering up to this point, and you've made it. Now you get to reap the reward—finally, you can be creative without fear of failure." Does that mean that the remaining majority of the population—those who get weeded out—are losers? I don't think so.

Every child has a potential for success, and deserves to fulfill that potential in his own way, on his own terms. Our society can't afford to produce any more failures. The people who fall through the cracks are acting out their anger and frustration by becoming violent. They have chemical dependency problems. They're committing the futile act of suicide (now occurring even among children under ten).

A Different Model of Education
Competition is a curse inside the classroom, as it is outside of it. The first time the *Mayflower* is introduced in a history lesson, I'd want to say to the children, "What do you think would've happened if everyone on board the ship had tried selfishly to get ahead of everyone else? The pilgrims would never have reached America, that's what!

And the same applies to this class. Either we all make it or none of us does. Yes, that's right—either the whole class passes or the whole class fails the semester."

I can imagine the gifted children gasping, "You mean *I* have to fail because *Joe* can't do math?"

But think what would happen in this situation if it were actually implemented and adhered to. Over time, the more gifted children would help the less gifted. The academically proficient kids might find that—once they were in the theater, in the music room, or on the basketball court—they were the ones in need of help. The game of mutual support would become fun. The children's natural inclination to play as a team would be revived, and their experience of school would rise to a whole new level of enjoyment.

Given this scenario, would the class's median score on standardized tests increase or decrease? If a parent or administrator were to ask me this question, I'd have no answer. I wouldn't know what to say to someone who held such an educational vision so divergent from mine.

If pressed, I could say that informal evidence suggests that graduates of progressive schools are as likely to do well as graduates of traditional schools. By "do well," I mean according to standard assembly-line criteria. In non-standard terms, though, my definition of success is living the exquisite life—discovering who you are and what you stand for and expressing this in every moment.

The ideal school, then, would be one with a project approach in which students get together with the outside community, voting on what they want to do and who should take what roles. They might landscape a field, paint a house, or build a bus shelter. Whatever the project, they would have to find out all the things they'd need to know about it by talking to mentors, doing Internet research, finding information in reference books, and so on. Give a child enough interesting projects to do, and she'll receive a full education.

What, in this scenario, would be the role of teachers? Teachers would learn right along with the children, modeling for their students how problems are solved and how learning is best accomplished. Teachers would serve as resources, either answering questions posed to them or pointing the questioners to needed resources for the answering of their questions. When projects were finished, the teachers could then assist their students in writing about the experience.

Education should be experiential. For optimal education at the high school level, we would need exceptional teachers for whom subjects are so compelling that they can make them come alive for their students. Whether it was American History or Biology, the students would actually do hands-on projects within a subject, rather than just reading about it in books. This is the only way to get students voluntarily involved in their subject matter.

I experienced this when I got to college and was lucky enough to be placed in an outstanding advanced program at Boston University called the College of General Education, where we sat down with Ph.D.s who cared about their students and taught in the way I've just described. We could discuss projects, carry them out, and pre-write papers with an advisor, someone who told you what they thought about the subject and inspired you to do hands-on things.

This was an integrated studies program, so that whatever you learned in one subject corresponded with all the other subjects. If we studied Ancient Greece, for example, we studied everything from that time period: art, music, drama, history, politics, literature, mythology, philosophy, geography, and so on. This approach brought together all the disparate elements so that the subject came alive in my imagination. It occurred to me at the time that I could have learned everything I'd learned up to that point in my life in six months, using this method.

As we saw before, our culture tends to view education as a way of supplying information to students in the form of "answers." The problem is, we keep giving young people answers to questions they haven't even asked! In the pleasurable-learning model of education, teachers would wait for children to ask questions, because when youngsters come to the point of asking, that's when they're most ready to learn. And in answering questions, the wise teacher would provide only enough information to encourage further inquiry. Open inquiry, rather than closure, is the emblem of good education.

Rhythmic Teaching

Musician Don G. Campbell, author of *The Mozart Effect: Tapping the Power of Music to Heal the Body, Strengthen the Mind, and Unlock the*

Creative Spirit, and educator Chris Brewer write about important educational uses of rhythm in their book *Rhythms of Learning: Creative Tools for Developing Lifelong Skills.*

According to Brewer and Campbell, "The methods used in rhythmic teaching enhance many aspects of learning. The changes in the cadence and intonation of our voices alter listening and concentration abilities. Rhythmic repetition of information allows for rehearsal of information, leading to increased memory abilities. The cycles within our presentation create a rhythmic entrainment. The preparation of the mind-body system creates a state of alert relaxation, and periodic changes of pace in instruction methods maintain an optimal level of attention. Our use of time cues during the day can help us maintain a synchronous flow with others. All of these techniques of rhythmic teaching blend together to create the dance of educational synchrony."

The ability, acquired early in life, to observe one's own inner state and clearly notice shifts in that state will later continue to provide internal anchoring for all learning. Ideally, noticing skills naturally evolve from a vague awareness of trial and error to a more focused ability to identify and respond to thoughts, feelings, and sensations. This evolution can be greatly enhanced by the use of Brain Gym, whether through private sessions or course work, for Brain Gym helps impart the language that can refine one's noticing ability.

Brain Gym in Schools

When Brain Gym is a part of each day, children and their teachers love to come to school. Teachers who incorporate the Brain Gym movements within their daily classroom routine rediscover that joy of teaching for which they originally chose their profession. And there is no need to coerce or control a healthy child who is learning in an optimal environment. Such children know when to move, when to rest, when to initiate learning, and when to practice new skills.

I originally designed the Brain Gym program as a series of movements for use in schools, and it continues to be successful in a school setting. Part of its appeal is that it can give rise to amazing improvements in all areas of academic performance, without conflicting with the school's established methodology. It works *with* existing programs, not against them. Even though most of our educational system has a way to go, in the meantime teachers can benefit from an effective tool that's easily implemented within their present system.

The Brain Gym program emphasizes the physical skills of learning, those body-based abilities that get short shrift when mental skills make up the curriculum. In Brain Gym, we recognize that learning is more about "how to" than "what's next." When children don't yet know how to point their two eyes on a line of print without seeing double or losing their place, what value is there in knowing the right answer? When they don't know how to write a "b" or a "d," what 's the point of a spelling test?

When students are introduced to Brain Gym, they seem to love it, request it, teach it to their friends, and integrate it into their lives without any coaching or supervision. When they have mastered the physical mechanics of learning, they've learned to trust their body; and the information they need is now easily acquired with minimal instruction or teacher intervention. When children have lit the flame of their own love of learning, I've seen them acquire as many as nine years of academic skills in one year. Whatever the subject and whatever the curriculum, I have witnessed countless times how Brain Gym brings the joy back into learning.

Knowledge of the Code

Reading is only incidentally visual and phonological. As the reader searches for structure on the printed page, he uses a hierarchy of clues. The number of clues needed is inversely proportional to his fluency as a reader: the more clues he needs, the less fluent he is. The less fluent he is, the less secure he will be in trusting his ability to find meaning and success in reading. On the other hand, the more fluent he is, the more his reading will be directed by structure and meaning, the printed clues becoming only redundant positive feedback for his linguistic hunches.

A skills program implemented by a teacher sensitive to the above assumptions can be an invaluable tool. It helps the teacher work with, not against, the child. The skills sequence guides the child away from making inefficient generalizations about the code as he internalizes its structure. It gives him a standard by which to verify what his own linguistic competence tells him is so. The point is not "Why is the child guessing?" but "What information must the child have to guess more accurately?"

Knowledge of the code is indeed important. Once internalized, this knowledge must be recognized and made secondary to syntactic and semantic clues. Teachers, directors, coordinators, and administrators of reading programs must remember that the "end" to these means is the growing child. His self-concept as a worthwhile human being capable of solving problems, finding order in chaos, and teaching himself is all a teacher needs to foster.

Beginning reading instruction in our schools is believed by most educators to be a mental activity wherein the child must master a written code, adapting her body to fit the task. Does this kind of instruction build upon a child's innate movement toward neurological organization or hinder it? I believe that, for each child, congruency of muscle proprioception, postural organization, and the visual mechanism should be established before reading instruction is begun. Otherwise the learner will develop visual stress and related compensatory habits. Tension, injury, or premature fixation of body postures can inhibit the child's natural joy of learning.

Over the centuries, our ancestors learned in a natural, uninhibited manner through example, movement, manipulation, and imitation. In order to survive, people had to gain physical mastery over their environment. Valued skills were passed from generation to generation, from father to son, from mother to daughter, and through apprenticeship. Oral language traditions, including storytelling, rituals, and song, kept history and its lessons alive. Art, music, and dance provided a visual, auditory, and kinesthetic context for the individual so that he knew where he belonged.

From the beginning of civilization, the printed symbol has helped people to represent their living experience for posterity. Symbols are important to our consciousness, in our waking and dream states alike, providing continuity and meaning to our lives. However, as we have seen, with the proliferation of books and electronic devices, modern educational practices have put the cart before the horse, forgetting that children must have real-life experiences and be permitted to recreate their own symbols and language.

Educators are now expecting children to read, to decode symbols and master facts, without having first developed a meaningful context for storing and retrieving the information—in fact, without even having had concrete experiences with which to connect the symbols.

The High and Low Gears of Reading

For each individual student, reading materials are grouped into three levels: independent, instructional, and frustration. When we read at our independent level, we are thoroughly familiar with both the vocabulary and the subject matter. We're reading in high gear, with little need for low-gear thinking. We add factual information or enjoy new plot material within a comfortable context. Independent-level reading improves our skills of word recognition and reading rate. It is relaxing and pleasurable, yet may not challenge us to work at our full potential.

When we read at our instructional level, we recognize most of the words and the context is familiar. We get into high gear easily, and the context helps us to anticipate where the text is going. When we come to new words, we're able to figure them out, using the language of the writer as well as other word-recognition skills. We learn the new words without losing our train of thought as we move our eyes easily over the page. We are able to shift from high gear to low gear to high gear automatically. We have the satisfaction of learning something new and of expanding our structure without losing control. This is integrated learning, in which low gear is readily available within the high-gear context.

When we read at our frustration level, we have too many new and unusual words and not enough context and information to reconstruct the code into meaningful language. We must decode the text one word at a time, with no pleasure or satisfaction. This is negative stress in a low-gear state that is not integrated.

For too many students in our schools, independent-level and instructional-level learning are not available and frustration-level learning is the norm. Driving in low gear without the option of shifting to higher gears is difficult, if not impossible. Ideally, when we drive, we are always aware of the possibility of high gear. Whenever we're in low gear, we do our concentrated work, looking for opportunities to get back into high gear so we can relax between operations.

Our schools should provide students with opportunities to

shift their learning into high gear, thus alleviating the negative physiological responses to continued stress that make concentration, comprehension, and recall impossible.

Education for the Whole Being

To achieve a more physical, natural education for our youth, we must start children out early with the whole-being experiences—such as music, art, and nature walks—described earlier in these pages. The potential benefits of any pursuits involving movement and creativity are limitless. It's said that, by age seven, a child's brain has been hard-wired with 80 percent of everything he or she will ever know. All subsequent neural growth is constructed on top of those early pathways.

A great architect, for example, might trace his success back to the toy buildings he made at age three with his uncle. Something experiential was established within his circuits at that time, something no lectures at architectural school could ever provide. We want to offer our children rich learning situations in which those kinds of neural pathways can be formed. We won't achieve this by overvaluing analysis, orderliness, and routine at the expense of play and imagination.

Speed, simulation, and virtual reality have replaced the natural world of the past, when people spent time singing, dancing, and sharing their lives with each other. Life took place then in the concrete world of playful interactions and genuine experiences. I wonder how we ever came to consider the schoolroom an assembly line from which we turn out "finished" products on graduation day.

Federally mandated testing programs with their call for "accountability" turn schools into factories. When teachers, principals, and school boards live in fear of low rankings on standardized tests, they end up valuing the test more than they value the child. When parents live in fear of their child's failure to perform on examinations, they put undue pressure on the child to achieve and conform, rather than creating an atmosphere conducive to natural learning at the child's own pace.

"Teaching to the test" amounts to cheating on the part of school systems. Giving children the correct answers to questions that will appear on tests, all for the sake of making a school look good, is cheating—especially when the questions are ones the children haven't even asked. In following these practices, we cheat our children, cheat the test evaluators, and ultimately cheat our society. Education is not about developing a populace that doesn't move, notice, or think for itself. Yet in current public education we have children who can't solve problems, make decisions and think for themselves, or come up with the meaningful questions that demonstrate real learning.

The ideal school is a place where young people *have* experiences instead of reading about them. Children naturally like to write about what they do, just as they enjoy reading about interesting things that others have done. But if the purpose of school is only to learn to pass tests and fill out forms—with no singing, dancing, or creative play—why should children see much reason to attend? They're being deprived of true education, and our society is bankrupting its future by wasting its most valuable resource.

Movement Is Life

By the time I had completed my Doctorate in Education, in 1975, I was exhausted and sorely in need of a lifestyle change. Between running my reading clinics, managing research studies, and writing my dissertation, I had physically deteriorated to the point of being overfocused, round-shouldered, and overweight. I remember seeing a chiropractor for my aching back. After the adjustment he said, "Don't move." He meant that the stability of my spine was so precarious that any significant movement would put my system out of alignment again. Sure enough, by the time I got back to my car in the parking lot, I needed another adjustment.

Clearly, something wasn't right with this picture. Clearly, I needed to move. The body is made of muscles that need to move in balance with each other, so that our organs, tendons, and bones retain their structure and integrity. Movement is life, and being passive or restricted in one's movement is like having no life at all.

By definition, living things move, grow, and reproduce, whether it's a plant's movement toward chlorophyll-producing light or the self-propelling of the tiny sea squirt within a tide pool as it seeks its best environment for survival. Movement is inherent to that dynamic evolution of life that we call learning. Where there's no movement, there's no life.

Learning, in our most basic understanding of the term, is the modification of responses to stimuli over time. Even a virus—on the borderline between animate and inanimate—adapts to changing conditions and thereby learns. Even in human beings reduced to a state of paralysis, learning never stops so long as certain systems of autonomic movement such as respiration and blood circulation continue to function. So learning is a constant of life, but in the realm of psychology it is life's preeminent feature.

Research shows that, within the womb, a fetus is already learning profound lessons about the nature of the external world. And a newborn is like a mad scientist, greedy for the data of sensory input, quick to modify neurological and other structures in response to such data, and tireless in the creation of evolving models for the way the universe works. As the newborn grows and develops, play becomes an increasingly central part of its behavior and learning. Even while asleep and in the dream state, a baby's consciousness sifts through images both literal and archetypal, ceaselessly making sense of things, endlessly building a structured order out of chaos.

From beginning to end (with few, if any, exceptions), learning is a defining characteristic of human life. Go to a park on a sunny day and you'll see this universal phenomenon at work. From the child playing with a ball to the elder doing a crossword puzzle, the human contingent in the park—and, to a lesser extent, the rest of the fauna—is one vast learning system.

Watch a baby crawling, a toddler taking his first steps, or a little girl balancing on a bicycle, and you're seeing the miracle of learning in action. Children and their patterns of growth have enthralled us since the beginning of time, but only recently have we developed the technology to explain the processes of learning from a neurological standpoint. Through the technologies of magnetic resonance imaging and positron emission tomography, scientists can now track how the human brain functions as it learns.

An infant is born with one hundred billion brain neurons, twice as many as in the adult brain; this ensures that the brain can adapt to any set of conditions or circumstances. Over time, the child loses this surplus of neurons, for only those reinforced through experience will survive. Certain critical learning periods in a child's life, once missed, can never return. Vision, language, social development, musical ability, and logical/mathematical development all have critical phases during the first ten years of life, and some of them before the age of five. In all these phases—in fact, throughout the rest of life—movement is the single most important component of learning.

Movement Is Learning

Most of us have come up through the public school system. As survivors of this institution, we've been marked by it. We believe we must perpetuate the system and teach our children to conform to a meaningless tradition in which teachers purvey information to passive students.

All learning—including that requiring abstract thought—occurs through movement, since abstract thought involves the internal repositioning of ideas. Movement is the primary way that we integrate our learning into expressive action. Because children and adults learn by practicing and doing things, by putting knowledge into action and feeling the process of growth, we need to allow our youngest generation to learn kinesthetically, in a natural way, instead of requiring them to learn by passive listening and rote memorization.

It's natural for children having a healthy, physical learning experience to move, laugh aloud, groan their displeasure, and speak to their classmates. Yet, as a public schoolteacher, I saw how only the children identified as gifted are allowed these freedoms within the classroom. Such freedoms are typically denied to children of lesser performance. We need to acknowledge that all children are gifted in their own way; that motivated, self-directed learners can have high self-esteem at any level of progress; and that society as a whole benefits when all children are trusted to learn in their own way and are given the freedom to move and be themselves.

Why is capability not nurtured and encouraged in all learners? Why discourage the very behaviors that are so crucial to the learning process? If learning is part of the essence of being human—and, as such, innately a joyful experience—how is it that our schools have become places where joy is the exception and stress and anxiety the norm? The answer is that we have institutionalized learning, and in so doing have allowed the system to become more important than the child. Few are asking: *If we imagined that all children are gifted, and capable of learning far beyond present expectations, how would we "do school" differently?*

If learning is defined by neuroscience as changed behavior, I submit that no learning can take place without movement. We change a behavior when we have emotionally imprinted some new learning; we are then able to perform more precisely and have more mastery of a skill. In the brain, movement takes place across synapses organized to connect several critical areas necessary for behavioral change . . . back brain to front brain, top brain to bottom brain, and right hemisphere to left hemisphere.

Whole-brain learning is the spontaneous interconnection, related to the learning event, of all the centers of the brain. It involves physical, emotional, and mental processes that result in permanent changes in skills, attitudes, and behaviors, because such learning is not superficial but fully internalized.

At a simple level, you can see in animals the connection between learning and movement. When kittens play, they're finding out how to respond to the different situations with wich life will present them. They romp around with their mother and discover what behaviors are acceptable. They chase after a ball and integrate all the reflexes necessary for hunting.

A more complex version of this takes place in humans. We think we can tell children what to do and they'll just do it, but we learn that this isn't so. Children need to feel what they're learning in their body. They need to play and, in their play, experience the nerve net that movement awakens, first imitating the behaviors they see around them and then, once the feeling of the behaviors is physically anchored, performing the actions proactively.

If we look inside any classroom, we'll see that the active learners are those who are lively and active. Such children physically reach for information and for opportunities to express themselves, barely containing themselves in their enthusiasm for knowledge as they write, turn pages, and relate with their peers. Meanwhile, the children who are not moving as they learn will appear stressed, passive, and bored. In either case, children can't hide their authentic feelings about learning. These feelings are apparent in their movement, demeanor, and body posture.

Factory-Style Education

Our schools follow a factory model of education that originated in Germany and Prussia and was then adopted wholesale by American educators during our industrial revolution. In this model, we place children in an environment that replicates what they'll encounter as adults in the workplace —a world of schedules and evaluations, much tension, and little time for creativity, spontaneity, or individuality. Walk the streets of any of the world's major cities during rush hour and see what a fine job the educational system has done: people wear identical clothes and identical worried frowns as they hurry to their interchangeable jobs.

If we measure the effectiveness of education by these standards, then we have succeeded perfectly. But if we dare to dream about the exquisite pleasure of learning, about seeing children access their true creative nature more and more fully, then we must see that this educational system has failed our children terribly.

We divide children into age groupings, thus implying that all kids should be doing the same things at the same ages. We divide things that are indivisible into separate subjects: reading is separated from writing, which is separated from listening, which is separated from speech, and that's just for starters. Around these separate subjects we then proceed to create schedules, curricula, and grades. Just because things have always been done this way, we think it must be the right way.

In this aberrant system of winners and losers, it doesn't matter into which category a child may fall. The kids who succeed (those who get good grades) still lose. They're stamped into a mold just like the so-called losers, for all are the products of a factory paradigm that stifles their creativity and ability to be the best they can be. They're confined into a certain shape until they lose contact with their deeper purpose, and with it their experience of joy.

It's an old educational saying that at the elementary level we teach the child and in high school we teach the subject. It would be wonderful for all children if the former were truly the case. But at the elementary level we now teach reading—not the child. Learning to read has come to be seen as more important than children's actual well-being, and becoming a young repository of information is more important than growing up in a safe, stress-free, nurturing environment.

Young adults graduating from college will do best (in terms of worldly success) if they have a marketable skill. My daughter graduated recently from the University of California at Davis. Since she had majored in an unmarketable subject, had she opted to do what she was trained to do, she would not have found a job. Her alternatives were to take an entry-level job at minimum wage or walk into the computer industry and immediately earn four times that amount. (She chose the former.) So this is what our schools are currently creating: people who know how to use computers.

Jane Healy, author of *Endangered Minds: Why Children Don't Think and What We Can Do about It*, makes this perceptive comment about the situation: "Schools will need to accept the fact that lectures and 'teacher talk,' which commonly comprise approximately 90 percent of classroom discourse, must give way to more effective student involvement. Today's learners must become constructors of knowledge rather than passive recipients of information that even the least intelligent computer can handle more effectively."

If education, which means to draw out (the best of) what's inside a person, is to become pleasurable, we must place students in situations that are meaningful and worthwhile to *them*. These are the situations that produce learning that will be useable beyond the classroom.

Learning Disorders

My friend, former student, and colleague Marilyn Bouchard Lugaro included the following quotation in *Hunting the Myth of the Hunter in AD/HD: An Educational Kinesiology Perspective*, her unpublished 2004 doctoral dissertation on attention deficit disorder:

> Hi. My name is Hunter. They say I'm ADD—and sometimes, when I wiggle and don't sit right in my chair at school, they say I have AH/DH too. I don't know what they mean and I don't know why everyone is always mad at me. My dad says I'm stubborn and he could fix me with a smack in the head. My mother says I'm lazy and I just don't try. I say I am fine, there's nothing wrong with me! School is boring, that's all. I am eight-and-a-half years old; I have brown eyes and brown hair.

When I hear a child speak like this, I feel like crying. I can't bear to see what we're doing to our children. In the United States alone, several million young people are taking medication for attention deficit disorders, although experts estimate that, of these children, only 5 percent actually need the medication. In any event, ADD is a not a Ritalin deficiency! It's an insufficiency in the ability to focus attention, one that can be eliminated by processes that integrate the functioning of the brain and body. In Brain Gym, we achieve the necessary focus of attention with activities that relax the tendon-guard survival reflex and help children feel safe in their body.

The main point I wish to make is this: If you or your child has been diagnosed with ADHD, please look for an alternative to the medications that are being too readily prescribed. Ritalin is a Schedule Two classified drug (along with cocaine, morphine, and opium), and its possible side effects include depression, irritability, hypertension, stomach pains, inhibited growth, social withdrawal, loss of appetite, and depletion of the immune system. The drug affects the basal ganglion and the corpus striatum, the brain areas concerned with motor control and the sense of time.

I should say a few words here about dyslexia. What I've discovered is that most children with reading challenges share the mixed-dominance profile (see Chapter Five), in which they inhibit the dominant left eye under stress and switch to the use of the right eye so it can follow the linear right hand and right ear. The right eye is associated with fine-motor control and seeks to "hold words still." The mixed-dominant children who inhibit their visual-recall ability can see only parts of words, so they stutter and sound them out. Often no connection happens between the sounding out and the recognition that generally occurs in the reader's right brain and left eye, so the child trying to read aloud says, "ta-er-toll," instead of "turtle."

Many educators believe that, if children sound out words for long enough, someday they'll spontaneously master the ability to read. In my own experience, they will not, for the dyslexic reader described above is experiencing a block in the visual/auditory learning process. Sometimes one Brain Gym session can help such a person do linear and recognition tasks simultaneously, thus overcoming the reading impediment labeled as dyslexia.

Secrets of Reading, Writing, and Doing Arithmetic

Our children rarely experience a nurturing environment at school. Time and again I see parents bringing their sons and daughters to Brain Gym sessions with spirits so broken that the children can barely function.

Many adolescents I've seen over the years are so blocked in math that they can't even do simple addition and subtraction. I'm not talking about children with "special needs"—only youngsters who have the intelligence to mentally subtract $1.25 from $5.00 but haven't had the concrete physical experience needed to develop their neurological wiring in order to do so. This means that they're leaving high school incapable of performing basic life skills.

Such young people have spent twelve years struggling to get to the point where they can solve $2y = 18$ (with the use of a calculator), but they can't balance a checkbook or estimate well enough to verify that someone has given them the right change. Only a little time in their early life spent playing with coins (maybe role-playing as vendors or cashiers making change) would have made higher math more real and available to them in their adolescence. These are not unusual students; millions of young people leave school each year with this kind of numerical limitation.

The same is true of reading. The illiteracy rate in the United States rivals that of some Third World countries. This alone is shocking, but an even more insidious statistic is the number of children who lose, or never acquired, a taste for reading. If young children are taught to read with the whole brain at their own level of skill, they'll naturally enjoy books. Why? Because good stories activate the imagination, and children, without exception, enjoy using their imagination.

Where we go wrong in public education is that we lead children through the correct steps to competent reading, but do this in the wrong order. First we teach children how to read, then we teach them to write, and finally we teach them to write stories about what they observe in the world. A whole brain doesn't function in this way.

The natural order of events is the opposite of what we practice. Ideally, a child first observes the world with her mind, heart, and whole body. As part of this observation, and while still unhampered by the technicalities of reading and writing, she creates stories about what she sees.

Next she writes about what she perceives and imagines by dictating her words to an adult serving as her scribe. She speaks what she wants to write, then learns to read back what she's said. In this way, a link is forged from the outset between her imagination and the printed word.

Now the child learns to write. She asks to see a word, and the teacher responds by writing it for her. She traces the word till she's formed a tactile, kinesthetic sense of it, then writes it for herself. She asks for another word, then another, gradually expanding her skills. She's learning how to start with a whole idea and then recreate it from pieces, instead of starting with the pieces (the letters and phonemes or speech sounds) and trying to make whole ideas out of them.

Finally the child learns to read words other writers have put together to express *their* thoughts, emotions, and observations, starting with the writings of her peers.

To put it another way, the child moves from love to speech sounds, not vice versa. You can't create love from phonemes, but you can generate phonemes as an expression of love. When children learn in this way, their reading, writing, and imagination become connected from the outset, as they properly should be.

Incidentally, when we bypass the oral phase of storytelling to head straight for the written word, we violate the natural laws of social evolution. Reading and writing walked onto the stage of human history relatively late. For tens of thousands of years before that, humankind was transmitting information from one generation to the next by word of mouth. Just as a developing fetus appears to follow certain biological phases of evolution (from reptilian to mammalian to human), the education of a developing child should be allowed to follow the sequential steps of social evolution.

The Value of Drama and Music

Drama—the writing and performing of plays—has great value as a means of bringing movement back into the curriculum. It's astounding what young people can do when they're placed in the realistic, movement-based learning situation that is the theater. They'll stay at school rehearsing until nine o'clock at night, and view this as completely normal. Only the factory-model mindset would prefer to see children planted at their desks in rows, passively taking in information as a lettuce patch absorbs water.

Music, too, should be an integral part of the curriculum. Music, rhythm, and song integrate the brain; we sing melodies with the right hemisphere and keep rhythm with the other side. Music and dance, meter and rhythm, tapping things out, developing active listening, receiving visual, auditory, kinesthetic, and tactile input at the same time—all of these create fundamental structures and pathways that are stored automatically in the brain and that underlie all later forms of endeavor for that individual.

Some Practical Ideas for Using Brain Gym in the Classroom

Thousands of teachers in the United States and around the world have incorporated some form of Brain Gym into their classrooms. I'm now going to provide some recommendations to give you a sense of how this can be done.

These suggestions for how to bring Brain Gym into the classroom are based on extensive experience, and have been proven to work. Nevertheless, the ideas are offered only as a springboard; I encourage you to discover further ways to manifest this simple and effective system in daily classroom life.

Bear in mind that, when teachers give their students an experience of this practical tool, everyone in the classroom experiences a more fulfilling day. Whether the subject is reading (using phonics or whole-word instruction), math, science, or physical education, if the class does Brain Gym for a few minutes prior to the lesson, each child's mind/body system will be ready to assimilate new information.

I recommend the following sequence for introducing the Brain Gym movements in the classroom. The order moves from simple to complex, each movement building developmentally upon the last. This program follows a weekly plan, however it could be monthly or could vary according to the age, ability, and motivation of the class.

Week One: An Introduction to Brain Gym
    Sipping Water
    Brain Buttons
    Hook-ups

Lazy 8s

The Lazy 8 design (see Chapter Two) is a repatterning for the visual system, in the same way that the Cross Crawl is used to repattern whole-body movement. Lazy 8s teach a person to use both eyes in both visual fields, and are therefore essential for enhancing reading skills.

Lazy 8s can be taught to children of any age. The teacher first demonstrates the movement, which involves tracing an infinity sign in a continuous movement. Students trace Lazy 8s on a variety of surfaces for different tactile experiences: e.g., on the carpet, on a window screen, on a smooth wooden surface. They feel the Lazy 8 drawn on their back by a partner, or a Lazy 8 track may be traced, a child's finger moving along a groove etched in the wood. Following a marble as it rolls along the Lazy 8 track teaches visual attention and improves the ocular motility skills needed for reading.

Alphabet 8s

Whether first introducing writing to beginners who are learning to print letters or to assist more advanced students make cursive writing more fluent, the Alphabet 8s help facilitate the process of learning. The Alphabet 8s involve writing the letters of the alphabet within the circles made by Lazy 8s—only lower case letters are used and a Lazy 8 is drawn after each letter. The purpose is to feel kinesthetically that alphabet letters either are round first and end on the midline, or they start with a down stroke line on the midline and move to the right. The Lazy 8 is the whole in which all letters are a part.

Dennison Laterality Repatterning

The teacher may lead a group Dennison Laterality Repatterning (DLR; see chapter 5) at any grade level as often as seems necessary. With a large class it may be necessary to repattern several groups within the class. In the timeframe of about forty minutes, the entire class can experience this repatterning, which integrates learning through movement. The intention of repatterning is to teach children to become more automatic new learning and to be more conscious and aware reflexive movements that do not support academic achievement. Make Dennison Laterality Repatterning a priority early in the school year so that the children can realize the benefits all year long.

The Double Doodle

The Double Doodle movement activates both sides of the brain and body at one time, supporting one hemisphere to lead while the other follows. Students love to draw pictures with two hands at the same time and a Double Doodle warm up prepares them to work at their desks with improved attention to the lesson. One seventh grader enthusiastically stated, "Oh, this stuff is fun!" The ease and immediate shift in the physical skills of reading and writing invite students into the "game" of doing the Double Doodle. Prior to doing this Brain Gym activity I might request that students write at their desks for one minute and, when the activity is complete, I again ask the students to write again for one minute. They are then directed to compare the before and after writing samples and discuss any changes or differences they have witnessed.

Brain Gym in Secondary School
If students are initially self-conscious and reluctant to do movements, I might show them the Alphabet 8s or the Double Doodle as described above. However, prior to the activity, I would offer information about recent brain research that reports the importance of the left and right hemispheres of the brain integration to able ease of communication. This background regarding the neurological stimulation provided by the movements creates curiosity and therefore willingness for the high school age student to readily do Brain Gym and thus notice for himself the rewards of these simple movements and activities.

Brain Gym Games

Children look forward to doing the Brain Gym movements. A box or bag with each of the 26 Brain Gym movements and activities written on cards can be placed in an easily accessible area. Class members take turns drawing the cards each day. A group of four students might have a set of these laminated cards at their cluster of desks. The teacher can instruct the students to choose a card from the box or bag prior to any given activity. Or the teacher may wish to divide the cards into the three categories of the Lengthening Activities, Midline Movements, and Energy Exercises, and request the students to choose from a specific category prior to engaging in a classroom assignment.

Learning Centers in the Classroom

To create a learning center in your classroom, refer weekly to the book *Brain Gym: Teacher's Edition* by Dennison and Dennison, in which the movements are grouped according to skills similar to the above. The book will give you good ideas about which movements and activities to include for your students' needs.

One method that has been successful in the classroom is one in which a game is played by the students. The students go to the learning center. The classroom teacher has made a cube out of a milk carton (or laminated construction paper). The die has a Brain Gym movement or activity on each side. The chosen activities that are placed on the die are congruent with the skill being developed.

For example, if a writing center is being developed, then Lazy 8s, Alphabet 8s, Arm Activation, the Calf Pump, the Footflex, and the Energy Yawn are placed on the die. Each student who comes to the center can view these activities pictured on the poster board, so that when the die is rolled he or she can refer to them as a reminder of how to practice the movement correctly. Each student seated around the table takes turns rolling the die and practicing the Brain Gym movement that shows itself. This is done for about ten minutes, then the students return to their desks to complete their writing assignment.

Group Balances

Children love whole group balances. They love to see how much they can improve a skill after doing the movements for a goal. For example, after doing PACE, have the students write a paragraph or simply one

192

sentence. Do the Brain Gym menu associated with the skill of writing and then compare the two writing samples. Each student will certainly notice a difference in either the tidiness of his or her writing or the ease with which he or she is able to express ideas on paper. This is great for physical skills during P.E. time. I'll never forget the class of fifth graders who balanced to do cartwheels!

Brain Gym Stories

Make up stories that have the Brain Gym movements incorporated into them. I like to invite students to play a game with me in which each student verbally adds a paragraph to a story that I start. Each student adds one or more Brain Gym movements to the story, along with their paragraph. For example, the following is the beginning of a story I told in a fourth grade classroom that I visited, with the Brain Gym movements added in parentheses.

A great big bear woke up from a deep sleep (The Energy Yawn), and decided to go outside (The Cross Crawl) to see the stars. As he looked up high, he saw them all twinkling above his head (Space Buttons). Somewhere in the distance, he could hear an owl hooting (The Owl). A playful young raccoon was hiding near the trunk of a large oak tree (Earth Buttons) . . .

The Energy Yawn

Put your fingertips against any tight spots you feel on your jaws. Make a deep, relaxed, yawning sound, gently stroking away the tension.

The story continues with the students adding their own ideas of what is to come. The teacher can assist, when needed, in adding in the Brain Gym movements. The story is finished when every student has a turn or when it is time to move along into the next activity of the day. This Brain Gym break "wakes up" the brain and allows the students and the teacher to move more freely and easily into the next assignment.

Quantifying Results in an Elementary School

Having found Brain Gym to a be an effective tool in her own classroom, my friend and Brain Gym instructor, Cecilia Koester wanted to validate the techniques she had been using by working on a small research project at her local school. Here is her account of the experiment:

Having formerly worked as a classroom teacher in a special day class for severely challenged students on this particular campus, I approached principal Paul Jablonowski at Saticoy Elementary School in Ventura, California, with the request to conduct this project with some of his students. I received his consent and was met with open arms and great enthusiasm for the project by the twelve teachers whose classrooms would be involved.

These teachers agreed to the following:

1. To meet for one hour after school every Monday throughout the school year.
2. To do a minimum of fifteen minutes of Brain Gym each, integrated into the daily activities of the classroom rather than in a fifteen-minute block of time.
3. To allow students-selected by each teacher-to leave class once a month for a thirty-minute session of Brain Gym within a small group, facilitated by a Brain Gym instructor.
4. To invite Brain Gym instructors to do classroom consultations a minimum of two times during the school year.
5. To allow students' test scores to be gathered for data comparison. An equal number of student scores were extracted from the school files to serve as a control group, with the permission of the teachers in those classrooms.

Throughout the school year, enthusiasm and follow-through remained high. All of the above agreements were carried out. We arranged a special Parents Night, which drew an astonishing crowd of 120, to inform the parents about Brain Gym and explain how their children were using it in the classroom. In addition, the participating classroom teachers papered their walls with suggested Brain Gym materials, instructed students in the task-appropriate use of the Brain Gym movements, and reminded the young people about which Brain Gym activities to do prior to undertaking a homework assignment. The teachers learned the Brain Gym exercises and subsequently taught their students.

As I passed through the halls, when we were only three months into the project, I saw children using Brain Gym throughout the school day, even without teacher direction. The students who continued to have difficulty with their reading skills were seen by a Brain Gym instructor in small groups of two to four. In these groups, balances were facilitated to remedy specific difficulties related to such areas as attention and comprehension, fine or gross motor coordination, or specific academic skills.

The results of this pilot project were phenomenal. Students' self-esteem improved, the classroom climate became calmer, the students reported how much easier their reading had become, and the teachers expressed deep gratitude for this simple, effective tool that enhanced their teaching strategies.

I also gathered test data from the Stanford 9. Students in each grade level who experienced the Brain Gym activities improved their test scores twice as much as did the students in the control group, who did no Brain Gym activities.

The following quotes were taken from conversations the Brain Gym consultants had with students after doing Brain Gym activities.

A third grader said: "I want to be able to read better." After doing Brain Gym she said: "I feel a lot different; like I'm ready to work now. It's easier to understand the words."

A fourth grader said he wanted to know how to take apart bigger words. He would point at each word as he read and did not finish words that he started to read. After doing Brain Gym he said: "It feels easier to read. What just happened?"

A fifth grader said that she wanted to "be able to read easier." She formed many of her letters of the alphabet from the bottom up. After doing Brain Gym she said: "Before, I felt like my eyes were jumping all over the page. Now, I feel like I can actually look at the page and read it!"

Shifting through the Ages

A paradigm shift can be defined as a radical change in perception and thinking, from one point of view to another that may be quite different. No part of one paradigm can predict what the next will be. As human society evolved from hunting and gathering to agriculture to industrialization, it went through many shifts that continually altered how we live and think. People in the Western world once believed the Earth to be the center of the universe. So the Copernican model of the solar system, with planets moving around the Sun, was at first a radically revolutionary idea.

In every age in history, when a pendulum has moved too far in one direction, a countermovement has emerged to restore balance. Brain Gym is an important component of a major paradigm shift occurring right now, the shift to brain-based, movement-based education that recognizes the child as a natural learner.

Chapter Ten

Passion, Purpose, and Right Livelihood

You Couldn't Have Known This Then

Finally, one day (unbeknownst to you)
you will have already begun living from
that immense dreaming part of yourself.
And, without knowing why, you will have
already begun letting go of the tightly
held reins you told yourself you would
never let go of.
You don't get to understand—and you wouldn't
have believed it had anyone told you—
but the day will come when you will actually
want to give up all that fighting
and all the important suffering.

You couldn't have known this then
and only now can you begin to trust
that the strange presence of gravity
in the bones and flesh of your body
and the strange sensation of solidity
from under your feet
is the forgotten blessing
that comes only when the passion of the
dreamer surrenders to the mystery of
being dreamed.
This is not the way we wanted things to be.
This is the hard-won maturity that comes
only from saying yes to being shaped by the
slowly sculpting hands and the slowly burning
fires of life.

                              —Richard Palmer

I define purpose as something innate within us, something divinely inspired. It operates on a larger scale than intention. For example, an individual's purpose may be to lead others, while his personal intention is to win a local election. When seen in this way, living becomes a delicate balance between directing our life and getting out of our own way.

The great scholar and mythologist Joseph Campbell wrote about the need to allow our divine purpose to manifest, saying, "We must let go of the life we have in order to have the life that is waiting for us." We're not mere puppets, though: while we must allow the divine plan to evolve naturally, within our overarching purpose we can still set our own goals and intentions and direct our own life.

A Sense of Infinite Possibility

Besides the onset of adolescence, something else happens to young people starting when they're around thirteen.

In my own case, I was recovering from the skull fracture I mentioned in Chapter Two. In the hospital, I had invoked the power of prayer to hasten my recovery. Many people had come to visit me. Even Norma, a waitress at the restaurant where our family sometimes went out to eat, came to sit by my bed. I had a new sense of belonging, and felt grateful to be alive and connected with other people. My father always said that bump on the head was good for me. He said that, after the accident, I finally joined the human race—I was no longer such a silent dreamer, off in my own world.

By the time I was out of the hospital and out of the temporary depression brought on by my brush with mortality, school had already begun. I started the sixth grade late, filled with a desire to catch up on what I'd missed and a new excitement about learning and exploring the world. Joe Pearce says the teenage years are the time of new neurological growth in the frontal lobes, giving teenagers a sense of infinite possibility as they fill their senses with a world waiting to be conquered. This was certainly true for me.

I eagerly caught up on class assignments and participated in the group discussions. My classmates were studying adult careers and doing research on various vocations in the process. I jumped in, with no idea what I really wanted to do in my future life yet knowing I had to make a choice. I read all of the resource materials and, contemplating the life of an attorney, ended up choosing the field of law. Our career studies culminated in each student writing a paper on success. Our class held a pageant in which many of us stood like a chorus and rhythmically read excerpts from our papers.

I remember that I had a crush on the petite and sophisticated Phyllis John, the cutest girl in class. The beauty of her words and lilt in her voice fascinated me as Phyllis softly chanted: "Success is something to strive for, something to cherish." Yet her goals sounded so lofty and far away. Perhaps this was my first experience of actually "reading" the body language of someone who wasn't accessing physical grounding, because even in my state of adoration I wondered if Phyllis knew what she was talking about!

By this time I had already been involved in the world of work for four years, and I was a witness to my parents' constant struggle to make a living. So my own contribution to the pageant was: "Success is earned by sacrifice and hard work." Somehow my young mind already understood the concept of sacrifice as a process of making dreams sacred. I knew that we need to make difficult choices and leave some things behind in the process of finding out what we feel passionate about doing, and I figured that hard work also came into the equation somewhere.

"I Thought I Could, I Thought I Could"

Ultimately, we don't want to be struggling all the time, but dedicated effort of the right kind is always needed until it's no longer needed. If you're learning the piano, you stick to your lessons until you master the instrument so well that you can forget you're playing the piano and simply enjoy the music. If you're going to run a marathon, you train hard and follow a schedule so that, on the day of the meet, you can enjoy the bliss of reaching that exquisite state in which you're effortlessly in the flow.

Life is a continual process of going from low gear to high gear. Low gear is the appropriate state for new experiences, as we consciously and methodically do whatever is necessary to learn them, code them, and follow through on them. It's the phase in which we climb the mountain with care until mountain climbing is installed in the body. Finally, when we reach the pinnacle of high gear, we enjoy the "I thought I could, I thought I could" experience of *The Little Engine That Could* (as detailed in the well-known 1940s storybook that came with a phonograph record; as a child, I played that record so often that I wore it out).

What gave effort a bad name is that, as children, we were expected to try hard for no reason—at least none that we could see or understand. When adults fail to nurture, at home or at school, a child's intrinsic interest in learning, they are compelled to replace it by external motivators that co-opt the soul in the name of education. This disconnection from our own inner sense of purpose and destiny carries on into adulthood and accounts for the well-known "mid-life crisis," triggered mainly by the heart's rising need to have its own frustrated purposes listened to.

Billy: A Young Musician Discovers How to Read

Too often, the people I work with assume that, if they're not successful, it's because they still need to put out more effort, discipline themselves more firmly, or promise themselves bigger rewards. And if their children are not doing well in school, they often make these same assumptions about their progeny.

Billy came to see me when he was fifteen and a sophomore in high school. When his mother, Lee Anne, first called me to set up an appointment, she quickly launched into a sad story of struggle, frustration, humiliation, and guilt.

"My son hates school," Lee Anne began. "All he does is hang out in the garage with his buddies all day long, practicing on the guitar. And now I think he's smoking pot. When he does go to school, he cuts classes, but this year he hasn't attended five days in a row all year long. He gets Ds and Fs; that's all he's ever gotten. We've tried everything, but he just won't even try. He's never liked school.

"When Billy was in the second grade," Lee Anne went on, "they said he had learning disabilities, so we got him some tutoring. Billy started getting in trouble at school. When he was in the fifth grade, we sent him to an expensive private school, but he got kicked out. One summer we sent him to a reading camp, but he just didn't catch on. I can understand, because I had problems reading, too. But I got through school okay.

"Billy's not stupid," the boy's mother pointed out. "He knows how to take care of his car and fix things around the house. He taught himself guitar without a lesson. He can also play the keyboard, and he taught himself to read and write music. His dad and I always thought he would grow out of the learning problems, but every year it gets worse. He's too big for me to yell at."

Although the Edu-K process works without my needing to know anything about a person's history, I sometimes find that letting parents talk about their process helps them get clear about their goals for their child—and sometimes for themselves. Even though parents may need to talk, when I start a session I do my best to let go of any preconceived notions about the person I'm working with and just start from where we are.

For the actual balancing session, because of Billy's age and the dynamics with his mother, I requested that Lee Anne wait outside while we worked. My first priority upon meeting Billy was to establish trust and rapport so he would enter the process with me. I wanted to show him that Edu-K wasn't just one more intervention that wasn't going to work.

"What's going on for you, Billy?" I began.

"Nothin'," he answered, looking away.

"This process works best if you have a purpose—a goal—for the session . . . something you'd like to do better," I offered.

Billy's response was a preoccupied silence.

"What would you like to have happen in your life?" I asked.

"Nothin'," he said again, this time looking squarely at me. "I don't like goals."

"Billy," I said, searching for a way to connect with him, "when I say 'goal' it doesn't have to be a big deal. A goal for the session is just something for the brain and the rest of the body to focus around.

Without a goal, you might feel better after the session but it might not help you learn. And if we don't learn, nothing really happens. Maybe we have some fun in life, but we don't really find pleasure."

Billy settled back in his chair and gave me a questioning look.

"Let me give you an example," I continued. "A woman was here this morning. When I asked her to choose a goal, she said she wanted more energy. 'But what would you do with more energy?' I asked her. She thought about this for a moment, then said, 'I would sing.' When she connected with singing as something that brings her joy, she suddenly had so much energy, she could barely stay in her chair. And you should have heard her sing after that balance!"

Billy mumbled, "I really like playing the guitar. But my parents don't like me to. They want me to do my homework."

"If I could help you to do your homework and still play the guitar, would you be interested?" I asked.

Billy looked curious.

"Billy, reading is what life's all about. A musician has to read the music, read the other players in his band, and read the room. It's just like when you're driving and you need to read the other drivers. It's called *noticing, awareness,* or *being in tune.* And no matter what you do in life, in our modern world you need to be able to read words. I can help you to be the best reader you can be, in every part of your life."

"Okay. What do we do?" he asked.

I asked Billy to read aloud from a fifth-grade-level book I had there, and listened as he struggled over the words in a flat monotone for a few paragraphs, with no apparent interest or comprehension.

"Okay, let's get started," I said, taking the book back from him and setting it aside. "Billy, I'm going to be straightforward with you. You're reading at about the fourth- or fifth-grade level. You need to read at about the seventh-grade level to be a literate adult. You're almost there. Once you get there, you'll be able to teach yourself to read, better and better as you go."

I tested Billy for crossing the visual midline, which caused him great difficulty. When he looked at an object (a pen) in the left visual field, his body was stable, yet the moment his eyes followed the pen across the midline and into the right field he became confused. Similarly, when he tracked the movement of the pen back into the left field, he again lost track of his object of focus. Yet, because of the way he was able to guess the unfamiliar words he read, I could see that Billy had received excellent training in sound-symbol correspondences. (And of course reading is a sound-symbol or phonological skill, following as it does the decoding of phonemes and graphemes.)

Because of my training with developmental optometrists, I've become convinced that, even though reading isn't primarily a visual skill, certain visual skills are basic to the acquisition of reading. These are (1) pointing the two eyes together (called binocularity); (2) crossing the visual midline; and (3) moving the eyes from one place to another (known in Edu-K as focus recovery). By the same token, I'm convinced that visual stress can prevent a successful linguistic experience, and that if any kind of stress *is* preventing the use of one's skills of vision, then one can't readily acquire abstract language abilities. The visual skills of a reader must be learned in such a way that they become automatic and vision becomes a non-issue.

I asked Billy to write his goal on paper, and could see by the way he held the pen and approached the paper that he was having difficulty with writing, as well. His hand-eye coordination for playing the keyboard or guitar—using both hands—was fine, but differentiating with one hand for the skill of writing was quite stressful for Billy, and thinking of what he wanted to say on paper was a nearly impossible task. I look at all these abilities as physical skills involved in the learning process.

For the most part, the young people I see are highly verbal, intelligent, and knowledgeable, and fully capable of obtaining the information they need from books and computers. But they have no idea that they have bodies, or how to organize their eyes, ears, hands, limbs, and thinking to communicate information effectively. This is why I'm concerned that, in our eagerness as educators to fill "empty heads" with knowledge, we're taking for granted the physical aspects of the learning process.

I spent the next thirty minutes with Billy using microinterventions, including Dennison Laterality Repatterning, the Calf Pump, Arm

Activation, Lazy 8s, and Alphabet 8s. Billy seemed to come to life, automatically unlocking his knees, relaxing his rib cage to deepen his breathing, and starting to organize his thinking and movement patterns around the goal of reading within the larger context of his passion to play guitar.

I tested Billy's visual tracking again, and he could now cross the midline as if he'd been doing it all his life. I handed him a seventh-grade-level book to read, and he read a passage with absolute clarity and comprehension, as if he had written it himself. (My definition of reading comprehension is the ability to make the writer's voice your own.)

Billy picked up a pen and wrote his goal, adding what he was going to do today, tomorrow, and next week to organize his band to be successful. Then we invited in Lee Anne to hear him read.

Teens sometimes don't like to read for their parents, but Billy said, "This is cool, Mom. You should hear me read."

Lee Anne was obviously moved by Billy's change of attitude and ability, her eyes tearing as she listened.

I explained the goal and some of what Billy and I had discussed: "Imagine that Billy is a professional guitar player who is going to go to school and get the skills he needs to function independently in society. Imagine letting go of the notion that Billy is a student who has a hobby of messing around with his guitar.

"Billy, if you feel full supported in your music, will you stay in school?" I asked. "No problem," Billy responded.

All this happened ten years ago. Billy graduated from high school and went on to become a guitarist in a world-famous band. He recently came in to see me, and brought his girlfriend with him for a balancing session.

I'm proud of the way Billy kept his commitment to himself and discovered how to reorganize the things he "had to do" around the things he "loved to do."

The Integrated X

The Visioncircles course, Edu-K's basic seminar on vision improvement (created by Gail with input from me) includes a statement of one of my favorite maxims: V = T x S (Vision equals time times space). What I mean by this is that vision is more than visual acuity skills; it is focus toward the horizon over a distant expanse, and involves an understanding of time (how long it will take to traverse that distance) and space (an all-encompassing awareness of the distance to be traversed).

As I have previously pointed out in these pages, our brains of today were created by the physical activities of our ancestors—hunters and long distance runners who were able to eventually overtake most animals. Humans have a prefrontal cortex developed to organize time and space around a purpose. Our vision represents our overall sense of purpose, the organizing principle behind how we move and take action in the world.

Homo sapiens lives in a body uniquely designed to move forward, and the forward momentum of running is a good metaphor for living a full life. The "running" of which I speak can be any forward-impelled activity that aims toward a focus or direction, a way to go (e.g., skipping, riding a bicycle, even the creeping of a baby after a rolling ball). Holding that focus in balance requires a sense of the elements of both time and space.

When we can cross the midline of the body, moving our arms and legs in contralateral synergy and firing the bundled nerve fibers of the corpus callosum that connects our cerebral hemispheres, we access time (the left-hemisphere real time of our movement) in space (the more right-hemisphere perception of our physicality). When we're "in space" (so to speak) and aware of time, we can move with rhythm, relaxation, and pleasure, as well as with a sense of purpose.

When we lose our sense of either time or space, we break stride, also losing our integration. Now moving as though we're beside ourself, we function from only one hemisphere at a time, losing our two-sided, multidimensional sense of a personal vision and our step-by-step movements within that vision. When we engage the whole brain with the rest of the body, we have a sense of oneness with our vision and a sense of movement and forward momentum that propels our exquisite bodies onward in the flow.

Yet stress can sidetrack us from our purpose. If we lose our sense of space, our muscles contract. We lose the aliveness of feeling and sensation, and disconnect from the heart. Our tissues and muscle proprioceptors respond reflexively, without awareness of the pleasurable sensations—of movement, warmth and coolness, pressure and tactility, and so on—that tell us we are in the body. If we lose our sense of time, we're overwhelmed by sensation and can't sequence our physiology to take action or even move effectively.

The integrated X of the runner exists even in our stillness, connecting each shoulder to its opposite hip across the midline, at the body's postural core. This is the lateral heart connection that unites time and space as we focus to follow our visions into the unknown future, feet on the ground and all the while noticing our head and our heart.

The Power of Purpose

As we saw in my discussion about the Land of Ahhhs in Chapter Four, purpose is larger than our intentions. The power of intention is our imagining and yearning, our setting our mind to something, our belief that it can be done. If intention represents the goal, purpose is the knowledge, the rightness, and the irresistible force that rises out of our life's experiences to shape, organize, and integrate us.

Purpose sweeps us up and says *Yes*. We need to have a purpose of our own as our reason for being alive; otherwise we may exist only to please others and life may become an empty existence characterized by drudgery. We are all here for a purpose, and we need to discover what that particular purpose is—why we're alive and what we want to put our energy into.

If a man is living someone else's purpose—his mother's, father's, or wife's—or if a woman has become so preoccupied by the raising of children that she has lost any sense of purpose outside of her family, then such individuals have lost their connection with the pleasure of learning. If they consult with me, I'll remind them about something that they used to feel passionate about. Often they'll cry when they think of it, and soon thereafter they'll take up the pursuit again—

whether it be landscape painting, playing the flute, or volunteering in a homeless shelter.

I use the goal-setting process (an important part of a Brain Gym session, as we'll see in the next chapter) to remind clients about their deferred dreams. I consider their identification of their life purpose to be half or three-quarters of the work. A clear sense of purpose musters and draws on all the resources of the brain and the rest of the body, which is why it's an agent of integration. When a client leaves a session with a new sense of purpose and a feeling of excitement about that purpose, I feel that our work has been successful.

When I conduct balancing sessions with clients here in the United States, many of them express an intention to make more money. This isn't surprising, because money and the culture of wealth are national obsessions in this country. But money is only energy, and the best way to attract it is to create a magnetizing energy field around oneself. You can achieve that spontaneously by finding out what you love to do and diving into it.

People who are both passionate and skilled are always successful, without any need to focus on money. It's possible to be gifted in an area that doesn't excite you; conversely, you can be enthusiastic about something you have no talent for. However, everyone has a passion and a talent in some area of life. If you don't believe this is true of you, it's only because you haven't yet discovered the thing that you're passionate about. Chances are you're still stubbornly looking in the opposite direction!

The Connection between Purpose and Pain

In my years of doing private balancing sessions, I've discovered an intriguing relationship between purpose and pain. When I ask clients to choose a goal and their first response is a reference to some area of physical pain, I encourage them to appreciate their own body for finding that way to make its needs known. Pain and goals are often connected, and time and again I've seen pain go away once an individual has gotten in touch with his or her life mission. There are countless possible reasons for the presence of pain, as pain is one of the body's best ways of communicating with us.

Pain is often stuck energy in the body—the body's way of saying *You're not moving properly.* Unfortunately, I far too often see people who've become stuck in the fight-or-flight reflex. They're unable to return to homeostasis, that state in which the body can heal and restore itself.

If our energy is blocked because we're not moving in the right direction in life—as it is when we're out of touch with our purpose— the body will cry out for help. It doesn't speak with words; its language is sensation, and pain is one of its messages. When seen from this point of view, pain can be our friend.

Often, in a balance process organized around a goal, a person has the opportunity to slow down and safely feel and sort through some of the messages that her body has been sending. And often the happy by-product of a balance is that it supports the individual in returning from a fight-or-flight state to a state of normalcy governed by the autonomic nervous system. This system has two main parts: an arousal system called the sympathetic nervous system and a calming and restorative system called the parasympathetic nervous system.

A physician in Germany who attended one of my courses in that country once commented, "There's one word to describe Brain Gym: effective." He explained his belief that many of his patients could get well if only they could find a way to restore the normalcy of the parasympathetic nervous system in balance with the sympathetic. He saw the Edu-K process and our empirical understanding of the relationship between the brain stem and the frontal lobes as offering an important clue to this balance.

I describe the sympathetic nervous system as our low-gear state, in which we're challenged to work with greater intensity; and the parasympathetic system as our high-gear state, which provides the context and momentum for our everyday movements.

It helps our understanding of this to remember that the autonomic nervous system oversees the supposedly involuntary behaviors of the body, such as heartbeat, circulation, respiration, blood pressure, elimination, sexual responses, adrenaline production, digestion and metabolism, and so forth.

When we get involved in a creative endeavor or some physical pursuit that gives us a sense of mastery or success, the body naturally makes the pain-killing, pleasure-enhancing hormones known as endorphins. And when the body shifts into a relaxation response, our natural production of endorphins increases.

Pain will often disappear as a person starts living life in the awareness of being part of the whole, the sacred, and the spiritual. I'm always thrilled to see people get so excited about their life that their pain goes away. And when people connect with something that really brings them joy, I sometimes see them make a shift from pain all the way to pleasure. When people are living fully, sometimes even cancer goes into remission, since tumors can be only another of the body's many ways of telling us our energy is blocked. It's useful to remember that everything is energy; if our energetic vibration is not in accord with the rhythm of life, we start to die.

Sally: Finding the Message in Pain

On the first day of a three-day workshop, into the room limps Sally, relying on a crutch for support. A scowl is etched into her face. During the introductions, Sally explains that she has undergone two surgeries in the last few months, and that at one point her doctors were not confident about her chances for survival. She experiences excruciating lower back pain twenty-four hours a day, and describes her life as a living hell.

In view of her evident distress, I don't wait long to invite Sally to be the subject of a demonstration balance. She readily accepts, and declares as we begin that her goal for the session is to get rid of her pain.

"I wouldn't advise that as an intention," I tell her. "Everything in life is valuable. And anything we can lose, we can find again! So I recommend that you express your goal in a more positive way."

Sally presents a new goal: "I'd like to be healthy and to be able to live my life more fully."

"What would that mean?" I ask her.

Sally seems to be having some difficulty formulating her intention,

209

so I invite her to do the PACE activities (see Chapter Twelve) with me. Sally then makes a few more attempts to describe her goal, and finally settles on this: *To honor who I am and know where my boundaries are.*

As the other course participants watch, we begin to do the balance. Sally comments on her goal, suddenly realizing that, due to her illness, her life has changed completely in the past year. Her ability to slow down and say *no*, she says, now requires a great deal of her attention.

I ask Sally if change is so overwhelming to her, and makes it so hard for her to cope with her work, that she has had to get sick in order to take a vacation. Sally meekly laughs, and agrees that—yes—maybe she's been taking vacations the hard way. I then ask her about the level of her pain, and she rates it an eight on a scale of one to ten.

For a pre-activity related to Sally's goal of knowing her boundaries, I ask Sally to say no to me as I approach her. Even in our role-playing, this is clearly difficult for her. We do a selection of movements that include the Positive Points, to bring Sally's awareness to her frontal lobes; some Lengthening Activities, to allow her to relax her tendons and reengage her muscle proprioceptors; and Hook-ups, to help her regain her equilibrium.

When the time comes for the post-activity, I again walk slowly toward Sally. This time, as I come too close, she blurts out "No!" so forcefully that the whole class jumps. Sally laughs heartily, the group joining in.

I ask Sally to repeat her intention in the first person: *I honor who I am and know where my boundaries are.* Sally does this in a strong, clear voice that reveals that the statement is now anchored in her body. I ask about her present level of pain, and she says it's now down from an eight to a three.

Sally and I select a group of Brain Gym movements for her to do daily for a month—some "homeplay" to help the new learning become a stable habit—and then she goes back to her seat.

The next day Sally returns to the class, her walking noticeably improved and her mood elevated. She says the pain is down to a one— it's now bothering her only slightly.

On the third and last day of the workshop, Sally walks into the conference room with no crutch, no limp, and a broad smile on her face. For the first time in four months, she is entirely free of pain and able to walk normally.

Gathering Our Intentions

Intention is the smaller sister of purpose and a key component of Brain Gym. To clarify the role of intention in our lives, I like to use the metaphor of a lake. Imagine a vast, crystal-clear lake full of pretty fish, colorful aquatic plants, and precious stones. This lake has everything you could possibly desire, and the water itself is a delight to the palate.

You arrive at the shore of the lake and a boatman waits there, ready to respond to your every need. This boatman is quite a character. He knows everything about the lake and can guide you to anything you want from within it, but he has one quirk: he will not take you anywhere or give you anything unless you make a specific request.

As great a lake expert as he is, the boatman shows absolutely no initiative in trying to comprehend vague commands. If you say to him, "Give me all the good stuff from the lake," he'll take you in the boat to the middle of the lake and then let the vessel drift around aimlessly. He shows you nothing, and brings nothing to you. If you say, "I want some fish," pretty much the same thing happens. You would swear there were no fish in the lake at all.

On the other hand, if you're very specific in your request, the boatman is marvelously helpful. If you say, "I want three rainbow trout for dinner," the next thing you know you'll be in exactly the right spot for catching trout. You'll see them gliding beneath the surface of the water as if waiting for you. Within minutes, your meal will be flopping around in a bucket.

Besides being specific, you need to put energy and enthusiasm into each request. Try saying to the boatman "I want a handful of diamonds" without meaning it, and see what happens. Perhaps you don't really want the diamonds. Maybe you want them but don't truly believe you can have them. Either way, the boatman ignores you completely. It's as if you had never spoken!

I can see this in my own life. If I'm half-hearted about a project, I usually get a poor result. If I'm enthusiastic, determined, and clear, not only do I work with greater focus, but it's also as if the whole world has decided to cooperate with me. The right person appears at exactly the right time, an unexpected check arrives in the mail to provide some funds I need, or someone calls me and happens to have exactly the information I was looking for.

Whatever the goal, a clear, energized intention helps us to achieve it.

My Own Experience of the Power of Purpose

Purpose is one of the most powerful elements of our lives. To paraphrase the poem that opens this chapter, when we disconnect from the heart and misuse, or fail to use, the energy we've been given with which to express purpose, then our energy stagnates, sometimes even turning to physical or emotional disease.

I consider it a mistake to say to oneself, *Once I've cleared away this or that difficulty, then I'll be in the correct state to find and pursue my purpose.* I don't see things working that way. I believe that the pursuit of our purpose is the very healing force we seek.

Let me give you an example from my own life. I had life-threatening pneumonia when I was born, and, ever since, my respiratory system has been a vulnerable area. Then, when I was a child, some kind of developmental delay affected my speech, which was marked by unusual cadences known as "cluttering"—a form of stuttering in which a person thinks faster than he can speak, so the voice can't keep up. People with this challenge have to learn how to breathe and speak at the same time. I was unable to fully connect my speech mechanism with my thoughts, and it was often hard for people to understand what I was saying.

As if having a speech impediment were not enough, life gave me a series of confirmations that I would never be able to perform in public. My parents, being as they were in the business of marionette shows, frequently did public speaking. I remember how Mama taught me, as a four-year old boy, to sing "California, Here I Come," imitating Al Jolson. She wanted me to perform this song in front of a big group.

When the time came for me to render my song, Mama painted me in blackface and came out on stage with me, holding my hand. I

212

looked out at the audience below and immediately panicked. Turning around, I pressed my face against her knees and sang the whole song with my back to the audience.

Later I was a Boy Scout in the Order of the Arrow, the Scouts' national honor society. Every Saturday night we'd do a ceremony around the campfire, with Order of the Arrow members playing the roles of various Native Americans. One of the older campers was a mentor to me, kind of like a big brother. One night he fell ill, and I was recruited to take his place. The ceremony involved my donning a loincloth, wearing a feather on my head, and giving a rousing speech.

I had only a few hours to learn my lines, and when the time came for the ceremony I was so scared that, as before, I forgot my lines. As I stood beside the fire, watching the audience on the other side, I froze. The person next to me had to whisper my lines to me, a few words at a time. It was a humiliating experience. To add insult to injury, when I got back to the dressing area, the young man I had replaced yelled at me, "Dennison, you stink!" I felt that I had failed a friend and let my buddies down, and that night I cried myself to sleep.

Recovering from those early experiences has called for a huge effort on my part. In my mid-twenties, I took speech lessons to try to overcome the "cluttering." This work involved connecting what I was saying with what I was feeling—in other words, actually experiencing the feelings and sensations of my body while speaking. Until that time, I hadn't realized that I couldn't blurt out everything I thought and still be understood.

The speech therapist would have me recite phrases that activated certain tones; for example, "Ho-ho-ho, I'm Santa Claus!" I was about to go to Los Angeles to take on a teaching job, and the therapist would ask me, "Why do you want to go there?" I'd reply, "I want to teach," and he'd say, 'No, no, no—you must say it with passion!"

So I would practice saying aloud, "I *want* to teach; I want to *teach*." Finally I reached the point where I was able to go to Los Angeles, find employment at an elementary school, and stand as teacher before a classroom on my first day without freezing and losing all credibility with the children.

Later, when my work in Educational Kinesiology became known, public speaking turned into an even bigger issue. I was required to give talks to large audiences, workshops to small but equally intimidating groups, and—most frightening of all—I sometimes had to give interviews on radio and television, media that put anyone's imperfections under a magnifying glass. I would see that red light on the TV camera and be thrown right back to the humiliating Boy Scouts speech. Again, I'd feel myself freezing up.

While in the studios, I watched accomplished TV personalities and wondered at their ability to be enthusiastic and emotive about everything, even the weather. Fortunately, by this stage of my career I had the tools to work with these kinds of issue. I did Brain Gym balances for myself that helped me emulate these television professionals.

I also did everything I could to experience giving one truly successful interview. One of my students in Toronto happens to be a brilliant TV host, rivaling Larry King in her talent for putting guests at ease and drawing them out. Moreover, she knows my work and loves it. I realized there would never be a better opportunity to create a positive broadcast experience for myself, so when she asked me to be on her show, I went for the opportunity. The interview went well, and this created a positive "marker" to bring to the next one, thereby replacing the campfire marker that had been burned into my memory as a Scout.

This remembering a time when we were more "in the zone" than at this present moment is an important feature of Brain Gym, as is bringing that body memory to a new situation. For example, if I'm working with a boy who's good at soccer, I'll ask him to remember the feeling in his body when he scores a goal. If possible, I'll create makeshift goalposts in my office and have the boy shoot a ball at me. We then take that in-the-flow feeling and transfer it to whatever low-gear situation we are currently working with.

Increasing personal mastery in this way is the key to high self-esteem, which is not measured by how nice people are to you or the good thoughts you have about yourself, but by what you can do. If we can't learn to do something better or have an experience of doing it better, then we don't care how nice someone is to us or what grades they may give us . . . we will always doubt our own competency. But if we can actually do it better, then we know who we are—we know our boundaries of skill and effort. This helps us to be grounded and ready to take future risks.

Purpose is a galvanizing force that propels, challenges, and ultimately heals. Today, I'm no longer intimidated by public speaking. My purpose in life—to teach others to become effective educators and whole people—forced me to work with my fears, since I couldn't fulfill my mission without overcoming them. The power of my purpose has taken me to a place of accomplishment that few who knew me as a young boy would ever have foreseen me reaching.

Bigger than Life

In our family marionette shows, my father played Paul Bunyan, the giant woodsman of the North woods. Papa Joe was six feet tall, so, to the children in our audiences, he appeared to be a real-life giant.

Boom! Boom! Boom! Boom! We heard the giant's enormous footsteps behind the stage. The children gasped as they saw Paul's enormous legs, wearing big black boots, step commandingly onto the platform while his upper body remained hidden behind the canopy of the set.

Paul's bellowing voice filled the theater and captivated the watching children as he said, "I'm Paul Bunyan, and this is Babe, my faithful blue ox."

My mother had designed an unusual marionette that was just Babe's head. The large blue ox turned and nodded his head, from the end of the stage, toward Paul. The other lumberjacks and the Indians— wonderful marionettes that Mama had made and costumed—looked like very small people as they interacted with Paul and Babe on the stage. No wonder the kids accepted that Paul really was a giant.

In the middle of the set was a giant tree that my father had built and my mother had painted. In one scene, Paul and several other "lumberjacks" would saw this enormous tree together. The audience saw only the upper half of Paul's body as he laid himself down on the stage, resting his head on one elbow. He held one end of the curved saw with the little finger of his free hand, while the string of marionettes, standing at the other end of the stage, held the other end. The small lumberjacks, breathing and bending in unison and seeming to huff and puff with the effort, followed the lead of the giant man as he cried out "Heave!" when they pulled on the saw and "Ho . . ." when it was his turn to pull.

My favorite scenes were the ones in which Paul talked to Babe, the giant blue ox. In one scene, my dad, as Paul Bunyan, would sit on the stage, squatting down in front of Babe's enormous, kind face, and brush Babe's teeth for the benefit of the children in the audience. "*Up* and down, *up* and down . . . never across . . . always *up* and down," Paul would chant, as he scrubbed the teeth of the blue ox with an oversized brush.

As the show ended, Mama and I and my younger brother, Peter, dressed in our black puppeteer costumes, would bring the thirty-inch-high marionettes—the Indians and the loggers—dancing on their strings to the edge of the stage. The children would chortle with delight, pointing at the marionettes and reaching out as if they could touch them. Suddenly they would gasp as Paul Bunyan appeared and jumped down off the stage.

They could now see his whole body, upright, for the first time, and they were in awe as this giant of a man stood before them. In a solemn, fatherly voice, my father would announce, "Remember these words from Paul Bunyan. Mind your mothers and fathers, be good boys and girls at home and at school, do your homework every night, and help your parents with the chores, so you can grow up to be good lumberjacks. And don't forget to brush your teeth every morning and every night . . . *up* and down, *up* and down . . . never across!" Every child listened with glowing eyes.

As I was growing up, my parents didn't have much money in the bank, yet we were rich beyond compare. We always had what we needed: music, play, and imagination. Our marionette shows were a gift from the heavens. What a blessing it was to be able to create such experiences and share them with others!

My father was bigger than life to me, and though he's been gone for years his passion to write scripts and perform with my mother remains a priceless inheritance. Those early memories are a repository of wealth such as few children ever receive from their parents.

Abundant Living

When I took my Touch for Health teacher training, I was asked to write a letter to myself, defining my goals for the coming year. In my letter, I stated that I would write a book about my work (which I then called Edu-Kinesthetics). This letter was sealed and put away for one year. When I eventually reopened it, I was amazed to realize that, in that year, I had fulfilled the promises I'd made to myself: I had written my first book and was growing the seeds of an exciting new profession.

Several years later, at a Touch for Health conference, Dr. Sheldon Deal, President of the International Kinesiology College and an inspiring motivational speaker, challenged us to "Get on fire with what you do with your life, and the world will come to watch you burn."

Sheldon's words that day affected my life. I began to risk doing the work that I love and feeling excited about what I do. And, as one outcome of this, I began to learn about financial abundance.

Money is energy. For me, it comes as needed, yet it isn't my focus. I don't worry about money; in fact, I seldom even think about it. Yet I never doubt that I'll receive what I need. If you like what you do, and like being in your body as you do it, then you'll attract what you need because you're open to the gifts of an abundant universe.

I've noticed that some people who don't have enough money are focused on scarcity and are worrying about survival, rather than living in creativity and that state of wide-open possibility that is available to us only from the prefrontal cortex. Even if such people acquire money by luck, the survival orientation of their brain stem will likely cause them to mismanage it and end up as broke as before.

We enter and leave this world naked, and I believe that all the abundance we may have while we're here is on loan to us as a form of energy for our life. My own attention isn't on receiving money but on giving of myself to serve the planet. I know what I do best, and I keep balancing to live, learn, and grow so that I can keep on giving.

How Purpose Leads to Abundance

Through the past twenty-five years, I have given hundreds of balances for abundance. I've assisted people in getting in touch with issues of worth, trust, and letting go that had formerly prevented their abundant living. I have learned, through my own balances, to believe in what I do and take the necessary risks to change self-limiting patterns into self-fulfilling strategies for success. I've learned from my students and have grown from their wisdom and loving support. I am absolutely, one-hundred-percent positive that life is abundant and that it will support authentic work.

To identify our life work, we need to know what we want to offer within the community we're seeking to serve. Each one of us has a unique gift to give. If we each did our own thing in life, according to our inner calling, there would be less misunderstanding, less destructive competition, and more cooperation. In the private balancing sessions I do with clients, I support people in finding their mission out of their pain, their loss, and their wounding so that they can turn these into their passion.

Do you work for money? If you answered yes, you may have thus far missed the most important lesson about abundant living. You can work for money, and you'll probably even get some this way. But the money won't satisfy you, it won't bring you happiness, and you may even lose it.

Having money is a means, not an end. It's not a substantial goal or objective because it isn't an intention that the body understands. Our bodies love to *do* things, not have things! The valid objective is abundant living, because money flows like energy when we do the work we love. Find out what you love to do—your rightful focus—and put your energy into it. Abundance, including money, will then flow for you like a fountain.

If you pour love into your work, then joy and satisfaction will come back to you a thousandfold. Gail and I like to express our gratitude for all that we receive by giving generously of our time and energy to causes we believe in. The universe supports us in wonderful, delightful ways. By putting ourselves into the flow of life, we've been able to receive life's bounty.

My First Work Experiences

I started working at age eight. Most of the other kids I knew received an allowance from their parents, but I knew that if I wanted spending money I'd have to earn it myself. I set pins in a bowling alley and delivered the Sunday paper in the dark hours of the morning, pushing a big wagon that creaked down the road. On rainy days, I covered the newspapers with a tarp.

One day, when I was twelve, I was selling newspapers on a corner when our landlord stopped to buy a paper from me. He hired me on the spot to be his assistant. Our landlord was a millionaire realtor who trained people to be brokers at his own real estate school. This wonderful teacher taught me many practical business skills that I still use. During the four years I worked for him, he trained me to pack books for his mail order business and even flew me on a trip with him for a workshop he was teaching. As his assistant, I learned how to run a school, and this mentor's influence later helped me conceive of my reading centers, and still later even helped me envision an international school for Brain Gym instructors.

Listening to My Calling

When I first started developing the program that would be known as Brain Gym, I had a calling. "Go and teach this work to the world," a small voice whispered in my ear. I knew that I wanted to follow this voice's urging.

I could have taken an easier road. I already had a secure, comfortable business that would have continued to sustain my family and me. My reading clinics had been established for more than a decade and were well respected in the community. By word of mouth, new students continually replaced those who were graduating. I didn't have to make any great effort; I could run the business and collect my paycheck blindfolded.

Yet deep down I had become restless and bored. I was ready for a new challenge to set me on fire. "Do *me*," the Brain Gym work said invitingly.

Brain Gym pushed me to face my "stuff," for it meant speaking in public, international travel, radio and television appearances, and abundant success. Was I ready for this new level of thinking and being?

I remember the balance I did with a goal of letting go of my old life and stepping into my dreams. With it came the thrill of realizing, "Of course I can do it. I am worthy. My work is valuable. I have something important to offer. It's a foregone conclusion that my work is an unqualified success."

Running a Business Like a Balance

During the last twenty-five years I've taught workshops, written books, spoken all over the world, run a publishing company, given private consultations, and cofounded an international nonprofit organization. I can say without hesitation that I have always loved my work.

I have sought to run these various enterprises like a balance, meaning that I have remembered to stay in touch with the three dimensions of focus, centering, and laterality and explore how they affect my interrelationships with employees, clients, and community members.

For me, a business isn't separate from a life purpose. Neither of these is about money, power, or control. Those elements may come into play, yet actually, in both business and life, it's all about the degree to which we can express our love.

When we think about our work, we can notice the Focus Dimension and ask ourselves: *Can I easily move forward in my work? Can I locate myself in space, in the here and now? Can I retreat as needed, restore myself, and keep myself safe? Can I hold my boundaries and protect what's valuable to me?*

Similarly, we can notice the Centering Dimension and ask: *Do I feel grounded in my heart, rooted in my passion? Am I connected with my community? Am I able to interact—to play and to feel love? Can I fight for what I believe in, what is true for me? Am I able to "fly," to soar in my work?*

When we're exploring and noticing the Laterality Dimension, we can ask: *Can I move between integrated high and integrated low gears, between information and metaphor? Can I bring more mastery to what has been unconscious or reactive? Conversely, can I make automatic what I have been trying too hard to do?*

The following are some of the key components of focus, centering, and laterality as they apply to running your business as you would a balance:

1. We create a safer place for everyone to work by really listening to our employees and clients or customers and by establishing trust with them. We are listeners, first and foremost, to the body's innate wisdom. We endeavor to hear needs, ideas, pain, passion, and aliveness as we hold space.

2. We are real with people. In this virtual, emailing world, we remember to touch, to hold, to play, to build, to break bread with our employees and clients. We roll up our sleeves and do something physical. We make intelligent movement— such as the Brain Gym activities—a part of each day.

3. We love our clients and coworkers and we make a heart connection with them. In Edu-K, the terms "centering," "grounding," and "being in the body" all mean being connected to the heart, not just the mind, When we make a heart connection, everyone feels it.

4. We dream and then set our goals, remembering that energy follows intention. Why are we here? We must know our own intentions.

5. We take our failures as pre-activities, reviewing our intentions on a regular basis, revising what is not working and renewing our commitments. We keep moving and we risk new experiences to create new pathways.

6. We honor others as well as ourselves, and in the process we dare to be magnificent. We include honoring as a primary means of evaluating. Any criticism is suspect. Honoring positive accomplishments is the only valid policy.

7. We create community, and keep it vibrant through celebration. We take the time to acknowledge growth and to celebrate all changes, expressing appreciation for the milestones. We create a community that loves to work and play together and that supports each individual's aliveness within the group.

Chapter Eleven

Vibrant Relationships

I Will Disappoint You

I need you to know I will disappoint you,
leaving you bewildered by the audacity of my actions

I need you to know that I will leave you,
whether in death or in the dust of my path

I need you to know that I cannot fix you
or solve your life's riddles

But don't you dare write me off,
brother, sister, father, mother, lover

For I am a tracker hunting down soul,
reclaiming all the heartwood that was lost by the wayside

To burn once again in the Fire of the Sacred

—Jeffrey Scharetg, © 2002

I treasure my relationship with my dear wife, Gail. Together, we have for more than twenty years built a precious jewel that glows through our lives, giving them a meaning we might never have known alone.

This jewel is sometimes a demanding teacher. By being open, though, to its lessons, we have learned important truths that have helped us to grow as individuals and to heal wounds that we would otherwise never have attended to.

Most people have the notion that a relationship passes through a honeymoon phase, and that the real marriage starts when the honeymoon ends. Gail and I feel that each conflict we face and resolve together brings us the possibility of rekindling our honeymoon at a deeper level.

I am still awestruck by the wonder and beauty of the brilliant, talented being called Gail, who greets me each day with her magical presence. Whenever I see Gail, or even hear a telephone message from her, I fall in love all over again. Like every couple, we have our difficult moments. Yet, by remaining present, we're able to keep alive an ever-new sense of mutual discovery.

My Relationship with Me

My first relationship is with myself. Am I comfortable in my own body, with my own choices? Am I at ease with the resistances and contradictions, the demands, doubts, and questions, that arise each day in my life?

Do I have work that I like to do, and can I learn to like the work that I have to do? Do I know how to slow down and relax? Do I feel calm and take the time to breathe? Can I take the time to leave the cares of the day behind and collect myself so that I can be there for my partner?

I use the Hook-ups and Positive Points activities from Brain Gym to help me settle in, notice any stress I might be holding that doesn't really belong to the relationship, and release it. Only when I'm okay with me can I be ready to hold space for Gail.

How Play Can Restore and Deepen Any Relationship

We grownups sometimes forget that play is just as important for us as it is for youngsters. And one important form of grownup play is the sharing of quality time with our mate or spouse. When we're in touch with our playful heart, we'll spontaneously reach out to connect with our partner.

Gail and I do our best to play every day. One wonderful structure for our play is a game Gail learned years ago, in which we each receive fifteen minutes of undivided attention from the other, during which time we have permission to ask for anything we want. As Gail and I play this game, we request many different things from each other—whatever's "up" for us. The cooperating partner generally wants to grant whatever is wished, yet always has the option to say no.

I might request a foot massage, or that the two of us spend some time just sitting silently together. Gail might request that I take a walk with her, or that I just listen attentively as she speaks. Sometimes one of us will quietly listen as the second partner speaks of things he or she admires or cherishes about the first partner.

Sometimes one of us will have us both singing together through the whole fifteen minute; at other times, we dance. Often we do Edu-K balances. We generally do these exchanges in the late afternoon or early evening, and Gail and I both look forward to them. Often we're having so much fun that we go past our allotted time. Even if a session begins seriously—perhaps even from a place of conflict or disagreement—we've usually created a feeling of play by the time the quarter hour has passed.

It's important that Gail's time is her time and my time is mine—that we don't mix them up. When Gail requests that I listen as she speaks during the whole time, I've learned to just listen. When I speak during my own turn, I know I won't be interrupted (a rare thing in human discourse!).

When we speak during these special times, we do our best to use only the first person and to talk only about our own feelings and experiences. We avoid blaming, shaming, or "you shoulds," focusing instead on what's going on for each of us. Our mutual commitment to this practice of listening and sharing sustains us and helps us stay aware of each other's needs, especially when times are challenging.

One-on-One Time Works Well with Children, Too

Gail and I wish we had known how to play this favorite game of ours when our children were young. Now that all five of our progeny are grown, we've been able to achieve some of the game's best objectives by spending special time with each of our kids and grandchildren on an individual basis.

The Reverend Wayne Muller, the author of *Sabbath: Finding Rest, Renewal, and Delight in Our Busy Lives*, said something memorable in a wonderful presentation I once heard him give: "We can tell children we love them and we can mean it. However, the only way the kids are ever going to know what we mean by 'love' is the time we spend playing with them on the carpet." As the good reverend pointed out, play, exploration, and real time with our loved ones are the sustenance of all relationships.

Suppose you have only a quarter hour to spare. You may wonder if anything much can be accomplished in only fifteen minutes. Yet I once read a study that found that, on the average, parents give each of their children only twenty minutes a week of quality time.

When our children are at home with us, it may seem that we're giving them time all day long. But maybe we just glance up to respond to them for a moment, and don't really listen or connect with them. Busy as we are with our projects and responsibilities, we parents too often listen with half an ear and look with half an eye when children are asking to be heard and noticed. A commitment to stop everything and be totally present for just fifteen minutes means everything to a child, and will help build a lifelong friendship as we mentor that young person into adulthood.

I remember the bonding that took place when my son Tom was little and I would give him his bath, entering his imaginary world with him as he played with his toys in the water. At other times the two of us would walk to a nearby zoo and enjoy watching our favorite animals together. I find I still connect most deeply with my kids when we have one-on-one time together—often, these days, over lunch. For me, this time set aside is a valuable way to honor and connect with any important person in my life.

Giving and Receiving

People in relationship need to be able to both give and receive. This is true not only for partners in a marriage but also regarding our relationships with children, parents, siblings, friends, and coworkers.

Yet, too often, the roles of "giver" and "receiver" get in the way of two people having a full exchange.

As a child, I learned that I should not be selfish and that it's more blessed to give than to receive. Yet, during my teenage years, an important mentor taught me something contradictory. This man was convinced that giving is easier than receiving, and that the real key to successful relationship is to learn how to ask for help, seek advice, and receive love.

The fellow had a favorite maxim that I've never heard expressed in quite the same way anywhere else: "We love those we serve. We despise those who serve us." I've since come to understand that this maxim holds a deep meaning beyond the simplicity of its words.

Have you ever seen your own loving intentions backfire and turn into pain and resentment? I have, many times. You may be a generous, giving, caring person who wants to support others. As such, you give, give, give, and naturally you expect love and gratitude in return. You may wonder, *How come they don't love me? Look at all I'm doing for them!*

In life, it doesn't work that way . . . not well, anyway. We all need to learn how to receive from others as well as give. For the sake of human harmony, a relationship needs to be one of give and take, of mutual giving and receiving. We helping types need to form connections in which we allow the other party to love us and do for us in return, in more or less equal measure.

If we want people to resent us and eventually learn to detest us, we need only keep taking care of them. When we notice ourselves caretaking others, it's useful to stop and ask, *Which one of us is this for?* We need to reflect on how our words and actions are being received by the other party.

As caregivers, we may be truly seeking only the pleasure of nurturing, mentoring, or helping another. While these activities may offer tremendous satisfaction, are we allowing a space for the receiver to give back, repay, or offer a gift in exchange for our sacrifices? If we don't allow ourselves to receive, it's worth considering whether we're expecting something in return, giving in order to control the other person, or wanting to keep him or her dependent on us.

Sooner or later a one-sided relationship will cause difficulties. Our caring and overdoing often sends the message that we really don't believe in the other person's capabilities. The more we're taking over for the person we care about, the less they're learning to believe in, and rely on, their own gifts and strengths. If we really want to help another person, we need to let him stand on his own two feet, or else fall and get up on his own. We can offer our encouragement, yet it's important that we not try to fix things or take charge.

In every balance session, I like to teach clients that we give a blessing to others when we let them give back to us. I teach people, through balances, to be open to receive love, to listen to others, to seek the counsel of elders, to ask for advice, and to graciously accept the generosity of others.

Because it's easier to give than to receive, learning to receive is, for many of us, the real goal of being in relationship.

Nonverbal Communication

Movements, gestures, and body language—our means of self-expression through nonverbal communication—have a profound influence on marriages and other relationships. People who live and work together learn to "read" each other, and can sense harmony or discord even when no words are spoken. When we're in the heart space, our words and body language match. When there's a mismatch of words and body language, exchanges become confusing and uncomfortable for both parties in the relationship, as what we say is belied by our out-of-sync signals.

In every interaction, whether it's a coherent or incoherent one, the limbic brain and the fight-or flight-system read the situation before words are even spoken. Suppose I'm with a friend, and standing with my knees locked and my fists closed in front of me, while looking away out the window. My friend's limbic system will spontaneously read my postural attitude. Once the emotional midbrain has had its turn, it will send a signal to the neocortex, resulting in the conscious thought *Paul's angry with me.*

Simultaneously, messages are sent from the amygdala of the midbrain to the motor cortex of my friend's prefrontal lobes, where a plan of action is being prepared. Other outputs to the endocrine system are altering stress hormone release, while cortisol production in the liver is increased, which could affect a person's physical state for hours or even days.

Because his instincts tell him the outcome of the interaction may be a fight and that his physiology needs to be prepared, my hypothetical friend's limbic brain will direct his brain stem to increase his heart rate, increasing circulation to his arms and legs. All of this will happen in the wink of an eye.

When I say, "I'm not mad at you," and explain that the reason for my own limbic-system-driven postural attitude is a phone conversation I just had with a difficult person, I may still have threatened the friendship almost as much as if I were really angry at my friend. In such a situation, it would be better if I took the time to do some Brain Gym movements and left my work-related stress at the office, where it belongs.

In this way, a nonverbal message can shift a relationship out of balance as much as any verbal message. For me, being in a marriage relationship means that I want to notice my physiology and return myself to my heart space, centering and grounding myself before each interaction.

A real dialogue and exchange consists of more than the words spoken. Conversation means to "create verse with the other." We relate with rhythmic language, with meaningful pauses, and through coordinating our movement and breathing. If ever Gail and I can't do this, we know it's time to do some Brain Gym movements and reconnect to our hearts.

If ever Gail asks, "What's wrong?" and I, in denial, hear myself say, "Nothing," this is a time for me to stop and notice what's going on with me. In such a case, I need to trace back to the disconnect by tuning in to my body's intelligence and asking myself what I'm feeling. Once I have reestablished my connection to myself and communicated from that place, Gail can, in turn, relate to my situation and show up for me.

Feelings of Overwhelm or Neglect

Two main themes come up repeatedly in human relationships. These themes can be summed up as feeling either overwhelmed or abandoned by one's partner. For me, feeling neglected or even deserted is sometimes an issue, as my childhood experiences of not belonging taught me to make sure I'm never forgotten or left out.

It helps me when I remember that the brain stem—center of our deepest level of survival—functions in terms of space and territory. Such questions as *Where am I in this relationship?* and *Where are the boundaries of our relationship?* always come up as we negotiate the space in which we live with another person. Knowing this, I've become more aware of the subtle communications that I make and receive from others about that dimension of focus and participation.

When I see a person withdraw, I've learned to read that nonverbal signal as a need for more space, or sometimes a feeling of overwhelm—a nonverbal request for a clarification of boundaries. When I'm feeling balanced myself, I can slow down and give my own gift of time and space to that person. Similarly, when someone I'm with begins to speak rapidly, with a sense of urgency, I've learned to distinguish between a defense, in which the person is requesting more space, or a request for my time and attention. When such nonverbal requests as these are not acknowledged, they sometimes become more extreme, expressing a feeling of either engulfment or abandonment.

We all need to help one another negotiate our space so that we can discover for ourselves what it means to relate.

Love Will Come

Our modern Western culture is one of the first in history in which men and women unite in marriage for no other reason than that they want to be together. In the past, marriages were arranged, either for economic, political, and social reasons or simply because the parents didn't trust their children's ability to choose wisely. My economics professor at Boston University always said, "Love will come" when we would ask him about the arranged marriages in other cultures. People married first, and later, if they were lucky, love came.

In the modern world, the celebration of romantic love has come to the fore. We marry for romance, and only later does real love come. When the endorphin-rich high of romantic attraction fades, which it always does, then the deeper purpose of the relationship reveals itself—namely, to heal each other's wounds.

Every hurt we've ever experienced, starting in the womb, is sure to be restimulated within an intimate relationship. The more intimate the relationship, the more "stuff" we'll have to deal with. Indeed, we can look at romance as a form of divine bait. Without its irresistible attraction, who would ever sign up to be dangled from the hook of a real marriage?

Marriage is not a compromise, but a living, breathing entity that builds on the full actualization of each partner. Ideally, the individual flowering of the two persons is enhanced by their joining together to create their sacred partnership. If either partner must self-compromise to accommodate the other, the marriage is out of balance and will be diminished.

Yes, couples do of course negotiate on small things by talking over options, such as vacation destinations or the color of a new couch. These conversations are essential to the give and take of cohabitation, yet there should be no sacrifice of the true nature of either partner.

Gail and I bear this in mind, aiming always to nurture each other's dreams and hold them sacred. We can look into each other's eyes and say from the heart that, together, we have created something much more beautiful and fulfilling than we could ever have realized on our own.

The Heart-Limbic Component

We know certain things about the brain and the heart that can help us to improve our relationships through an improved understanding. As we contemplate entering a new relationship, are we prepared to take care of our own needs and also be there for another? Because it is economically and socially permissible, in today's society, to break up a marriage, an alarming percentage of couples never make it past the romantic stage. The result can be a catastrophic breakdown of the family structure.

Children learn by modeling themselves after their parents, and this modeling runs deep—into the very core of the brain. As my friend Joseph Chilton Pearce, the world-renowned advocate of heart-based child-rearing practices, so poignantly describes in his book *Magical Child Matures*, young children perceive information about their parents not just through the medium of the five senses. They also pick up attitudes, beliefs, and emotions through the limbic system, that heart link with the parents that connects them like an invisible umbilical cord.

As Joe Pearce says, if we are going to live together in growthful relationship, we must learn how to stay in touch with the resonance of that heart intelligence, innate in all of us and only waiting to be accessed.

The Brain-Heart Connection

The defining structure in human consciousness is the emotional mammalian brain. Like all mammals, we give birth to live young and feed them with loving care. The parental instinct to nurture and play with our offspring is part of a biological imperative that includes the ability to find a mate and be in relationship. This instinct underlies the heart-brain connection and the midbrain, as discussed earlier in this book. If we don't learn as children to connect and relate and play, we are often unprepared to cohabit lovingly as adults.

The older, more physical, and less emotional survival brain is more akin to the world of the snake, the turtle, or the bird. The typical reptile has a strong instinct to reproduce, yet ends its relationship with its young once it has laid its eggs, slithering away. Any instinct to nurture or love is not apparent. A snake will watch the death of its offspring with no interest apart from evaluating its chances of turning the predator into prey. Among reptiles, cannibalism is the norm.

We all have this snake part within ourselves; it shows up as a reflex to save ourselves at all costs. Without the survival reflexes we wouldn't learn to move, stand, set boundaries, say "no," and know when we feel safe.

The need to reproduce and survive as a species began long before mammals appeared on the planet. The brain stem, the survival system that regulates such autonomic functions as breathing and swallowing, also controls sexuality. According to Paul D. MacLean and Joe Pearce, this older, more "reptilian" part of the human brain is even more fundamental than the midbrain. Pearce explains that we need to develop all aspects of the brain so that we can access the highest part of our nature, to become fully loving and creative beings. He explains how the mother provides the emotional midbrain for the infant, as the infant explores the sensorimotor world of survival. Thus, at each stage of our development, our mentor or teacher can support us by anticipating the next step we'll be moving into.

Unlike reptiles, mammals protect their young—sometimes at the cost of their own lives. They play with their offspring, teach them, and communicate with them vocally until the little ones are sufficiently strong and resourceful to fend for themselves. Sixty five million years ago, when the first mammal set foot on the earth, life took an amazing leap forward.

Evolution's nonnegotiable requirement is that enough members of each new generation survive long enough to reproduce. Reptiles fulfill this requirement statistically: enough offspring are produced that some individuals remain after the majority have starved, been eaten, or perished through being frozen or overheated.

When mammals came on the scene, something beautiful happened: playful connection replaced sheer numbers in the struggle for survival. The neurological manifestation of this new component of life— emotion—resulted in the heart-brain connection.

Human beings are the flower of this mammalian evolution; and, just like our ancestors, we are animals of feeling. As with all mammals the limbic brain is the emotional generator for human beings, and it reigns over our every aspect of our lives.

Being the "rational creatures" that we are, we might prefer to think we are governed by the neocortex, which houses the higher-status processes of thinking, language, and reason. However, we must ultimately admit that we are first and foremost emotional animals who must always balance our emotionality with as much reason as we can find available.

If you're in a relationship, take a moment now to select any reaction you tend to have to the other person that carries with it a strong emotional charge. Maybe you can't contain yourself each time your partner leaves dirty dishes in the sink, or you feel jealous if he or she pays attention to another person at a party, or you become furious when your partner addresses to you what you perceive to be a critical remark.

Once you find a strong emotional habit, try to figure out a way to do something about it. Chances are you'll find reason a poor way to balance your feeling brain.

Why? Because, as powerful and esteemed as our conscious minds may be, they have little power in the realm of emotion, where the limbic brain reigns supreme. We can muster all the willpower and determination we like, but, until we can learn to move in new ways, the minute our partner repeats the offending pattern of behavior, our limbic system will be triggered.

Certainly we can use the conscious mind to block our expression of an emotional reaction, but we can't stop the reaction itself. Only the outer manifestation can be suppressed. Moreover, this kind of suppression creates a whole new set of difficulties: the biochemical soup that has been heated up inside now has no outlet, and may turn itself against us in the form of illness or disease.

Joseph Chilton Pearce tells us that the limbic systems of a mother and infant are connected in the near-magical process known as heart resonance. This means that the child is immediately aware of his mother's emotional state, independently of normal sensory cues such as frowning, smiling, or verbal alarms. Indeed, research has shown that, during the first phase of infant maturation, he is unable to distinguish his own emotions from those of his mother.

In a famous experiment, a baby crawls to the edge of a box, where there is a ledge of Plexiglas. He is now faced with an ambiguous situation, since he perceives danger signals and indications of safety at the same time. The infant looks to his mother and intuits her emotional state. If he sees alarm, he stops; if he senses encouragement, he continues.

Emotional connectedness through heart resonance crosses species. For instance, a friend of mine can communicate with his dog through his own posture. When Bonkers senses his master's feelings, his own internal state aligns itself accordingly. If my friend folds his arms and clears his throat, Bonkers knows he has been a bad dog and slinks away, sometimes literally with his tail between his legs. When my friend comes home and reaches out for Bonkers, the dog comes running and practically jumps into his master's arms. (Incidentally, research has proved how important owning a pet can be to human health, as people living alone are far less susceptible to illness and early death if they have a pet in the house.)

Heart resonance is the phenomenon at work when lovers sit silently together and speak volumes of feeling to each other. It is at work when women's menstrual cycles become synchronized; we know this to be a limbic process because the phenomenon is more common among good friends and family members than among roommates who are only acquaintances.

Liz and Jens: Finding Balance As a Couple

I have balanced hundreds of couples and families, and it's always a joy to see the dissolution of fear, separation, alienation, and isolation on the part of family members as heart resonance is restored to the family system. Often people seem to see and hear each other for the first time. An example that comes to mind is a balance I facilitated with Liz and Jens.

Liz hosts a television show. She is bright-eyed and full of irrepressible enthusiasm. Her boyfriend, Jens, from Germany, is a dance instructor. He spends several hours a day doing his routines. One day he plans to open his own school, but for now he accepts financial support from Liz. Both are in their early thirties.

Liz and Jens come to see me with the intention of improving their communication. Liz shares that they have some of the usual couple difficulties: trouble listening and giving full attention to one another, as well as difficulty in honoring each other's need for alone space, plus hesitation to create a long-term commitment. Liz is especially concerned about what she feels as a lack of intimacy, as Jens isn't expressive of his feelings. The plusses are that they both love to cook, enjoy their mealtimes, and do dance well together.

First I have us all do PACE together (see Chapter Twelve). As we complete these four simple activities, I notice that we're all laughing now, breathing easier, and feeling more at ease with one another.

We discuss some of the couple's goals around relationship and improved communication. I notice that the two don't make much eye contact, so I ask them to sit opposite one another and do a pre-activity of looking into each other's eyes. As they do this, I suggest that they simply notice any thoughts or feelings that pass through them, without judging themselves or their partner.

After a few minutes, I ask each of them to notice their body postures (as described in Chapter Three). Liz says she realizes that she now feels flighty, unable to settle down and relax. I explain to her and Jens that this feeling relates to the up-and-down dimension of emotional centering and heart resonance, dependant in part on how we relate to gravity and the ground that supports us with our posture.

Liz now offers that, as she and Jens made eye contact, she'd noticed what felt like a huge chasm in front of her. I explain that, when we're not centered in our bodies, we often lack a feeling of connection to the world; sometimes we seek to obtain that feeling from our relationships, perhaps depending on words instead of feelings to ground us, or depending on others to help us feel that we belong.

I ask Jens what he notices now about his body posture. I can see that his posture is pulling back, as though withdrawing, and that his knees are locked and his body rigid. Jens keeps looking toward the door. He comments that he sometimes feels pushed into things and that makes him feel resistant and overwhelmed, and even a little afraid, as though he doesn't know what is happening. He doesn't know what he's supposed to do, and is unable to concentrate on what's happening in the room. I share that the inability to concentrate our attention is related to our ability to focus and our movement forward and back across the participation midline of the body. Part of Jens wants to be there with Liz; another part of him has already left the room.

Two people looking into each other's eyes represents the intimacy of relationship. I help Jens notice that, as he looks into Liz's eyes, his body begins searching for a way to feel safer by withdrawing. I explain that locking his knees and withdrawing is a useful strategy that has probably helped him survive in previous relationships, but that it keeps him from being able to access his balanced sense of focus and give his attention to Liz. It also prevents his accessing his balanced sense of laterality, so he can speak and listen with greater ease and make good choices for himself.

Now that Liz and Jens have completed the pre-activity and had a physical experience of what they're doing as they relate, we start the movement part of the balance. The two now interlock fingers and create an X with their thumbs. They look at each other through the X and then do synchronized Lazy 8s while gazing into each other's eyes.

I encourage them to experience the sensations in their bodies as they move, and to express their love to each other if they feel like it. Liz says, "Jens, I love you." He tells her, speaking in German, that he loves her, too. There is heart in the words, and they both start to cry.

Jens and Liz face each other and touch their hands together. They now do the Double Doodle movement, with Jens leading and then alternating the lead with Liz. They move their whole body, and, as they stand, the movement turns into a dance. The two of them are so flexible that they look like strands of seaweed swaying together in the ocean.

When the movement activity has been completed, they go back to their post-activity and look again into each other's eyes. This time their rigid patterns of movement seem to have melted, and they shift back and forth between smiles and tears.

"How does that feel?" I ask.

"Wonderful!" Liz replies. "It feels like home—like Jens is a support."

"Jens," I say, "you are the earth to her rock. Give her the sweetness and the contentment she's asking for. All feelings are welcome in this relationship. Liz will hold the space for you, but you've got to show up for her."

I turn to Liz. "Your homeplay is to remember to ground yourself with Positive Points and Hook-ups. When you're more grounded, you'll be better able to hold a space for Jens to feel safe and come forward in himself. Then he can get in touch with his feelings."

Liz turns to Jens and says, "I know I'm so expressive of my feelings. Maybe I've been a little impatient, expecting you to do what comes to me so naturally." She cradles Jens in her arms.

"That's right," I say. "You can support Jens in feeling safe in the child so he can feel safe as a man. And Jens, your homeplay is to do Lengthening Activities, such as the Gravity Glider, so you can respond to Liz rather than pulling away or reacting to her."

I expect that, as Jens continues to practice interacting from a more forward place in his body, he'll gain a sense of inner direction and take more charge of his life.

From the session, Liz and Jens are realizing the value of slowing down, taking more quality time with one another, and being playful. Jens now leads Liz through some dance steps and twirls her into a resting pose.

"You may kiss the bride," I tease. In fact, many couples report that a balance like this one enable them to feel their connection in the body and to read one another's nonverbal communications as in no other ceremony.

Once we see a relationship as a dance in which each partner helps the other become balanced, we see what a truly beautiful part of life relationship is. There is no right and wrong inherent in our behavior . . . only imbalance and the opportunity to grow into greater balance.

When viewed as an opportunity for personal growth and a context in which a wonderful experience of cooperation can arise, a relationship can shift from heads to hearts and from fear to love.

Chapter Twelve

Brain Gym in Action

. . . Our deepest fear is that we are powerful beyond measure. . . .
As we are liberated from our own fear, our presence automatically
liberates others. . . .

—Marianne Williamson

Let's now take a closer look at the Brain Gym approach to life and
learning, in order to understand just how it helps us enter into the
exquisite pleasure of learning.

As I have explained earlier in these pages, Brain Gym is a series of
simple movement activities that optimize brain activity and integrate
the mind and body. It provides a "menu" of twenty-six different
movements from which to choose, and some individuals enjoy doing
all twenty-six movements every day. But the majority of people who
use Brain Gym select just a few movements pertaining to whatever
new ability they're currently wanting to enhance.

This new ability may be practically anything, e.g., a skill such as
reading or roller blading that they wish to improve, a personal quality
of character that they'd like to enhance, or some emotion that's been
coming up that they're wanting to understand and integrate.

For general purposes, and especially if you're new to Brain Gym,
I recommend a flowing sequence called the Action Balance that will
help you get maximum benefit from your use of this program. Many
people learn to do this balance on their own, but in order for you to
have optimal results from this potentially life-changing process when
you first experience it, I recommend that you choose a licensed Brain
Gym practitioner in your area to be your facilitator.

Establishing Rapport

When I begin an Action Balance with a student or client, my first responsibility as facilitator is to create a safe space for learning—a container within which the one being balanced can get in touch with his or her feelings, needs, and aspirations. I hold that safe space so the individual can look at issues more objectively, and I endeavor to inspire the kind of trust that allows for an optimal teacher-student interaction.

Energetically, the two of us involved in the balance meet as learners in a single context in time, joining together interactively to explore possibilities until we're both in touch with our aliveness, the fire that sparks us all and sustains our souls. We have a conversation through body wisdom. Each of us honors his or her own unique process as we set aside intellect and go into our innate intelligence, reminded in a deep, experiential way who we really are. This movement toward authenticity is the essence of my work.

For example, a woman named Susan comes to me feeling anxious about an impending relocation to Chicago. Her spine speaks volumes as I notice her arching backward in her dread of making the move. I'm sensing the emotion she feels at having to give up everything she knows in order to make this change in her life.

The success of the balance process with Susan, or with any of my students, will be due less to technique than to the fact that I'm trained to listen to the language of movement, and thus able to be there for the person in the now moment.

Susan says, "My boss really needs me at the new office he's opening in Chicago. My husband says he supports me, but I know he doesn't really want to move. He'll have to find a new job, and the children will have to change schools in the middle of the year."

I ask, "Where are *you* in the midst of all of this chaos?"

Susan answers by slumping forward and starting to sob. In the matter of her move to Chicago, this may be the first time she has truly been heard (or, perhaps, even heard herself) at the body level. I am there for her, in respect and appreciation of her honest response. As I hold the space and fully listen to her, the balance has begun before we've even started the actual process.

Susan is now able to relax into the feeling that she has nothing to do, no place to go, and nothing to change. She sees that this whole thing is not just about her husband and the kids; she must include herself in the picture. She needs to take into consideration her own spirit, and let it become a part of the dance.

In a safe space of this kind, no rejection, competition, or abandonment can occur. And when the true self is allowed to blossom, there's no telling what miracles may happen.

Witnessing this emergence in Susan, I say in celebration, "I see how much you care. And I know you can make this move, because I feel the passion you bring to your situation."

Step by Step through the PACE Process

Jason is a freelance writer; he has come to see me because he's received an assignment to write a children's story and is feeling intimidated and blocked.

"It's not my specialty," he explains. "I'm used to writing adult nonfiction, and I feel old and dull when I try to fire up my creative juices and imagine what a ten-year-old would like to read."

Following the usual sequence of the Brain Gym Action Balance, I invite Jason to begin with the four steps of PACE, an acronym that stands for "Positive," "Active," "Clear," and "Energetic." Each of us has an innate rhythm and timing uniquely our own, yet there are times when the stress of life jolts us out of this natural flow. Being in PACE reconnects us with our sense of intrinsic pace, and moves us in the direction of our pulsing, ardent hearts, as if we are slowing down and stepping back into ourselves.

When doing the four steps of PACE, we always start with the "E" and work backwards through the word.

Sipping Water

To become "Energetic," we take the first step of the PACE process and do something remarkably mundane and ordinary: we drink a glass of water. Most of us drink water only when we're thirsty, and fail to realize how H_2O benefits our brain function, ability to move, and general health. The water we drink is the medium that increases electrical potential across our cell membranes, and it is therefore essential for nerve net function.

When I'm feeling low in energy, instead of pouring myself a cup of coffee or eating a candy bar, I'll sip a glass of pure water. I wait a few minutes for my body to absorb the fluid, and then am always impressed by the result, for I'll inevitably feel more alert and have more energy for whatever task I need to do next. If I had been feeling hungry, the hunger pangs will usually subside, since very often the brain confuses the sensation of dehydration with that of low blood sugar.

After all, the brain is 90 percent water. And water is more than just an inert medium within which the real action happens; it's a vital part of brain functioning, and unperceived thirst is a key element in impaired mental functioning. Few of us drink enough water, mainly because the body's thirst usually goes unheeded. So it's a good idea to structure a conscious water-drinking routine into our day. Many teachers—and especially those who know the Brain Gym system— advocate that their students have water bottles at their desks to drink from throughout the school day.

Health authorities recommend that we all drink eight to twelve glasses of water a day, depending on our body weight. This is in addition to any other drinks we may consume, such as bottled sodas, and should also be over and above any drinks containing water, such as coffee, tea, and juices.

It's impossible to overestimate the nervous system's need for water. Frances Meiser and Nina Anderson conveyed this succinctly in their helpful book, *Overcoming Senior Moments*:

> Minerals in the brain create sparks called electrolytes. These charged particles are responsible for signals being delivered from one cell to the other. A salmon swimming upstream, when confronted with a waterfall, swims in circles at the base of the falling water. This helps the fish absorb the electrical charge created by the falling water and ultimately facilitates its miraculous leap up the waterfall. If electrolytes can do this for a fish, just think what they can do for your brain.

It's important to consider not only the quantity of the water we drink but also the quality. Municipal drinking water must always be considered suspect, since research suggests a link between chlorine and cancer.

Incidentally, in no area of nutrition do I advise you to wait for scientific proof that an additive to food or water is harmless. Just because an additive has not yet been shown to be harmful doesn't mean that it's harmless. I prefer the commonsense approach: if nature doesn't add chlorine to water, then I don't want to drink chlorinated water.

Trust nature, and don't be too quick to trust human interference with nature. In spite of marvelous advances in the last century, science is still in its infancy with regard to its understanding of human physiology.

I find spring water, with its purity and mineral content, to be perfectly designed for the human body. Unfortunately, buying spring water isn't always the best solution. It's expensive for some budgets, and there is concern in some quarters about the danger of contamination, both from plastic bottles and from microorganisms multiplying in the water while the bottle sits on the shelf. Well water is a good option, provided it's pure. Otherwise, I suggest purifying municipal water with a five-stage reverse osmosis filter. You can buy one for your home or obtain filtered water from the dispensers located outside many supermarkets. An undesirable side effect of filtered water, however, is that it lacks mineral content; consequently, it may be advisable to add trace minerals to your water before you drink it.

Brain Buttons

Jason looks suspiciously at the glass of water I hand him, but drinks it without saying anything. Then we move on to the next component of the PACE process, the one that represents "Clear." In Brain Gym, we call this second part of the sequence "Brain Buttons." To teach this activity, I show Jason how to place the thumb and first finger of his right hand on each side of his sternum, under the clavicle, to stimulate the reflex points located there.

The purpose of the Brain Buttons activity is to release inhibited eye movement by relaxing tension in the muscles in the back of the neck, muscles originating in the visual/occipital area. This improves visual perception and facilitates reading across the midline.

Brain Buttons

If you want to try this for yourself and don't know exactly where to place your thumb and finger, use your own body sensations to guide you. Approximate the correct position by pressing in below your collarbone, in the soft tissue area to the left and right of your sternum, then move your fingers around a bit until you feel a release in your neck. If you pay close attention to the sensations in your neck, you'll notice a pleasant feeling of letting go when you find the pressure points. Once you locate these points, massage them deeply with one hand while placing the other hand over your navel, continuing this for thirty seconds.

Though the brain accounts for only 2 percent of the body's weight, it uses 20 percent of the body's oxygen. Because the Brain Buttons lie directly over the carotid arteries, which supply freshly oxygenated blood to the brain, our stimulation of these points stimulates the carotids to improve their work of delivering oxygen. This in turn stimulates the brain and facilitates the transmission of messages between the right and left hemispheres, leading to greater integration of the linear, analytical side of the brain and the holographic, intuitive side.

Placing a hand over the navel reestablishes the gravitational center of the body, balancing the stimulus to and from the semicircular canals (the centers of equilibrium in the inner ear). This activates the ears' vestibular system—the door to learning—and improves the mind-body connection.

The Cross Crawl

Next, Jason does the exercise that represents "Active," for this activity literally activates the brain. Called "The Cross Crawl," the movement is a fundamental one in Brain Gym, for it coordinates the left and right brain hemispheres as they work together at the same time. This simultaneous hemispheric activity is an essential aspect of mind-body integration, which we'll examine in more detail in the next chapter. In brief, it helps us to access the spatial, big-picture part of the brain—the right hemisphere—opening us to new experiences, and it facilitates learning by making a linear process out of what we do—the province of the left hemisphere.

The basic concept is to move in such a way that, when one arm moves, the leg on the opposite side of the body moves too. For beginners, it's easiest to start by simply touching your right knee with your left hand and then alternating this with touching your left knee with your right hand, continuing from side to side in this way.

This movement is a very natural one for the body. We discover at an early age to interweave our opposite sides through crawling, walking, and eventually running. Experts theorize that contralateral movements, as activities of this type are called, work to activate the speech and language centers of the brain. In addition, the integration of the receptive (right) and expressive (left) hemispheres is an important element, since it facilitates learning, stimulates the imagination, and activates creativity.

As you grow more confident with the exercise, you can play some of your favorite music and turn the movement into a dance. The only requirement is that you move one arm and its opposite leg together, then alternate with the other arm and leg.

Hook-ups

Part One **Part Two**

The final component of PACE is known as "Hook-ups." This activity is designed to invite a "Positive" attitude by allowing us to let go of the fight-or-flight reflex that responds to any hazard perceived as life-threatening. The Hook-ups exercise shifts electrical energy from the survival centers in the brain stem to the reasoning centers in the midbrain and neocortex, thus activating hemispheric integration, increasing fine-motor coordination, and enhancing formal reasoning.

The Hook-ups activity also restores equilibrium after emotional or environmental stress, activating the frontal lobes (the goal- and movement-oriented "CEO" of the brain) and opening the heart. Most importantly, it grounds us in the body. As a result, we feel clear, optimistic and peaceful. This is a balance posture that fully activates the vestibular system. The crossed hands and feet stimulate the motor cortex in both hemispheres and simultaneously activate all the motor control centers of the brain, thus overriding any inappropriate responses of the survival reflexes, stress hormones, or sympathetic nervous system.

I first introduced you to this activity in Chapter Two, but let me repeat it here. The exercise is in two parts. First, place one ankle over the other. Next, extend your arms and cross the left wrist over the right; then interlace your fingers and draw your hands up toward your chest. Hold the position for one minute, breathing deeply, with your eyes closed and your tongue on the roof of your mouth. (The tongue pressing into the roof of the mouth stimulates the limbic system, for emotional processing, and the frontal lobes, for a more complete overview of a given situation.)

You may wish to do the Hook-ups exercise standing up, since that position activates the balance structures of the inner ear (the vestibular system). It is equally effective done standing, sitting in a chair, or lying down.When you have finished, uncross your ankles and put both feet on the floor. Place your fingertips together in front of your chest and breath deeply for another minute, with your eyes closed.

PACE, then, is a preparatory set of exercises designed to put your mind and body into a Positive, Active, Clear, and Energized state, so that you're in high gear for learning.

Pacing the Goal

When a student and I are both in PACE, I ask, "What's going on for you?"

In posing this question, my intention is to identify a goal or focus for the learning session. My strategy is always to shift students' mindsets from the fixing, solving, and remedying they think they need to the joy and aliveness of living life more fully. A student needs to reconnect to his or her mission and purpose and to state a goal in the present tense, as if it is already happening.

When a student can claim her life and see herself living it now, in the present session, she'll be able to do it later. The purpose of the balance is not to go backward to some earlier period when we might imagine life was easier. The purpose is to move out of the present situation and into a space of more possibilities by connecting one's body, mind, and heart.

The next step is to identify the goal that the student wishes to achieve. We call this "pacing the goal," because the goal must also be Positive, Active, Clear, and Energetic. Setting a goal has to do with intention, and intention is a key element in Brain Gym, for it ignites positive change in a person's life. When we have a clear intention, the mind and body come rushing to our aid, as does the whole universe—the exterior manifestation of the inner state. So we talk to the student until we hear in her tone of voice and see in her body language that she has formulated a goal she's truly excited about and willing to work for.

In Brain Gym, the PACE activities and pacing the goal put the student into the state of mind to express her intention in a way that her mind and body, and the whole world, will respond to. They put her in such a safe place that she can choose life changes as if they have already happened, rather than pushing changes through out of conflict or stress.

When I ask Jason to express his goal, he says, "I want to get creatively unblocked."

"Can you express that intention in a positive way?"

"I want to write a good children's story."

"What would the qualities of that story be?" I ask.

"It would be lively and imaginative."

"So can you put that together into a clear, positive intention?"

Jason takes a deep breath and says, "My intention is to write a book proposal for a lively, imaginative children's story that will delight my publisher!"

The intention has been expressed in positive language that's clear enough for a child to understand. I can see that Jason's statement of intention has made him feel energized and ready to move, so we're now ready for the step called "the pre-activity."

The Pre-Activity

In a Brain Gym balance, we want to identify those skills that are already in place and those that need drawing out. We do this by asking the subject to perform some task that involves using the skills in question.

In Jason's case, I ask him to write the first paragraph of a story on a piece of paper. He sits quietly for a while, deep in thought, then finally writes the following:

> Once upon a time, there was a young prince who wanted to marry a beautiful young lady. The only problem was that the girl was the daughter of a woodsman, and the king and queen disapproved of the match.

Although, theoretically, this introductory paragraph could develop into an intriguing story, as first stated it is ordinary and lacks flair. Jason sees this for himself, which is why he has been feeling so anxious. Somehow he has been unable to access his creativity and enthusiasm.

The pre-activity allows us to freeze a moment in time so that we can dissect the pattern or process that is Jason's strategy when he writes under pressure. In Brain Gym terms, Jason has disconnected from the imaginative faculty associated with the right brain hemisphere and has also disconnected from the passion and joy that are characteristics of the heart. We might say he is hard-wired for survival rather than creativity. This will remain Jason's strategy until he learns to reconnect his mental patterns for writing with the joyous physical movements of childhood that will allow his creativity to flower.

The Learning Menu

I now suggest a "learning menu" of Brain Gym exercises for Jason to choose from, activities that I expect will serve to connect his mind and heart and balance the left and right sides of his brain.

A learning menu is a series of movements derived from the master list of Brain Gym activities. This menu, selected for the purpose of activating the subject's mind and body circuitry to achieve a desired goal, is either chosen by the individual receiving the balance or suggested by the one facilitating the balancing session.

If you're doing an Action Balance as you read this, you can follow along with Jason or use your own awareness to find appropriate exercises for yourself. In Brain Gym we call this use of awareness "noticing" to emphasize that the process is an aspect of normal, everyday human functioning. Everyone can do this. Trust your body and your intuition; they are extraordinarily intelligent mechanisms. Just as they will tell you exactly what food you need to eat, they will also tell you the exact set of Brain Gym exercises called for by your current situation. The following is a list of those Brain Gym activities that I've chosen to include in this book:

Alphabet 8s - page 190

Arm Activation - page 65

Brain Buttons - page 243

The Cross Crawl - pages 90, 244

Cross Crawl Sit-ups - page 251

The Homolateral Crawl - page 90

The Seated Cross Crawl - page 89

The Double Doodle - page 191

The Elephant - page 250

The Energy Yawn - page 193

The Footflex - page 107

The Gravity Glider - page 148

The Grounder - page 149

Hook-ups - pages 45, 245

Lazy 8s - pages 35, 189

Neck Rolls - page 158

The Owl - page 252

Positive Points - page 70

The Rocker - page 252

Sipping Water - page 240

Think of an X - page 158

The Thinking Cap - page 251

The Elephant

For his goal, Jason considers the master list and then chooses to start out with "The Elephant."

    To do this movement yourself, stand with your knees slightly bent. "Glue" one ear to your shoulder and point that same arm across the room, focusing on some arbitrary area that will serve as the midpoint of an imaginary figure 8 that you're going to draw horizontally. Use your ribs to move your entire upper body as you draw the "Lazy 8" with your extended hand, up and around to the left, across the midline, and then up and around to the right. Do this three times on each side, pressing first one ear and then the other to its corresponding shoulder. You're looking past your fingers as you move, to let your eyes follow the 8 you're drawing.

    This movement has many benefits, including helping us listen to our own speaking voice, which is an important aspect of successful writing. It stimulates attention, perception, and discrimination, and helps integrate vision, listening and whole-body movement by fully activating the vestibular system.

Cross Crawl Sit-ups

Next Jason chooses "Cross Crawl Sit-ups." I ask him to lie on his back on a padded table, with his hands behind his head, and alternate touching each elbow to its opposite knee.

This movement facilitates the integration of the left and right brain hemispheres as it centers and grounds the student. One's mind and heart become connected and the channels of creativity are opened.

The Thinking Cap

Jason's next selection is called "The Thinking Cap." This activity involves gently unrolling your ears from top to bottom, which serves to stimulate more than four hundred acupressure points related to every function of the brain and body. Among other benefits, the Thinking Cap activates neural reticular formation, keeping the brain awakened and active. It's also thought to assist integrative thinking, making word meanings and associations more readily available as sounds, rhythms, and images become interwoven. The activity helps the whole body to listen and remember better, since the hearing sense is more directly associated with memory than seeing or most of the other senses.

The Owl

The next movement Jason chooses is called "The Owl." An owl turns his head and eyes at the same time and is able to rotate 180 degrees, giving him an exceptionally wide field of vision. The owl also has remarkably acute hearing. When we do this movement, we develop those same qualities of breadth of perception.

The Rocker

Jason's final exercise is "The Rocker." For this movement, sit on the floor on a firm, cushioned surface (an exercise mat is ideal), with your knees bent and feet up off the floor. Lean back with your weight on your hands and massage one hip at a time against the padded surface, by rocking forward and back for about thirty seconds. Avoid putting any weight on the delicate area of your tailbone.

Among other benefits, the Rocker stimulates the circulation of cerebrospinal fluid within the spinal column, and this in turn nourishes the brain, assists clear thought, and serves to connect the brain with the rest of the body.

The exercises just described are very simple. Conditioned as some of us are to believe that there's no gain without pain, it may seem hard to believe that such a small amount of effort can give significant results. (Jason has spent about ten minutes doing his movements, none of which are at all strenuous.) But the fact is, the movements are amazingly effective. The reason for this is that the mind and body are by nature already connected and balanced when we feel relaxed and safe. The Brain Gym activities simply activate whole-brain functioning, taking the system out of stress so it can function in the optimal way it was designed to do.

The Post-Activity
With the movements from the learning menu completed, it's now time for Jason to do his "post-activity."

The post-activity is a way of measuring how well we've succeeded in assisting the system to change to a more optimal strategy or pattern. The subject simply repeats the pre-activity and takes note of the changes.

In Jason's case, this means writing the first paragraph of his children's story again. I tell him that he is free to copy the original word for word or to make any changes he wishes.

Jason writes another paragraph, then looks up with a smile. He reads his first attempt aloud, and then, with an unmistakable air of pride, reads the new version:

> Once upon a time, there was a young prince who loved a beautiful girl. He wanted to marry her, but his father, the king, said, "Never," and his mother, the queen, said, "Absolutely, positively not." Even the prince's dog, Fluffy, had a look of severe disapproval in his one good eye (he had lost the other in a hunting accident). Why? Because the girl was the daughter of a woodsman and, when you are a prince, the daughter of a woodsman is the last person on earth you are supposed to marry.

I think you'll agree that the improvement was impressive. Unlike his first attempt, Jason's new paragraph is entertaining, creative, and three-dimensional. There is feeling in the story, and the narrator has a distinctive voice. And all this after just ten minutes of Brain Gym!

Jason is delighted. He feels the exquisite elation of a challenge met and a job well done, which, when the whole experience of one's life focuses on a single performance, is experienced in the left frontal lobe. He now feels confident of his prospects for writing a saleable story.

I tell Jason that he will need to do the movements once a day for the next month or so, which seems to be the amount of time it takes for the mind and body to fully anchor and learn new behavior patterns.

A few weeks after our session, Jason telephones me, very excited. He tells me that he has completed a book proposal and submitted it to his publisher, who promptly accepted it.

Empathy and Other Life Skills

Brain Gym will help you in any dimension of your life, such as sports, reading, painting, mathematics, and organization, to name just a few. Additionally, it can enhance many desirable human qualities—the ones available to all of us when we've made the connection to our own heart. I'd like to give you an example of the way Brain Gym can evoke one of the most important human qualities: empathy, or heart-to-heart emotional connection.

An empathic person is someone who is able to feel what another person is feeling. This is the foundation of the Golden Rule: "Do unto others as you would have them do unto you." We can't follow the Golden Rule unless we're aware of another's emotional experience. The extreme opposite of an empathic person is a psychopath, who has no sense of another's feelings and therefore has far fewer internal constraints on his behavior. Think how different the world would be if we all allowed ourselves to truly experience the pain and suffering of others! Within weeks there would be no more war and famine, social inequalities would be corrected, and human rights would be universally respected.

This is the highest vision of what empathy can bring. But it also works wonders on a more mundane level, because it facilitates our interactions with our family members and close associates. What a person is feeling is a much more accurate indicator of his relationship to us than what he's saying, so it's very much in our interest to pay attention in this area. How many husbands or wives have seen their spouse walk out on them, yet had no prior inkling of the looming disaster?

Empathy is also a vital skill in the workplace. The role of emotion is usually underestimated in business, where logic traditionally rules, yet feelings truly constitute the foundation of any business. In sales and marketing, for example, consumers' purchasing choices are influenced far less by the mind than by the heart; thus price cutting is a successful strategy only when competing firms have not successfully engaged their customers' hearts. In the area of personnel management, the realm of emotion is equally important. Employees whose feelings are acknowledged and understood are more loyal than employees who are simply well paid. We are sentient beings, and we blossom when our feelings are recognized and accepted.

The Ease That Is Your Birthright

How can a few minutes of simple exercises produce such amazing results? How did Brain Gym help Helen make such a dramatic shift in her ability to empathize? How did it so quickly unlock Jason's playfulness and creativity? How can something so easy help us to achieve whatever we desire? I hear such questions often.

The answer is that, when we're in our body and connected to our heart, every aspect of our life is enhanced. When functioning from the mind alone, and often using only a small part of it (usually the disconnected left brain), we see just a fraction of the situation at hand. Our range of responses is thus severely limited, as if we were trying to conduct a symphony with only one musician. Brain Gym, in effect, brings back the whole orchestra. When this happens, we can work, play, study, create, and relate to others with the full force of our being.

The Brain Gym program achieves this with very little effort, because all the elements are already in place. All the intelligence you'll ever need is already inside you, waiting to be drawn out. It's as if you're the owner of a luxury sports car that has the finest engine, radiator, battery, distributor, suspension, and tires, as well as a gas tank filled with high-octane fuel. Yet the car won't move by itself; you have to push it wherever you go. One day a mechanic appears and shows you how to connect the electrical system. It doesn't take long to do this, and the results are staggering. You turn the key in the ignition and the engine begins to purr; soon you're cruising down the freeway listening to some of your favorite tracks on the CD player.

Most people are born with the whole physical system in place: left brain, right brain, heart, and the rest of the body. All you need do is connect these elements—not a difficult task—and a whole new world of possibility will open as if by magic. This ease is your birthright, and its source is the playful movement that will reconnect you to natural learning.

Before we conclude this chapter, let's look at several case studies that show the power of Brain Gym in the areas of reading, sports, and learning to ride a bicycle.

Katie

At fifteen, Katie has scarcely ever read a book that wasn't imposed on her as a mandatory part of an English class. The Harry Potter series is an exception: like millions of other young people around the world (and many young-at-heart adults), Katie has found J. K. Rowling's books to have a magical power to awaken even the most dormant enthusiasm for reading.

At the point of the pre-activity in her balancing session, Katie is holding the latest Harry Potter book open at a random page, and she glances up at me for instructions. I nod to her, signaling that she can begin reading a paragraph. She reads aloud accurately and without hesitation, but her tone is flat. She sounds as if she is reading something vaguely distasteful, like directions to the dentist's office. She's holding the book at arm's length, as if the pages have a bad odor. I look over at Katie's father, who is valiantly trying to appear interested in the paragraph she reads. All three of us are relieved when the reading ends.

I do some simple checks with Katie, and determine that she has a "mixed dominance" profile. Among other mixed pairings, she is dominant in the left ear and the right eye; as a result, she's not using both sides of her brain and any reading is stressful for her.

Katie is a highly intelligent girl with an exceptionally quick analytical mind. At school, she can easily go through the motions of reading well enough to get by. However, apart from Harry Potter and a few of the wonderfully imaginative books written by Roald Dahl, she has been unable to find much joy in reading. This is because she has not been fully using her brain's right hemisphere and corresponding left eye, which together serve as a gateway to imagination and feeling—the faculties that give color to our endeavors and make the written word come alive in the body (and therefore in the mind).

I take Katie through an Action Balance, choosing with her a learning menu of Brain Gym activities designed to balance the brain hemispheres so that she can perform tasks with her whole brain. The process takes about half an hour. As always, the movements are simple and easily learned. For example, as we saw in Chapter Two, Lazy 8s involve tracing an infinity sign three times with the left hand, three times with the right hand, and three times with both hands.

I can see Katie's father sitting in the corner, and I can guess what he's thinking: *How can a movement this elementary and unexceptional have any effect on what appears to be a life-long, deep-rooted challenge for my daughter?*

Once she has completed the Brain Gym activities from her learning menu, Katie reads another paragraph from the Harry Potter book. When she has finished, she looks up with shining eyes.

"How did it sound to you this time?" I ask.

"Okay, I guess," she says with feigned nonchalance.

Katie's father can't contain himself. "Okay? Are you kidding? It was amazing! While you were reading, I could see the whole scene in my mind, just like a movie. It was like hearing an actress read."

Katie and her father drive from my office to the airport. Katie is leaving for a year as an exchange student in Switzerland. She is taking two suitcases. One contains clothing, a small CD player, toiletries, several bags of tortilla chips, and other necessities for an extended stay abroad. The other case is filled with books: in lieu of eleventh-grade

English, her California high school is having her read twenty classic novels while she's away. I know that, earlier in the day, Katie's attitude would have been that they might as well have asked her to climb Mount Everest.

"We bought two sets of books," Katie's dad tells me. "I'm going to read the novels too, and discuss them with her on the phone. Perhaps that'll motivate her, and our discussions will also prepare her for writing book reports."

Six weeks later, Katie's father calls me on the telephone to say, "I simply can't believe it. Katie has already finished all twenty novels. I'm only on the second one. There's no way I've been able to keep up with her. It's a miracle."

As Katie's experience demonstrates, it's not hard to help a disorganized reader become a unified thinker. Five months after our first appointment, I see Katie again when she comes home for Christmas. She is now a different girl: witty, self-assured, and quite verbally astute.

Seeing the changes in Katie was a moving experience for me. No doubt her shift was partly due to her increasing maturity and the experience of living abroad, yet I knew that the shift was also due in large part to that hour we spent together before her departure.

Enhancing Sports Abilities

The Brain Gym movements are a natural resource for all those interested in athletics. What athlete doesn't benefit from being more in the body and focused, and from accessing a greater range of perception? The following account is from a case study that shows the assistance Brain Gym was able to provide to one young person whose abilities needed a boost.

Erin

"I have been an athlete for more than ten years, competing in a variety of sports. I have been decent in sports, although I was never a stellar or standout type. I wasn't the go-to person if we needed a quick goal in soccer, a home run in softball, or a buzzer-beating three-pointer in basketball.

"As I grew and enhanced my skills, my roles on teams increased, but I never really experienced the pressure of being a star performer. Then, in the seventh grade, I discovered track—and especially the high jump—and for the first time I participated in an individual sport.

"When I began doing Brain Gym, my skills improved. A typical session went like this: First, I would go through a four-step series of simple exercises called PACE, which included drinking water. These activities really helped me to focus. I could feel a definite physical difference in myself after I did them. My anxiety would fade, the butterflies would disappear from my stomach, and my heartbeat would slow to a more normal pace. Then I would state a positive goal aloud and do a muscle check to see if this was the best goal for me. Then we would role-play the situation. We would also look at aspects of my jump and discuss my goals and how to achieve them.

"Immediately following my first session, which I did right there on the track, my mind was calm and focused. I attempted to jump the same height I had tried at the beginning of the session, and this time I cleared it easily. The difference astonished me. I went on to participate in the Washington State High Jumping Championship."

(Brain Gym Journal, July 1999)

Dean

In this book I've spoken a good deal about balance, because it's one of the fundamental concepts in Brain Gym. A balanced person has a real chance to reach his or her full potential. The following is an example of a small victory in balancing that made all the difference in a young boy's life.

A boy named Dean was facing challenges in elementary school in the areas of focusing, following directions, and participating in sports. Writing was especially difficult. Yet, for Dean, the most humiliating thing of all was not being able to ride his bicycle.

During Dean's balance, his Brain Gym Instructor focused on this all-important goal of learning to ride a bike. She and Dean did a bicycle role-play and some fun balancing activities. They then used Brain Gym movements, including a Dennison Laterality Repatterning, along with spontaneous play, to assist Dean in integrating his fear-induced reflexes.

A few months later, Dean's mother sent her son's Brain Gym Instructor this email:

"Two days after you did that Brain Gym balance with Dean, he took off on his bike all by himself. His dad, who had been trying to teach him for two years, sat down and wept. You can't even imagine how proud Dean was and still is. He shows every person who comes to our house how he can ride by himself. He tells them he learned to balance after doing Brain Gym. It lifted his self-esteem higher than ever. He really needed that. He is now doing very well in the classroom. His teacher said he is paying attention rather than daydreaming and fidgeting. My husband and I are so pleased. Dean will ask to do Brain Gym almost every day. That alone is rewarding for us."

When I see young people like Katie, Erin, and Dean experience the pleasure of learning, it gives me a bittersweet feeling. On one hand, I'm delighted when Brain Gym empowers a student to make such a huge shift so easily. On the other hand, I'm saddened by the awareness that so many others could just as easily be transforming their learning experience, if they could be given the kind of exquisite education that provides the tools to help them do so.

Dean's success, like Erin's accomplishments and the apparent miracle that happened for Katie, is simple to explain. When people tackle a given endeavor with their whole brain (which involves integrated functioning of the cerebral hemispheres, the whole amounting to more than the sum of the separate parts), they experience a dramatic improvement in their performance. They can think the words, experience them, and say them all at the same time.

The real miracles will happen when this understanding became common knowledge—and its application standard practice—in schools and in our society as a whole.

Notes

Bibliography

Adams, Marilyn Jager. *Beginning to Read: Thinking and Learning about Print.* Cambridge, Mass.: MIT Press, 2001.

Amen, Daniel G., M.D. *Change Your Brain, Change Your Life.* New York: Three Rivers Press, 1998.

————. *Healing ADD: The Breakthrough Program That Allows You to See and Heal Six Types of ADD.* New York: Berkeley Books, 2001.

————. *Healing the Hardware of the Soul.* New York: The Free Press, 2002.

Armstrong, Thomas, Ph.D. *The Myth of the A.D.D. Child.* New York: Dutton, 1995.

Ballinger, Erich. *The Learning Gym: Fun-to-Do Activities for Success at School* (translated from the 1992 German language edition). Ventura, Calif.: Edu-Kinesthetics, Inc., 1996.

Batmanghelidj, F., M.D. *Your Body's Many Cries for Water.* Falls Church, Va.: Global Health Solutions, 2001.

Baum, Frank. *The Wonderful Wizard of Oz.* New York: Modern Library, 2003.

Benton, Debra A. *Lions Don't Need to Roar.* New York: Warner Books, 1992.

Berman, Morris. *Coming to Our Senses: Body and Spirit in the Hidden History of the West.* Seattle: Seattle Writers Guild, 1998.

Bradshaw, John. *Hemispheric Specialization and Psychological Function.* New York: John Wiley and Sons, 1989.

Brewer, Chris, and Don G. Campbell. *Rhythms of Learning: Creative Tools for Developing Lifelong Skills.* Tucson: Zephyr Press, 1991.

Caine, Renate N., and Geoffrey Caine. *Making Connections: Teaching and the Human Brian.* Alexandria, Va.: Association for Supervision and Curriculum Development, 1991.

Carrigan, Catherine. *Healing Depression.* Santa Fe, N. Mex.: Heartsfire Books, 1997.

Childre, Doc, and Howard Martin with Donna Beech. *The Heartmath Solution.* San Francisco: HarperCollins, 1999.

Chopra, Deepak. *Quantum Healing: Exploring the Frontiers of Mind/Body Medicine.* New York: Bantam Books, 1989.

Cohen, Isabel, and Marcelle Goldsmith. *Hands On: How to Use Brain Gym in the Classroom.* Ventura, Calif.: Edu-Kinesthetics, Inc., 2002.

Coren, Stanley. *The Left-Hander Syndrome.* New York: Vintage Books, 1993.

Damasio, Antonio. *Descartes' Error: Emotion, Reason and the Human Brain.* New York: Quill, 1995.

————. *The Feeling of What Happens: Body and Emotion in the Making of Consciousness.* San Diego: Harcourt, 2000.

Dennison, Gail E., and Paul E. Dennison. *Vision Gym®: Playful Movements for Natural Seeing.* Kirchzarten bei Freiburg, Germany: VAK Verlags GmbH, 1999.

Dennison, Gail E., Paul E. Dennison, and Jerry V. Teplitz. *Brain Gym® for Business: Instant Brain Boosters for On-the-Job Success.* Ventura, Calif.: Edu-Kinesthetics, Inc., 1994 and 2000.

Dennison, Paul E. *Switching On: The Whole-Brain Answer to Dyslexia.* Ventura, Calif.: Edu-Kinesthetics, Inc., 1981.

Dennison, Paul E., and Gail E. Dennison. *Brain Gym®: Simple Activities for Whole-Brain Learning.* Ventura, Calif.: Edu-Kinesthetics, Inc., 1985 and 1998.

————. *Brain Gym® Teacher's Edition.* Ventura, Calif.: Edu-Kinesthetics, Inc., 1989 and 1992.

————. *Educational Kinesiology in Depth: Seven Dimensions of Intelligence.* Ventura, Calif.: Edu-Kinesthetics, Inc., 1984.

————. *Edu-K for Kids.* Ventura, Calif.: Edu-Kinesthetics, Inc., 1987.

————. *Personalized Whole-Brain Integration.* Ventura, Calif.: Edu-Kinesthetics, Inc., 1985.

Eccles, John C. *The Evolution of the Brain: Creation of the Self.* London: Routledge, 1996.

Freed, Jeffrey, and Laurie Parsons. *Right-Brained Children in a Left-Brained World: Unlocking the Potential of Your ADD Child.* New York: Simon & Schuster, 1998.

Glasser, William. *Choice Theory: A New Psychology of Personal Freedom.* New York: HarperCollins, 1999.

Goldberg, Elkhonon. *The Executive Brain.* New York: Oxford University Press, 2001.

Goleman, Daniel. *Destructive Emotions: How Can We Overcome Them? A Scientific Dialogue with the Dalai Lama.* New York: Bantam Books, 2004.

Goleman, Daniel. *Emotional Intelligence: Why It Can Matter More than IQ*. New York, Bantam Books, 1995.

Hannaford, Carla. *Awakening the Child Heart*. Captain Cook, Hawaii: Jamilla Nur Publishing, 2002.

————. *Smart Moves: Why Learning Is Not All In Your Head*. Salt Lake City: Great River Books, 2005.

————. *The Dominance Factor: How Knowing Your Dominant Eye, Ear, Brain, Hand and Foot Can Improve Your Learning*. Alexander, N.C.: Great Ocean Publishers, 1997.

Hawkins, Jeff, with Sandra Blakeslee. *On Intelligence*. New York: Henry Holt and Company, 2004.

Healy, Jane. *Endangered Minds: Why Children Don't Think and What We Can Do About It*. New York: Simon and Schuster, 1991.

Hinsley, Sandra "Sam," and Linda Conley. *Brain Gym Surfer*. Stuart, Fla.: Hinsley and Conley, 1989.

Holt, John. *How Children Learn*. New York: Delacorte Press, 1995.

Koester, Cecelia K., and Gail E. Dennison. *I Am the Child: Using Brain Gym with Children Who Have Special Needs*. Ventura, Calif.: Edu-Kinesthetics, Inc., 1998.

LaBerge, David. *Attentional Processing: The Brain's Art of Mindfulness*. Cambridge, Mass.: Harvard University Press, 1995.

Levine, Peter A. *Waking the Tiger: Healing Trauma*. Berkeley, Calif.: North Atlantic Books, 1997.

Lewis, Thomas, Fari Amini, and Richard Lannon. *A General Theory of Love*. New York: Vintage Books, 2001.

Madaule, Paul. *When Listening Comes Alive: A Guide to Effective Learning and Communication*. Norval, Ont., Canada: Moulin Publishing, 1994.

Marshall, Marvin. *Discipline without Stress, Punishment, or Rewards: How Teachers and Parents Promote Responsibility and Learning*. Los Alamitos, Calif.: Piper Press, 2001.

McManus, Chris. *Right Hand, Left Hand: The Origins of Asymmetry in Brains, Bodies, Atoms and Cultures*. Cambridge, Mass.: Harvard University Press, 2002.

Mendizza, Michael, with Joseph Chilton Pearce. *Magical Parent—Magical Child: The Optimum Learning Relationship*. Nevada City, Calif.: In-Joy Publications, 2003.

264

Montessori, Maria. *The Absorbent Mind*. New York: Henry Holt and Company, 1995.

Muller, Wayne. *Sabbath: Restoring the Sacred Rhythm of Rest*. New York: Bantam Books, 1999.

Neil, Alexander S. *Summerhill: A Radical Approach to Child Rearing*. Great Falls, Va.: Hart Publishing Co., 1960.

Ornstein, Robert, and David Sobel. *The Healing Brain: Breakthrough Discoveries about How the Brain Keeps Us Healthy*. New York: Simon & Schuster, 1987.

————. *The Right Mind: Making Sense of the Hemispheres*. New York: Harcourt Brace & Company, 1997.

Palmer, Parker J. *The Courage to Teach: Exploring the Inner Landscape of a Teacher's Life*. San Francisco: Jossey-Bass, 1998.

Pearce, Joseph Chilton. *Evolution's End: Claiming the Potential of Our Intelligence*. New York: HarperCollins, 1992.

————. *The Magical Child Matures*. New York: E. P. Dutton, 1985.

————. *The Biology of Transcendence*. Rochester, Vt.: Park Street Press, 2002.

Pearl, Eric. *The Reconnection: Heal Others, Heal Yourself*. Carlsbad, Calif.: Hay House, 2001.

Pearsall, Paul. *The Heart's Code: Tapping the Wisdom and Power of Our Heart Energy*. New York: Broadway Books, 1998.

Pert, Candace. *Molecules of Emotion: The Science Behind Mind-Body Medicine*. New York: Simon & Schuster, 1999.

Piaget, Jean. *The Grasp of Consciousness: Action and Concept in the Young Child*. London: Routledge & Kegan, 1977.

Pinker, Steven. *How the Mind Works*. New York: W. W. Norton, 1999.

Promislow, Sharon. *Making the Brain-Body Connection: A Playful Guide to Releasing Mental, Physical and Emotional Blocks to Success*. Vancouver, B.C., Canada: Kinetic Publishing, 1998.

————. *Putting Out the Fire of Fear: Extinguish the Burning Issues in Your Life*. West Vancouver, B.C., Canada: Enhanced Learning, 2002.

Ramachandran, Vilayanur S., M.D., and Sandra Blakeslee. *Phantoms in the Brain*. New York: First Quill, 1999.

Ratey, John J., M.D. *A User's Guide to the Brain*. New York: Pantheon Books, 2001.

Restak, Richard, M.D. *The Secret Life of the Brain*. Washington: Dana Press and Joseph Henry Press, 2001.

Shaywitz, Sally, M.D. *Overcoming Dyslexia: A New and Complete Science-Based Program for Reading Problems at Any Level*. New York: Vintage Books, 2003.

Schiffer, Frederic. *Of Two Minds The Revolutionary Science of Dual-Brain Psychology*. New York: The Free Press, 1998.

Shiller, Francis. *Paul Broca: Founder of French Anthropology, Explorer of the Brain*. Berkeley: University of California Press, 1980.

Springer, Sally, and Georg Deutsch. *Left Brain, Right Brain*. New York : W. H. Freeman & Co., 1989.

Sweet, Win, and Bill Sweet. *Living Joyfully with Children*. Atlanta: Acropolis Books, 1997 and 2002.

Swope, Sam. *I Am a Pencil: A Teacher, His Kids, and Their World of Stories*. New York: Henry Holt and Company, 2004.

Teplitz, Jerry V., and Norma Eckroate. *Switched-on Living*. Virginia Beach, Va.: Happiness Unlimited Publications, 1994.

Thie, John F. *Touch for Health: A Practical Guide to Natural Health with Acupressure Touch*. Marina del Rey, Calif.: DeVorss & Co., 1979 and 2005.

Tolle, Eckhart. *The Power of Now: A Guide to Spiritual Enlightenment*. Novato, Calif.: New World Library, 1999.

Trager, Milton, M.D., and Cathy Guadagno. *Trager Mentastics: Movement As a Way to Agelessness*. Barrytown, N.Y.: Station Hill Press, 1987.

Walsch, Neal Donald. *Conversations with God: An Uncommon Dialogue, Book 3*. Charlottesville, Va.: Hampton Roads Publishing Company, 1998.

Wilson, Frank R. *The Hand: How Its Use Shapes the Brain, Language, and Human Culture*. New York, Pantheon Books, 1998.

Wolfe, Patricia. *Brain Matters: Translating Research into Classroom Practice*. Alexandria, Va.: Association for Supervision and Curriculum Development, 2001.